EAST ANGLIAN ARCHAEOLOGY

The South-West Fen Dyke Survey Project 1982-86

by C.A.I. French
and F.M.M. Pryor

with contributions by
M. Armour-Chelu, A. Challands,
J. Downes, D.A. Gurney, D.N. Hall,
R.H. Middleton, R.G. Scaife
and M. Taylor

illustrations by
C.A.I. French, A. Challands, J. Downes
and R. Parkin

and photographs by
C.A.I. French and F.M.M. Pryor

East Anglian Archaeology
Report No. 59, 1993

Fenland Archaeological Trust

EAST ANGLIAN ARCHAEOLOGY
REPORT NO. 59

Published by
Fenland Archaeological Trust,
Flag Fen Excavation,
Fourth Drove,
Fengate,
Peterborough, PE1 5UR

in conjunction with
The Scole Archaeological Committee

Editor: Stanley West
EAA Managing Editor: Jenny Glazebrook

Scole Editorial Sub-Committee:
David Buckley, County Archaeologist, Essex Planning Department,
Keith Wade, County Archaeological Officer, Suffolk Planning Department,
Peter Wade-Martins, County Field Archaeologist, Norfolk Museum Service
Stanley West

Set in Times Roman by Joan Daniells using Ventura Publisher
Printed by Derry, Nottingham

©FENLAND ARCHAEOLOGICAL TRUST 1992

ISBN 0 9520616 0 0

for details of *East Anglian Archaeology,* see last page

This volume is published with the aid of a grant from the Historic Buildings
and Monuments Commission for England

Cover Illustration
The buried peninsula at Crowtree Farm, Dyke 14 (Site 1)
(Photo: Francis Pryor)

Contents

List of Plates

List of Figures

List of Tables

List of Microfiche Photographs

Contributors

Miranda Armour-Chelu, B.A., M.A., Ph.D., Dept of Palaeontology, Natural History Museum, Cromwell Road, London, SW7 5BD.

Adrian Challands, B.A., F.G.S., M.I.F.A., The Old School House, Helpston, Peterborough, PE6 7DG.

Jane Downes, B.A., A.I.F.A., c/o Department of Archaeology, University of Glasgow.

Charles French, B.A., M.A., Ph.D., M.I.F.A., Dept. of Archaeology, Downing Street, Cambridge, CB2 3DZ

David Gurney, B.A., M.I.F.A., Norfolk Archaeological Unit, Union House, Gressenhall, Dereham, Norfolk, NR20 4DR.

David Hall, M.A., F.S.A., M.I.F.A.,

The Fenland Survey, c/o Dept. of Archaeology, Downing Street, Cambridge, CB2 3DZ.

H.R. Middleton, B.A., M.A., M.I.F.A.,
Lancaster University Archaeological Unit, Physics Building, Bailrigg, Lancaster, LA1 4YB.

Francis Pryor, M.A., Ph.D., F.S.A., M.I.F.A.,
Fenland Archaeological Trust, Flag Fen Excavations, Fourth Drove, Fengate, Peterborough, PR1 5UR.

R.G. Scaife, B.Sc., Ph.D.,
c/o Department of Geography, University of Southampton, Southampton

Maisie Taylor, B.A., Dip. Ed., M.I.F.A.,
Fenland Archaeological Trust, Flag Fen Excavations, Fourth Drove, Fengate, Peterborough, PE1 5UR.

Acknowledgements

The major funding for this project has been and is being provided by the Inspectorate of Ancient Monuments, DoE (1982-83) and English Heritage (1983-86). We are grateful for the support shown in this project by Dr G.J.Wainwright and P.R.Walker of English Heritage.

This project would not have been possible without the invaluable assistance given by the staff and Commissioners of the North Level Internal Drainage Board, and in particular P.Charnley and D.Hunt. The advice and assistance of our colleague, David Hall, the Fenland Project Field Officer, has also been invaluable.

Many landowners in the North Level have been particularly helpful; special mention must be made of Mr N.Harris (Borough Fen), Mr and Mrs G.Little (Eye), Mr I.R.Plummer (Speechley's Drove), Mr E.Martin (Flag and North Fens), Mr M.S.Smith (Thorney), Cllr J.Whitsed (Borough Fen), the Cambridgeshire County Council land agents and the Anglian Water Authority (Oundle Division).

The authors would like to acknowledge Tim Malim for the original drawings of Figures 11 and 52.

The acknowledgements of the various authors of this report have been assembled below, in the interests of continuity in the main text.

A.Challands:
I wish to acknowledge and thank the following people for the material help, good advice and encouragement given: M.Armour-Chelu, British Museum (Natural History); J.Bartington, Bartington Instruments; A.J.Clark, A.David and D.Haddon-Reece, Ancient Monuments Laboratory; P.L.Drewett, I.Graham and K.Thomas, Institute of Archaeology, London; R.Evans, Soil Survey of England and Wales; C.French, F.Pryor and V.Taylor, Fenland Archaeological Trust; F.Oldfield and G.Yates, University of Liverpool; H.Parslow, Huntingdon Technical College; I.Plummer, farmer, Crowtree Farm site; L.Rollo, Nene Valley Research Committee; W.Sillar; E.Standen; and P.Williamson, Agricultural Estates Ltd.

J. Downes:
I would like to thank Mr and Mrs Foster, Mr and Mrs Beckon, Mr Hart, Mr B.Jones and members of the Soke Metal Detectors Club, particularly Mr M.Redding, Mr C.Simons and Mr P.Tointon, for making new finds available; M.Taylor, K.Gdaniec, H.R.Middleton, A.Challands and M.Howe for providing unpublished information; C.Richards and F.Pryor for discussion, and C.French for inviting me to contribute to this volume.

C.A.I. French:
I would especially like to thank D.R.Crowther, Area Museums Officer, Suffolk Museum Service, who began the dyke survey with us in 1982; Dr R.I.Macphail, Institute of Archaeology, London, without whom the interpretation of the thin sections would not have been possible; Dr R.G.Scaife, University of Southampton; Dr J.Zalaciewicz and Dr A.Horton, British Geological Survey; Dr R.G.O.Burton, Soil Survey of England and Wales; and Dr I.H.Longworth, Keeper of Prehistoric and Romano-British Antiquities, British Museum.

D.A. Gurney:
The equipment for pH measurement, phosphate spot-test and magnetic susceptibility measurement in the field and in the laboratory was kindly loaned by the Ancient Monuments Laboratory. Dr H.C.M.Keeley and Dr A.Clark provided invaluable guidance. For providing the equipment for phosphate analysis, the help of Dr P.Craddock and the British Museum Research Laboratory is gratefully acknowledged.

F.M.M. Pryor:
Apart from my co-authors and those mentioned in the general acknowledgements, I owe a special debt of gratitude to Drs Roel Brandt and Sander van der Leeuw (then of the Albert Egges van Giffen Instituut voor Prae-en Protohistorie, Amsterdam) who showed us how it could be done.

Summary

This report presents the results of survey along freshly cleaned Fen drainage dykes, mainly in the North Level. The dyke survey is augmented by selective excavation coupled with environmental, geophysical and geochemical surveys. The work was carried out by staff members of the Fenland Archaeological Trust and colleagues. The dyke survey is a continuing small-scale project which examines drainage dykes following mechanical recutting carried out by drainage authorities during the autumn, winter and early spring months. The cleaned dykes provide linear transect sections through otherwise invisible buried landscape(s).

Chapter 1 sets out the aims and techniques of the project, and the environmental background of the area.

Chapter 2 briefly presents past and present archaeological work, including a summary of the results of David Hall's field survey work (for the Fenland Project) in the North Level. The chapter also includes a study of Bronze Age metalwork found in the locality in the past two centuries (by Jane Downes).

Chapter 3 presents the detailed results of the dyke survey in the North Level up until the end of 1986. The results are given by fen name area and by period.

The report concludes with a synthesis of the archaeological and environmental evidence, and a discussion of possible future research.

The microfiche enclosed inside the back cover contain an additional stratigraphic record in the form of a selection of 35mm colour slides of important dyke profiles.

This volume is dedicated to Dave Crowther

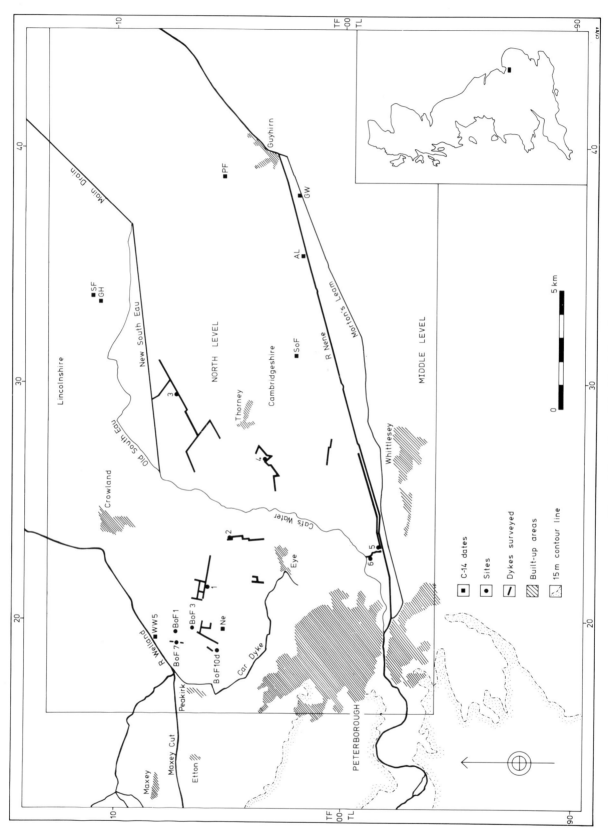

Figure 1 Location of the North Level.

Chapter 1. Introduction to the dyke survey project

I. Dyke survey: its aims, potential and limitations

by F. Pryor

Preamble: Fenland studies, some pitfalls and possibilities

It is probably as true in archaeology as in daily life that anything worth doing is rarely straightforward. Nowhere does this apply with greater force than in the study of past wetland landscapes. The biases and distortions caused by our necessarily partial understanding of the taphonomy of as complex a region as fenland *ought* to impose so restricting a straightjacket on our assessment that it would be impossible to say anything of significance at the end of the process. This simply will not do: all archaeological data are partial and it is the duty of the archaeologists to create something on the basis of what is available. A good example of this is the almost universal use in archaeological research of radiocarbon determinations at a confidence level of one standard deviation, whereas the accepted statistical practice should be two. The range of the latter is simply too large for most purposes; accordingly, as archaeologists, we make allowances for using less secure statistics, but we use them nonetheless in preference to the sounder, but often meaningless security offered by the the more extended date range.

It will be evident, in the detailed dyke-by-dyke discussions of Chapter 3, that the taphonomic problems are enormous. By the same token the physical complexity of the changing fenland landscapes is more than equalled by the complexity of the various human communities living there, a point that has recently been discussed by C. Evans (1987); it is a topic that could not have been discussed without an over-generous imagination prior to the large-scale excavation and survey projects of the past twenty or so years. Campaigns such as Fengate, the Welland Valley Project, the Fenland Survey, Stonea, Haddenham and its environs (*e.g.* the Upper Delphs) have provided some of the secure data we require for inter-regional comparisons, but we are still only at the outset. Nonetheless, ten years ago it would have been impossible to compare the Neolithic Bronze or Iron Ages of fenland with those of similar regions on the Continent: the Rhine/Meuse delta, the lower-lying parts of the North European Plain or the Alpine and sub-Alpine regions of southern Germany, Switzerland, France and Italy. Detailed formal studies have yet to be attempted, it is true, but much informal comparison takes place at conferences and colloquia — and this would have and this would have been impossible until quite recently. So progress has most decidedly been made.

The completion of the main, first, phase of the Fenland Survey (which the dyke survey is complementary to) has clearly shown that fenland has distinct physiographic regions. It has also demonstrated that certain areas would not repay close archaeological attention either because they have been so severely damaged by agriculture, quarrying or drainage, or because the archaeological deposits of real interest are too deeply buried. Accordingly archaeologists are beginning to define their own areas of study, perhaps they could be called 'territories'. It should not be forgotten, however, that these territories are defined by largely modern criteria, such as travel costs, recent farming, mineral extractive or housing practices; accordingly they may bear scant relationship to ancient patterns of settlement and land-use.

Three problem areas have been touched on: taphonomy, social complexity and regional definition. There is of course one other: personal bias. All of us involved with fenland archaeology are products of the twentieth century and we see the past from a modern standpoint. This has been a long-standing theoretical objection (*e.g.* Hodder 1982, 211) to the supposed objectivity of much empirical archaeological research, such as that offered in the present volume. We acknowledge it, but proceed nonetheless. There is in addition a more practical interpretive problem that could also be termed 'personal': the once vast wetlands of Europe have been drained or at best greatly restricted. We may visit the Camargue or Wicken Fen or even the Blackwater estuary, but that is not the same as having been born and brought up in these places. Indeed it is probably fair to say that the Bronze Age landscape of fenland would seem as foreign to us today as Saharan Africa, for no amount of reading can replace actual experience; this is a point that Petrequin (*e.g.* 1984), seemingly alone, has fully realised. Accordingly, the interpretive perils of simplistically applying dry land models, or even our own dry land common sense, to wetland situations are very real and have recently been pointed out clearly (Barrett 1987).

Dyke Survey: an Introduction

The fens are, or rather were, Britain's largest wetland. They formed in a large basin and consist of various layers of water-borne and water-influenced deposits. These different beds are discussed in detail elsewhere in this volume (see Chapter 1, Part IV), but their origins are essentially twofold: freshwater and marine. The former include finer particle clastic deposits such as alluvial clays or silts and peats of various types, the latter are mainly silts or fine sands nearer the Wash.

The various fresh- and salt-water deposits accumulated through time and buried old land surfaces beneath them. The vast acreages of ancient buried soil provide one of the most under-studied archaeological resources yet found beneath the sediments of fenland. Whilst these soils have often been subject to natural and man-induced erosion, they are generally sufficiently well preserved (and dated) to discern their *original* soil type and history of development, including man's role therein. These soils, moreover, are often waterlogged and therefore allow the preservation (for analysis) of pollen. In short, these extensive areas of buried soils could provide unparallelled information and on a grand scale.

Usually buried land surfaces become partially visible when material from them appears on the modern land surface, following deflation of superficial material. By then it is usually too late to recover much usable archaeological information, other than the fact that the material is there: a flint scatter, or whatever. In certain cases buried upstanding monuments, such as barrows, are seen to protrude through the modern ploughsoil, as the land 'shrinks' following drainage. This provides an excellent indication that a buried soil lies intact and often not far below the surface.

The example given above illustrates the potential of the region: not only will the barrows in question be untouched by antiquarians and others, as most of the ground 'shrinkage' is very recent, but many may also be waterlogged. This is not all, however, for the land *between* and not just that *beneath* the barrows is intact and this allows 'off-site' studies to be undertaken with some confidence, provided, that is, the overburden can somehow be 'seen through' or removed.

Organic material is, of course, preserved in wet areas and aspects of past technology usually denied to the dryland archaeologist may readily be studied there (Coles 1984). However, another aspect of fenland which is not always appreciated is its relative alkalinity. The principal rivers that drain into the fen basin carry calcareous run-off, and most of the gravels or the fen-edge and 'islands' are either calcareous or circum-neutral. Thus most 'damp' (*i.e.* partially waterlogged) and truly wet sites also produce well-preserved molluscan and bone remains, thereby adding important components to the already environmentally-rich spectrum of available evidence.

The history behind the development of the current dyke survey's methods is described in a recent publication (Pryor 1985) and it need not be repeated at length here. Similarly the project's original research aims and theoretical rationale are outlined in another, joint, paper published in the same year (Crowther *et al.* 1985). Suffice it to say that the present project arose after a period of trial and error; in essence, the problem boiled down to 'seeing through' or removing overburden. 'Seeing through' essentially employs geophysical and geochemical techniques or remote sensing (especially heat-sensitive media). Various of these techniques have been employed and not all successfully; all however are relatively slow and expensive, especially given the size of the buried fenland landscapes, which may sometimes cover many square kilometres. Indeed, survey techniques that 'see through' overburden are generally not suitable for conventional site prospection unless the area involved is small and well delimited. They are, however, very well suited for defining the boundaries of sites revealed in other ways. They are virtually useless for 'off-site' archaeology where the finds or features may be very small and widely separated.

The digging of drainage ditches, or dykes, necessarily involves the disturbance of *in situ* material, but it is not completely divorced from its original context. Most upcast from drainage dykes is mechanically dragged back from (and at right-angles to) the dyke brink. Generally, there-

fore, finds made on the field surface as far away as twenty metres or more from the dykeside, can have their original position in the ditch located quite accurately. Furthermore, most dykesides contain just a single horizon that produces archaeological material, so relocation of disturbed items can often be relatively precise.

The walking of spread, or unspread, spoil heaps alongside dykes is a useful adjunct to the much more effective technique in which the freshly exposed strata in the dykesides are closely examined. Here finds and features are both revealed and it becomes possible to examine the buried soils both in, around or between settlements or other types of site. This requires the ability to walk at 45 degrees on a slippery dykeside and is not as straightforward as it sounds, but it is nonetheless very effective. The recording of the buried strata revealed in the dykeside and the various sampling and levelling procedures are discussed in Part III of this chapter.

The principal drawback of dyke survey is that it is haphazard, rather than random, in the sampling theory sense of the word (Cherry *et al.* 1978). Furthermore, the direction and layout of dykes will tend to respect the drainage history of a given area and this in turn will usually have been a response to various engineering problems. Engineering problems themselves may be caused by 'running silts' or particularly low-lying stretches of fen, to name but a few. In other words, the layout of dykes will often ultimately reflect the original micro-topography of the fen. So the arrangement of dykes is most decidedly not haphazard in engineering terms and will bear some relationship to the pre-existing landscape.

Water is most efficiently removed via the shortest distance, and with the greatest possible slope. Dykes are accordingly often arranged at right angles to the contours and will often therefore provide a good selection of landtypes to examine. There is a tendency for shorter dykes to radiate from around the edges of relict 'islands' in a distinctive pattern, whereas deep clay or silt-filled basins are traversed by long straight dykes running parallel to each other in a rectilinear fashion; if, as usually happens, choices have to be made, the former, radial-pattern, dykes will be examined more closely than the latter, rectilinear, group.

Viewed as an exercise in probabilistic sampling, the dyke survey is haphazard indeed everything that a good sampling design should avoid. However, the dykes are there and they have revealed an extraordinary series of buried sites and landscapes (*i.e.* 'off-sites'). In these circumstances we must recognise the limitations and potential biasses of our sample, insofar as this is possible, and we try to redress obvious imbalances when time and finance permit. For example, experience has shown that most ancient activity is concentrated around and on relict 'islands' or the 'wavey' edge of the fen itself, hence the attention paid to radial-pattern dykes. These are the areas where buried soils can be expected and where habitation sites of all periods can confidently be predicted. The survey of these dykes is seldom uneventful.

The long, straight dykes of the deeper silt fen or the large peatlands around Whittlesey Mere, for example, are very different. One may walk for days, carrying heavy equipment, and record little else than the level of the water and the dyke surface at selected profile locations. But when discoveries are made in these otherwise unprepossessing regions they are often unusual and unexpected: the

Guy's Fen trackway (Chapter 3, Part III) or the Flag Fen Bronze Age platform (Chapter 3, Part IV), to name but two. It must, however, be admitted that it is the possibility of discovering something unusual that encourages the survey of less archaeologically promising areas, rather than the knowledge that one is helping to redress a sampling bias.

The archaeological objectives of the survey are now becoming better defined as our knowledge of the fen and fen-edge in the Peterborough region accumulates. The various regions selected for special attention are discussed in four parts in Chapter 3. Inevitably attention has focussed around the two areas of most of the intensive recent archaeological research, namely the lower Welland Valley and the Peterborough Fen-edge at Fengate and Flag Fen. We have also moved further afield, to the deeper fen deposits of the east, and in so doing it would appear that the two regions might soon be drawn together. Ten years ago it was thought that the way to unite the two lay west of Peterborough, across the uplands. We now know (Pryor and French 1985) that this route is not available, due to the depredations of agriculture in fragile limestone soils. Ironically the same processes are enabling us to examine the buried landscapes to the east; thereby allowing us to attain the same goal via a different road.

The dyke survey then has clear archaeological goals which are also reflected in future plans (see Chapter 4, Part II). But it also has an important site management function: namely the monitoring of the effects of desiccation on the various deposits, buried and surface, encountered in the dykes. This is why all deposits are levelled-in and why the drawn outline profiles (see Chapter 2, part II) are backed-up by a comprehensive collection of colour slides a selection of which is included in the microfiche accompanying this volume. In twenty or thirty years' time this will provide a very important record of fen stratigraphy. Incidentally, most profile slides are accompanied by wider views along dykes to establish relative locations; these wider views, housed in the project archive, will provide an important record of fenland topography for future students of landscape change.

II. Background to the project
by C. French and F. Pryor
(Figs 1-3)

The southwest fen-edge or dyke survey project arose from the extensive fen edge excavations at Fengate in the lower Nene valley (Pryor 1974, 1978, 1980a, 1984) and at Maxey (Pryor and French 1985) Etton (Pryor et al. 1985) and elsewhere, in the lower Welland valley. Recent work in the deeper fen by David Hall, then the Fenland Project's field officer, demonstrated that the cropmark landscapes of the fen-edge extended further east than was once supposed (Hall 1987); at the same time contacts were established with Dutch colleagues of the the Instituut voor Prae- en Protohistorie, University of Amsterdam, who were carrying out a form of dyke survey, as part of the Assendelver Polder Project (Brandt et al. 1987).

It was soon apparent that immediately east of the Peterborough fen-edge there lay a vast buried landscape, protected by recent sediments, which was largely unexplored, except where upstanding monuments protruded through its eroding surface (Figs 1–3). Furthermore, this untapped prehistoric landscape would provide new data,

hopefully free from the worst of the post-depositional distortions that normally affect the interpretation of surface field survey data (Crowther et al. 1985). Significant buried environmental deposits were also anticipated and it was hoped that these could be assessed in close conjunction with the palynological survey being undertaken by the Fenland Project's palaeoenvironmentalist, Dr Martyn Waller (Waller forthcoming). Given the extraordinary nature of the buried landscapes, special emphasis would also be given to the monitoring of post-drainage effects, such as the shrinking, truncation or distortion of buried and surface sediments. These general objectives have remained constant throughout the survey, although there have been minor modifications brought about by changing circumstances; they have been further discussed in two earlier papers (Pryor 1983b, 1985; Crowther et al. 1985).

It is probably fair to say that prior to the 1970s, the fens of Cambridgeshire had received surprisingly little attention from prehistorians. There are several reasons for this. Fenland consists of extensive spreads of superficial and relatively recent deposits that effectively obscure surface distributions, except around the fen-edge and 'islands'; in addition, only the largest earthworks can protrude through this blanketing material, and even these are rare: doubtless many still remain totally buried in the deep fen. Pre-Roman cropmarks are generally absent on true fen soils, and the region is one of the most intensively farmed in modern Europe. Consequently it is very difficult to 'do' conventional prehistoric archaeology in such an area. Studies of site distribution and hierarchy, for example, are made difficult because of the unknown quantity of missing sites. Thus most studies tend to be site-specific in archaeological, if not in environmental scope. Indeed, the only attempt at a regional synthesis has concerned the Roman period, where occupation is generally visible above the blanketing deposits (Phillips 1970). Indeed in some places Roman earthworks survived intact until the 1950s (Potter 1981), and their many cropmarks are still clearly visible, following ploughing (Phillips 1970). Nevertheless, even this record can now be shown to be incomplete, following Hall's most recent fieldwork (Hall 1987). All fieldworkers are agreed, however, that the threat to these buried landscapes from agriculture and land drainage continues unabated.

The practical problems outlined above determined that we should follow the long-established archaeological principle of working from the known to the unknown; in the present case this meant that we should proceed from the comparatively well-understood fen-edge, eastwards into deeper, and more obscure, fen deposits.

The Fengate and lower Welland valley projects referred to above gave us an impression of the archaeological potential of the deeper fen, but they were only a small, and relatively elevated, part of the landscape that was available to prehistoric communities. It is now apparent, for example, that the Peterborough fen-edge, which slopes gently eastwards over the terrace gravels and merges with the Fen gravels over a vast tract of largely arable landscape, is particularly important as it involves a necessarily gradual transition first from dry, then to damp and finally to wet environments. The bulk of this landscape is protected by blanketing and quite recently deposited alluvium with peat towards the eastern fen-edge proper. These are the type of surroundings where one might expect to find the earlier Neolithic landscapes which are only just beginning to be identified in the lower Welland valley (French and Pryor, in preparation).

Moving deeper into the fens, the former, largely dry, Flandrian landscape is buried by a succession of relatively well dated, mainly marine, superficial deposits. They provide a series of fixed chronological horizons, which may be used to date other, more ephemeral, episodes with some precision. Needless to say, the work of the Fenland Project's environmentalist, Dr M. Waller, has revealed that the sequence and dating, even of the well-established and widely occurring deposits is far more complex than hitherto realised (see Part IV below).

The widespread occurrence of the various 'marker' episodes (usually marine transgressions and associated freshwater back-up) allows closely dated stratigraphies to be studied over wide areas, and to a certain extent it also has predictive value: sites of various periods are often found to cluster around certain levels above OD. One would not, for example, expect to find Iron Age settlement much below 1–2m OD, nor wet Neolithic sites above that level.

The vast acreages of prehistoric soil that lie buried beneath superficial deposits are still largely unstudied. Whilst these soils have often been subjected to both natural and anthropogenic erosion, they are generally sufficiently well preserved (and dated) for it to be possible to discern their original soil type and subsequent development. These soils, moreover, are often waterlogged and contain pollen.

Finally, it is not always appreciated that the soils of fenland are primarily base-rich. The principal rivers that drain into the great fen basin carry calcareous run-off, and most of the gravels of the fen-edge and 'islands' are either calcareous or circum-neutral. Thus most 'damp' and wet sites also produce well preserved molluscan and bone remains, thereby adding greatly to an already rich spectrum of environmental evidence. It should be mentioned here that the term 'damp' has a specific meaning when it is applied to archaeological sites with high ground water tables, where deeper features penetrate to permanently waterlogged levels.

Despite their environmental potential, the major archaeological problem of the fens remained one of accessibility, but the answer lay close at hand, unappreciated for many years. Each spring and autumn the various drainage boards both clean out, deepen and widen drainage dykes on a regular basis, approximately every five to seven years. In effect, these works often expose long sections through buried landcapes and allow the selective examination and sampling of significant deposits. Clearly the selection of dykes for recutting or maintenance is an engineering decision, not related to archaeological criteria in any way, but dykes are selected by the Commissioners of the various internal drainage boards, usually for sound agricultural reasons. In other words, the drainage authorities know best where the wettest parts of the fen still survive, as that is where their efforts are concentrated. It therefore behoves archaeologists to examine those areas closely, before they are de-watered. Finally, the approach to dyke survey must be flexible and adaptable in the field, able to allow anything from simple recording and levelling, to augering, or even to small-scale problem-orientated excavation.

III. Techniques of dyke survey
(Figs 12, 75)

Dyke survey arose from the simple observation that farmers and drainage authorities clean out or enlarge their drainage ditches in the autumn, winter and early spring. Almost every field in the fens is bounded by four dykes, and these are cleaned out periodically, perhaps every five to seven years. Each time a dyke is cleaned mechanically it is deepened and widened to give a clean, open V-shape. This type of cleaning is ideal for archaeological purposes as it reveals a complete section of from c.2–4 m depth. The drainage authorities also carry out drainage improvements which involve the production of complete and often new profiles. Ditch bottom maintenance or 'slubbing out' is rarely of much archaeological use.

Initially the dyke survey was confined to the fen and fen-edge immediately northeast and east of Peterborough and to the lower valleys of the Nene and Welland. Since then the whole of the North Bedford Level (known as the North Level and comprising the Peakirk/Newborough/Eye/Thorney area between the River Nene and the Lincolnshire border) has come under scrutiny, and more recently the Middle Bedford Level (the Whittlesey/March/Ramsey area) and the remainder of the Cambridgeshire fens. These areas of dyke survey will be reported upon in future reports. The area and scope of the survey has enlarged as techniques have improved and as funds for drainage work have become harder to obtain; this in turn has meant that fewer dykes are currently being renovated so that a larger area can be covered adequately by a single team.

The basic record is composed of five elements:
1. 25-inch base maps.
2. 35 mm colour slides.
3. levelled-in sketches of dyke-side sections.
4. levelled-in dyke profiles at appropriate intervals .
5. notes on the stratigraphy and the nature of the buried soil, which are entered on a proforma dyke record sheet (Fig. 75).

Every cleaned dyke is examined along its entire length, but only selected profiles are noted in detail. The base map locates every dyke examined and records the position of all profiles. The position of archaeological artefacts and of any samples taken are similarly recorded. The slides taken include general views of the dykes and the landscape around them, as well as the profiles themselves. Water surfaces are also levelled-in and dated.

Experience has shown that it is impossible to make hard-and-fast decisions about the spacing and recording of dyke-side profiles. Initially 50m intervals were tried, but when we were confronted by several kilometres of featureless expanse of marine silts (where human occupation was obviously impossible), much wider intervals of about 150m were employed. In other cases, for example around the eroding fringes of buried 'islands', profiles were recorded at every 10 or 20m, depending on what was encountered; and in a few cases such as Crowtree Farm (Fig.12) the system of narrow profiles was replaced by a more conventional continuous (or linear) section drawing. It should be noted that whatever the sample or profile interval chosen, the full procedure must be carried through: photograph, level, draw, note and map. The levelling is crucial as a means of relating profiles in different parts of the fen; accurate levels are also essential to the correlation of buried land surfaces, occupation horizons and marine transgression episodes.

The apparent lack of a stated sampling strategy is deliberate, but nonetheless requires some explanation. The network of dykes is haphazard, but does conform in its fundamental layout to the region's topography and geology. Therefore it cannot be considered as 'random' in the strictly probabilistic sense (Stuart 1976); if it represents a judgement sample, then the judgement exercised was not ours. It seems best, therefore, to treat the dyke network as haphazard and this does not constitute a proper basis for probabilistic sampling procedures. Although the basis of the survey might be seen by some as fundamentally flawed, an attempt is nonetheless to achieve a reasonably balanced coverage of the whole area: for example, every dyke, no matter how short, is at least sampled at the beginning, middle and end. This also allows an estimate to be made of the rise and fall of the subsoil or buried soil layers. The approximate maximum sampling interval of 150m also helps to maintain balance.

A pragmatic approach is also employed in the selection of soil samples for phosphate analysis (Appendix III), magnetic susceptibility (Appendix III), molluscan analysis (Appendix I), soil micromorphology (Appendix II) and pollen analysis. Putting it crudely, if the terrain looks promising, samples are taken. It was originally intended to take samples for geophysical and geochemical analyses at regular intervals in every dyke, but this intention was quickly given up as the time and resources were simply not available, given the large numbers of dykes that were being machine-cleaned (some pilot studies were however made before the approach was modified). The techniques employed are discussed in more detail in Appendix III. Although the results are promising, much more experimentation with different kinds of apparatus and methodologies is required before worthwhile geophysical or geochemical surveys are feasible on an extensive scale.

The initial years of dyke survey in the North Level area, have made it possible to isolate several potential sites and to do more intensive fieldwork to ascertain their true nature. The latter has involved two stages of further research. The first stage is an intensive augering survey at intervals of 5 or 10m moving outwards from the suspected site as revealed in the dyke-side, in conjunction with the levelling in of each stratigraphic change in the boreholes. The numerous borehole logs made available by the British Geological Survey have also proved to be of valuable assistance. It has been possible to delimit the probable extent of the site concerned, and if done in sufficient detail, also to produce contour maps of the archaeologically relevant surface. In a few cases, it has been possible to follow this stage with small (c.2 × 2m) test excavation trenches. This has enabled the retrieval of artefacts and the taking of undisturbed soil and pollen samples in particular. In effect this is the 'Phase Two' currently envisaged by the Fenland Project Committee as the follow-up to the extensive field survey. Experience has shown that it is only by a variety of techniques, such as those described in more detail below, that a prospective site may be assessed in terms of its archaeological and environmental potential, the degree of waterlogging and preservation, and the possibilities for future preservation or conservation.

In conclusion, dyke survey identifies potential sites which are generally not recoverable by surface survey or remote sensing techniques. Once discovered, it then becomes possible to define their size and place them in their landscape contexts (a process that may often involve 'off-site' procedures). Once defined, the sites' potential may be assessed and their continuing survival monitored. Finally, an informed decision may then be made on future management.

IV. Geology, soils, environment and dating
by Charles French

Present day climate and vegetation
The region under review is on the western fen margin of East Anglia and situated where the sub-oceanic British climate is becoming more continental. When compared with the average for Britain, annual and diurnal temperature ranges tend to be greater, and annual precipitation less, but with a summer convectional maximum higher. The climate figures given below were obtained from RAF Wittering and Abbeyfields, Peterborough, just outside the study area to the west, and refer to the years between 1955 and 1974. The mean temperature range has a low of 3.3°C in January and a high of 15.9°C in July. There are air frosts during the months of November to April inclusive (Burton 1981).

The mean annual rainfall for the area is low, 577mm for Wittering and 563mm for Abbeyfields, Peterborough, in comparison to the west of Britain. Six months of the year (June to August, November to January) have an average in excess of 50mm rainfall. The June to August maximum of 28.6% of the annual average rainfall is associated with the continental character of the area. February to April are the driest months with 20.9% of the annual average rainfall (Burton 1981).

The daily mean duration of sunshine in hours varies from 1.63 hours in December to 6.9 hours in June. The sunniest months of the year are May and June (Burton 1981).

The study area today is dominated by arable land, almost entirely of classes 2 and 3, but ranging from classes 1 to 5 (after Bibby and Mackney 1969; Seale and Hodge 1976). The fenland landscape is flat and dominated by large arable fields delimited by drainage dykes. Trees such as willow and poplar, tend only to be around farm buildings and along road verges and ditches. Hedges and stands of trees are now generally absent.

Prior to recent drainage which began in the mid-17th century, this part of the fenland landscape would have looked markedly different. The peat fen surface would have been c.2.5 and 4.5m above Ordnance Datum, as opposed to the present day level of between c. -1.0 and +1.0m OD. It would have been drained by a series of winding channels, with the surface otherwise broken only by small sand and gravel 'islands' and peninsulas varying in size from a few hundred square metres to several thousand hectares.

Geology of the North Level
(Fig. 3)
The area can be divided into three broad topographical categories: lowland terrace (alluviated and non-alluviated gravels), fen-edge (or 'skirtland' covered by thin peat and alluvium) and fenland basin (infilled with peat, fen clay or Barroway Drove Beds, Terrington Beds).

Pre-Flandrian deposits

Before discussing the geology of the fen basin itself, it is necessary to discuss the two main Pleistocene drift deposits in the study area: the river terrace sands and gravels and the less extensive marine/estuarine gravels.

The river terrace deposits of sands, gravels and alluvium are the most extensive drift deposits in the area on either side of the present rivers Welland and Nene (Fig. 3). They consist of varying thicknesses of current-bedded sand and gravel made up of limestone and flint with Bunter pebbles and ironstone (Burton 1981). The Welland river terraces (mainly First Terrace) widen out into a broad fan to the east of Maxey and coalesce with the fen margin gravels to the east of Etton forming an extensive flat around the western edge of the fenland basin (Burton 1981). This flat could have formed as alluvial fan deposits of First Terrace age (Booth 1982). The gravels overlie Oxford Clay or Kellaways Sand or Clay. These same geological substrates sweep in a wide arc from the south to the north side of the Nene valley around the east side of Peterborough (Horton *et al.* 1974). First Terrace deposits are found on the eastern margins of present day Peterborough, and consist of limestone and ironstone debris containing flint, quartzite and other erratic pebbles derived from glacial drift. They may also contain seams of sand and clay. The river terrace gravels represent predecessors of the present river system (Horton *et al.* 1974).

Skertchly (1877) originally described three types of exposed sand and gravel deposits in East Anglia as 'Fen gravels'. More recently, this term has been applied specifically to the extensive flat northeast of Peterborough (Horton *et al.* 1974). The term 'Fen gravels' was also applied to gravels beneath later (*i.e.* Flandrian) fen deposits by Skertchly (1877) and Horton *et al.* (1974).

The Fen gravels were all originally thought to be of marine origin (Skertchly 1877) because of the occurrence of sporadic non-fluviatile shell fragments. They were also correlated with the March Gravels on the basis of a similarity in molluscan faunas. But it is now suggested (Booth 1982) that both these shelly gravels are marine/estuarine in origin, rather than exclusively marine.

The survey by Booth (1982) confirms the two-fold sub-division of the Fen gravels and demonstrates that they may be differentiated by height into two divisions, each of which has a fluviatile and a marine/estuarine facies. The low altimetric level consists of alluvial river gravels of the Nene (and Welland) First Terrace to the west and Fen (or marine/estuarine) gravels to the east, for example at Northey 'island' and between Eye and Thorney. The high altimetric level consists of alluvial river gravels of the Nene (and Welland) Second Terrace to the west and the March (marine/estuarine) gravels to the east, for example at Eye, Thorney and Whittlesey 'islands' (Booth 1982). Moreover West (1987) has also suggested that the term 'March Gravels' may include both Ipswichian (interglacial) sediments and Devensian (last glaciation) sands and gravels.

The long peninsula of marine/estuarine gravel (or March Gravels) which extend northeastwards from Eye to The Engine (TF 52593079) may represent a former watershed between the Rivers Welland and Nene during First Terrace times to the northwest, First Terrace deposits are thin or absent except for a southwest to northeast gravel-filled channel reaching as far as Crowland. These thin First Terrace deposits may be attenuated examples of a large fan-like spread of gravel deposited into the Fen basin by the River Welland (Booth 1982).

A relatively thin (*c.* 0.4–2.0m) spread of loamy sands and silts with scattered gravel pebbles overlies much of the First Terrace gravels. They are interpreted either as the final stages of aggradation, or an older alluvium (A. Horton and R.J. Wyatt pers. comm. to Booth, 1982), or as a soil resulting from the weathering of the terrace surface (A.J. Dixon, pers. comm. to Booth, 1982). Soil micromorphological analysis of the upper surface of these deposits is discussed below (Chapter 3: Parts I, II and IV).

The gravels in the fen basin are often overlain by a thin heterogeneous deposit of silty, sandy clays and clayey sand containing scattered gravel pebbles. This deposit is called the 'Crowland Bed', and probably correlates with the older alluvium/soil mentioned above (Booth 1982). Although its origin is uncertain, Burton (1987) has suggested that it may be a solifluction deposit.

Flandrian deposits: the fen basin
At the beginning of the post-glacial period, the fen basin was dry land whose substrate comprised Jurassic deposits: mainly Oxford Clay and Cretaceous formations in the south, mainly chalk and sand with glacial clays and gravels overlying these in other places (Fig. 3). The Oxford Clay comprises bluish grey and greenish grey mudstone which weathers to a pale grey plastic clay and produces a heavy clay soil (Booth 1982). The surface geology and soils of the fen basin differed little from the adjacent uplands, although the basin contained a number of low knolls which are now the fen 'islands'; rivers probably had narrower floodplains than at present (Perrin and Hodge in Steers 1965, 68–84).

During the post-glacial climatic amelioration, a deciduous forest established itself in the fen basin (Godwin 1975). It is now believed that lime was very abundant in this forest (Grieg 1982; M. Waller pers. comm.). Throughout, the sea level continued to rise, although probably in a fluctuating manner, from a possible lowest point at the end of the Devensian, to reach its present height more or less during the 1st millennium AD (Jelgersma 1966; Simmons and Tooley 1981; Shennan 1982b) (see below for a discussion of sea level change). Consequently, the drainage of the fen basin became severely impeded and resulted in freshwater flooding and the formation of a marsh. A eutrophic wood/reed peat began to form in this freshwater fen as a regional response to rising base water levels. The earliest dated basal peat is at Elm Tree Farm, Tydd St Giles, in the northeastern corner of the North Level with a date of (SRR1757) 7690 ± 400 BP at *c.*-9.10m OD (see Appendix V.I), and there is evidence of early peat growth by (Hv10011) *c.*6575 BP at Adventurer's Land in the southeastern corner of the North Level (Shennan 1986 a). There are also peat accumulations in buried channels which do not relate to regional base levels. For example, there is a date of (Q588) 8620 ± 160 BP at *c.*-4.3m OD at Peacock's Farm (Shippea Hill), Littleport.

There are problems in continuing to use the term 'lower' peat as a stratigraphic unit defined by radiocarbon dates. Traditionally the lower peat has been assigned a date span of *c.*6800-4700 BP (Godwin 1975). However, there are now many dates for basal peats which occur after 4700 BP, for example at Lade Bank, Feltwell, Flaggrass and Werrington. It is now best to use the term 'basal' peat, and to consider each profile as an individual unit.

6

There is now evidence to suggest that there were shallow incursions of the sea prior to the main deposition of the fen clay; these marine or brackish sediments would have been limited in extent and probably only extended along the valleys of the major fen rivers. Silty clay sediments were deposited shortly after 6415 BP and again at c.6200–5600 BP at Adventurer's Land for example (Shennan 1986 a, b). Peat growth would have continued further 'inland', for example at sites such as Holme Fen and Shippea Hill (Shennan 1986b).

Growth of the 'lower' peat was later interrupted by the deposition of a marine/brackish silty clay or the fen clay which inundated most of the fen basin. This is the 'buttery' clay of earlier authors (cf. Skertchly 1877, 173). The fen clay consists of soft, wet, bluish grey clays and silts with occasional silt laminae (Booth 1982), which range from silt loams to silty clay loams to silty clays (Shennan 1986a). Beyond the landward limit of the fen clay, peat formation continued.

Prior to recent research, the fen clay marine incursion was dated to the Neolithic period in the South Level of the fens, c.4800 to 4200 BP. More recently, however, it has been recognised that the incursion 'event' comprised a number of smaller episodes which were not necessarily synchronous across the whole of fenland: the marine sediments in the March/Ramsey/Whittlesey area to the north, for example, were attributed to a later date and apparently a separate episode from c.4200 to 3300 BP (Shennan 1986b). However, recent investigations by the Fenland Project within the Shippea Hill basin at Feltwell, on the southeastern fen-edge, suggest that the onset of marine conditions away from the incised river channels, and close to its maximum extent, are later than generally supposed, from c.4135 to 3815 BP (Waller pers. comm.).

The fen clay or Barroway Drove Beds has been variously described as indicative of lagoonal, salt marsh or mud flat conditions. Each is a different environment capable of giving rise to very fine-grained deposit, not unlike the fen clay. The evidence suggests that the fen clay was probably deposited in a low energy, high tidal salt marsh environment. The silty clays may have been deposited in quiet water between more silty ridges formed by the drainage creeks (Godwin 1940), and would only be flooded by high energy spring tides (Shennan 1986b). Indeed the marine or brackish deposits were probably gradually infilling an embayment. Seawards, the environment would tend towards more silty and sandy salt marsh; whereas landward, pools would be fringed by Phragmites reedswamp with a gradual transition to areas of peat accumulation (Shennan 1986b).

The fen clay salt marsh was drained by a network of roddons (or rodhams) which were channels infilled with silt and fine sand; they are usually interpreted as fossil tidal or salt marsh creeks. Like most present day salt marsh creeks (and in contrast to tidal flat creeks) they show little evidence of channel migration through active meandering. Their incision and infilling, however, must be regarded as two separate events. Between these two events, the balance shifted from erosion and scouring of the roddon floor (maintaining it as a channel), to landward transport and deposition of silt and fine sand (leading to the blocking-up of the channel). The reasons for this are as yet unknown (Zalaciewicz 1985/6), but Zalaciewicz and Wilmot (1986) have suggested the possibility that regional sedimentary accumulation may be affecting the tidal geometry, thereby causing roddons to silt-up. They also argue that there may be a causal link between the apparent coincidence of the silted-up roddons and the transition from fen clay to peat. The silting-up of the roddons meant that the clay supply from seaward had ceased, and this may in itself have initiated peat formation. This model satisfactorily removes the need to invoke sea level fluctuations as the direct control determining clay/peat transitions.

Subsequent to the first marine transgressions represented by the fen clay, an upper peat (the Nordelph peat) began to form. It is mainly formed under eutrophic conditions, from the earlier Bronze Age (from c.3500 BP) until recent times, only ceasing with the drainage of the fens from the mid 17th century onwards (Godwin 1975; 1978). The upper peat is now desiccated and much reduced by deflation, and tends to be a very humified, detrital/reed peat, with alluvial material often intermixed with its upper surface.

The fen to the north and northwest of Thorney in the North Level was subject to a second marine transgression phase subsequent to the fen clay (or Barroway Drove Bed) episode and coincident with the growth of the upper peat elsewhere in the fens. This phase of marine flooding deposited a grey silty clay, very closely similar to the fen clay itself, but less sticky and plastic in consistency and containing a greater proportion of silt. Although this deposit has rarely been differentiated from the fen clay by previous workers, it has been observed and mapped in Hall's (1987) field survey, the dyke survey by the present authors and in the British Geological Survey's recent survey (Zalaciewicz 1985/6; Zalaciewicz and Wilmot 1986) and has been termed the 'younger' or 'upper' Barroway Drove Beds. Parts of the previous (fen clay) dendritic channel system were still functioning, as small amounts of this younger Barroway Drove Bed material have been observed in the centre channels, otherwise almost completely infilled with Barroway Drove Bed deposits (Hall 1987).

The approximate date of the younger Barroway Drove Beds is believed to be late 2nd/early 1st millennium BC or the later Bronze Age (Hall 1987; Waller pers. comm.). Dyke exposures in Thorney parish show the silty clays overlying Barroway Drove Beds (or fen clay), with later (Iron Age) Terrington Bed silts above.

Recent radiocarbon dates from sites on the Wisbech A47 bypass indicate the onset of a late Iron Age marine phase after c.2000 BP, but only in the Wisbech area. However, it is still not yet possible to link the Wisbech area marine episode to the main Terrington Bed marine phase which occurred widely in south Lincolnshire (Waller forthcoming).

The northern fens (predominantly in south Lincolnshire) received a later series of marine transgressions which deposited silt (the Terrington Beds) during the late 1st millennium BC/very early 1st millennium AD (Godwin 1975; Hall 1987). Terrington Bed silts are only found in the North Level to the north of Thorney in the vicinity of Crowland (Fig. 3). But the southern fens (mainly Cambridgeshire) were probably rarely affected by this incursion, possibly due to the development of the upper peat which prevented significant marine penetration inland. There is some evidence of another transgression between the 5th and 7th centuries AD (Hallam 1970), designated by Shennan (1986b) Wash VII. Further possible wet episodes occurred in the late 13th, 14th and

15th centuries AD (Darby 1940a; Hallam 1961; Ravensdale 1974). All these later marine episodes are confined to the Wash coastal areas, as there are no marine deposits in Cambridgeshire after late Iron Age times (Hall 1987).

Alluvium
Extensive areas of the Welland and Nene river terrace gravels are covered with alluvium. In the lower Welland valley where the river crosses the gravel terraces with diminished gradient, alluvium has been deposited in former channels or on shelves cut into the gravels (Burton 1981). In the lower Nene valley, the alluvium fills a channel in the gravels of the First Terrace, which was probably cut by the lateral migration of major river meanders (Horton *et al.* 1974). This event probably began in the later Neolithic period and continued throughout the last two millennia BC (Horton *et al.* 1974).

Extensive areas of fen-edge 'skirtland' are covered with varying thicknesses of alluvium to the east of where the two major rivers enter the fen basin. This great alluvial fan was deposited in the area between the high ground (above the *c.*5m contour) to the west, now mainly occupied by the city of Peterborough, and the silty clay and peat fen deposits of the fen basin to the east. This deposition occurred because of insufficient gradient of the river outfalls and was exacerbated by poorly draining peat fen; it resulted in the ponding-up of freshwater and the consequent laying-down of alluvial sediments along the western fen margin.

Alluvial deposition on the western fen margin, or the western edge of the North Level area, mainly occurred during the last two millennia, and certainly since the Roman period. Few radiocarbon dates are available, but there is corroborative evidence from several archaeological sites. Although there is some evidence to suggest that alluvial material began to be deposited at Etton on the lower Welland valley/fen margin interface, as early as the later Neolithic period, the main period of alluviation probably began during the Roman period and continued until 1953 (Pryor *et al.* 1986; French 1983, 1988a). Similarly at Fengate, on the lower Nene valley/fen margin interface, alluviation began during the later Roman period (Pryor 1984).

The nature of the alluvium itself is largely determined by the original source material. The sediment in river channels is mostly entrained in overland flow, or derived from bank scour and collapse, while only a small proportion comes from the river bed itself. The sediment load consists of bedload or the material which slides or rolls along the stream bed, saltated and suspended load. The sediments may be deposited as gravelly, silty and/or clayey alluvium. Sediment load increases with the rate of discharge which in turn implies a greater capacity for transport. Conversely, as the water level falls the velocity and river bed stress increase, and the capacity for transport is consequently lower (Stratham 1979). A major contributing factor to the sediment load in rivers is the material added by a combination of extensive clearance and agriculture, especially on hill-slopes upstream (Limbrey 1978). Alluvium thus generated would have been deposited in a floodplain of shifting river and stream meanders, with old channels being cut as the water sought alternative drainage routes. As a consequence, considerable depositional distortion of the earlier landscape (with its associated archaeological settlement pattern) may occur.

The so-called 'skirtlands' occur on the western fen margin of the North Level. The term is used to refer to landscapes whose mineral soils (of any type) were previously covered by peat and/or alluvial deposits. The upper edge of the 'skirtland' probably represents the medieval fen-edge (Hall 1981). A band of 'skirtland' surrounds the whole fen on the landward side, with its width varying from a few metres to several kilometres according to the slope of the old land surface into the fen basin (Hall 1987).

Drainage patterns
Throughout the post-glacial period a complex of meandering natural channels continued to drain the fen basin, with greater or lesser efficiency. However, following the widespread drainage of the 17th century and consequent peat wastage, the now-infilled late Neolithic/Bronze Age dendritic watercourses are left upstanding as roddons; in the field they show-up as pale, sinuous banks composed of silts and fine sands (Chatwin 1961; Hall 1981; Zalaciewicz 1985/6). Recently Evans (1979) has attempted to discern earlier courses of the River Nene, which he now believes was split into several channels south of Whittlesey; near March it forced a new channel, probably as a result of blockages caused by the fen clay (Hall 1987). Possible former courses of the River Welland have been found in the form of late Neolithic meandering streams in the vicinity of Maxey and Etton on the north-western fen margin (Pryor *et al.* 1985; in prep.). However, by the Iron Age the Neolithic levels must have been at least two metres below the peat fen surface of the day. Consequently, the previous dendritic system of channels must have long since been infilled, and a new system developed, often where none had existed before (Hall 1987).

A natural fall in the water table during the early Roman period is thought to have caused peat shrinkage and a reduction in the size of old watercourses (Hall 1987; Phillips 1970). This was interrupted in the earlier 3rd century AD by the backing-up of freshwater in many areas and the deposition of alluvial silts at sites such as at Fengate, Earith and Hockwold-cum-Wilton (Churchill 1970; Hall 1987; Pryor 1984; Salway 1967, 1975). This freshwater from the fen hinterland had to find outlets, so a new drainage system was formed in the growing peat fen; a system which probably existed as late as the 17th century. Hall (1987) has identified at least two changes in the drainage system during this latter period: first, the River Nene was diverted away from Elm and through the centre of March possibly in the 10th century AD; second, the Twenty Foot River (or the Elm River) was cut at some time during the medieval period. The cutting of the canalised parts of the River Nene by Bishop Morton *c.*1478 marks the beginning of the modern, drained fenland landscape in the study area (Darby 1940b; Hills 1967; L.E. Harris 1952).

Radiocarbon dates and the stratigraphic sequence of Flandrian deposits in the North Level
(Fig. 2; Table 1)

Previous Research
Before we consider dates produced for the survey by the University of Cambridge Godwin Laboratory (Switsur in

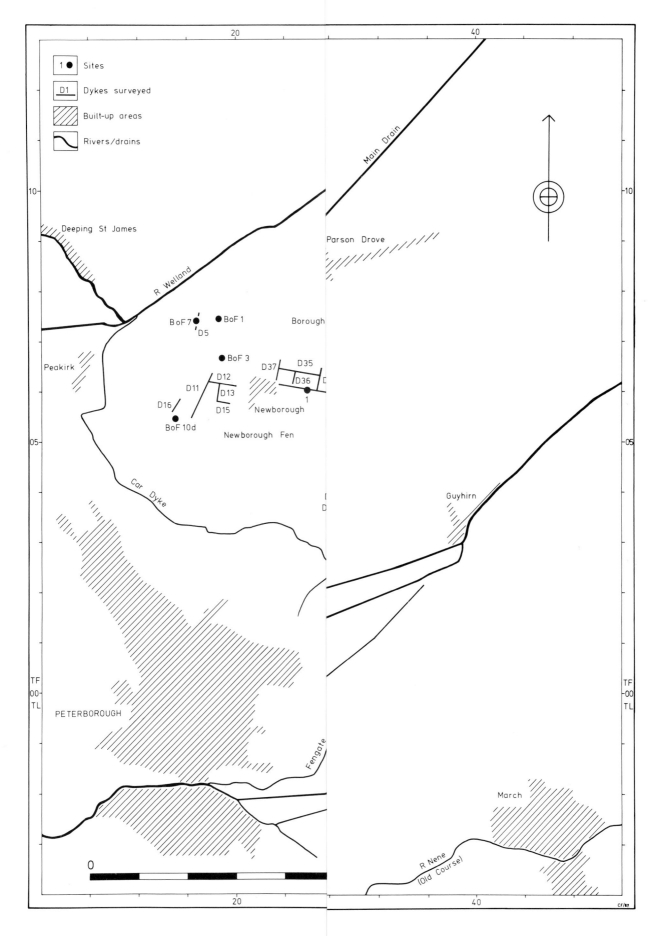

Figure 2 Dykes su

Date BP	Cal.BC*	Location	Grid Reference
Basal peat:			
7690±400		Elm Tree Farm	TF 54010 31487
(SRR-1757)		(-9.12 m OD)	
6575± 95		Adventurer's Land	TF 53567 30182
(Hv-10011)		(-7.89 m OD)	
6415±185		Adventurer's Land	TF 53567 30182
(Hv-9263)		(-8.15 m OD)	
6275±125		Adventurer's Land	TF 53567 30182
(Hv-9262)		(-8.06 m OD)	
6080± 60		Plash Farm	TF 53873 30530
(SRR-1761)		(-8.45 m OD)	
6010±200		Sycamore Farm	TF 53370 31113
(SRR-1763)			
5580± 70	4590-4345	Adventurer's Land	TF 53567 30182
(Hv-9261)		(-8.0 m OD)	
5140± 60	4050-3800	Welland Wash 4	TF 52459 31432
5000± 70	3985-3645	Welland Wash 4	TF 52459 31432
3390± 40	1835-1555	Newborough	TF 51953 30524
(SRR-1768)			
'Middle' peat:			
4520± 70	3425-2945	Plash Farm	TF 53873 30530
(SRR-1760)		(-4.13 m OD)	
4500± 50	3365-3000	Adventurer's Land	TF 53567 30182
(SRR-1590)		(-4.29 m OD)	
4460± 80	3370-2915	Sycamore Farm	TF 53370 31113
(SRR-1762)			
4340± 60	3105-2890	Guyhirn Washes	TF 53810 30198
(SRR-1765)			
4310±140	3355-2545	South Farm	TF 53024 30210
(SRR-1766)			
4180± 75	2925-2540	Adventurer's Land	TF 53567 30182
(SRR-1589)		(-4.08 m OD)	
4030± 80	2865-2380	Welland Wash 4	TF 52459 31432
3860± 80	2535-2120	Welland Wash 4	TF 52459 31432
Upper Peat:			
3250± 50	1680-1420	Gedney Hill	TF 53344 31084
(SRR-1758)			
3080±200	1780- 840	Guyhirn Washes	TF 53810 30198
(SRR-1764)			
3050± 50	1430-1160	Park Farm	TF 54018 31608
(SRR-1756)		(-0.5 m OD)	
2510± 50	810- 420	Plash Farm	TF 53873 30530
(SRR-1759)		(+0.1 m OD)	
2270± 50	415- 205	Plash Farm	TF 54018 31608
(SRR-1750)		(+0.3 m OD)	
2220± 50	410- 160	Newborough	TF 51953 30524
(SRR-1767)			
1845± 50	AD25- 245	Adventurer's Land	TF 53567 30182
(SRR-1588)		(-0.7 m OD)	

* The calibrations quoted are 95% probability, and were supplied by V.R.Switsur, Godwin Laboratory.
Cambridge University.

Table 1. British Geological Survey's Peterborough district radiocarbon dates (A.E. Horton pers.comm.).

Waller forthcoming) a number of earlier determinations require discussion. Attention will be given to a series of dates from Adventurer's Land (Shennan 1986a & b) in the southeastern part of the North Level, and ten sets of radiocarbon dates that are available from the British Geological Survey (A.Horton pers. comm.) (Table 1; Appendix V.I). Dates exist for the lower peat, 'middle' peat (or peat within the fen clay as bands), and the upper or Nordelph peat. These dates were supplied by the Natural Environmental Research Council's laboratory at East Kilbride (SRR), for the British Geological Survey.

The dates for the 'lower' or basal peat range from as early as (SRR1757) 7690 ± 400 BP at Elm Tree Farm, to the northwest of Wisbech, to as late as (BGS) 5140 ± 60 BP (4050–3800 Cal. BC) at Welland Wash Site 4 to the northeast of Peakirk (Table 1). As mentioned previously, the early growth of peat was probably largely confined to the valleys of the major fen rivers (Shennan 1986b). These dates suggest that the onset of growth of the lower peat in northwestern Cambridgeshire occurred during the 5th, 4th and 3rd millennia BC, or throughout the later Mesolithic and Neolithic periods, with the dates becoming later further inland. There are also several much more recent dates for basal peat formation, indeed as late as (SRR1768) 3390 ± 40 BP (1835–1555 Cal. BC) at 'The Firs', Werrington, in Newborough Fen (see Appendix V.I).

Dates for the 'middle' peat refer to a phase or phases of peat growth intercalated within the fen clay. Intercalated peats in the North Level give a variety of dates such as (SRR1760) 4520 ± 70 BP (3425–2945 Cal. BC) at Plash Farm, (SRR1762) 4460 ± 80 BP (3370–2915 Cal. BC) at Sycamore Farm, (SRR1766) 4310 ± 140 BP (3355–2545 Cal. BC) at South Farm and (SRR1765) 4340 ± 60 BP (3105–2890 Cal. BC) at Guyhirn Washes (Appendix V.I). Elsewhere in the North Level, there are two dates from Adventurer's Land which put peat growth between (SRR1590) 4500 ± 50 BP (3365–3000 Cal. BC) and (SRR1589) 4030 ± 80 BP (2865–2380 Cal. BC) (R.J. Wyatt pers. comm.). This group of dates appears to be relatively consistent, although their contexts, height OD and differing topographical locations throughout the northern fenland area are less consistent.

The available dates for initiation of growth of the upper or Nordelph peat range from c.3250–2055 BP (Table 1; Appendix V.I). It is probable that peat growth continued throughout the last two millennia BC in more landward areas of the fens which were beyond the influence of the fen clay and the younger (upper) Barroway Drove Beds.

Soils of the North Level
(Fig. 3)
There are four principal soil associations relevant to the North Level area (Seale and Hodge 1976) (Fig. 3).

The first soil association is the organic soil or fen peat of the Adventurer's 1 Series. It is a deep peat, from c.30cm to over 3m, which produces an organic, generally non-calcareous soil. The land is flat, and the groundwater levels are artificially created and controlled by ditches and pumps. As it is highly desirable agricultural land and it is well drained, it is subject to wind erosion. This soil association may more or less be equated with the distribution of the upper or Nordelph peat. Its land use capacity class may vary from 2 to 4.

The second soil association is the Downholland 1 Series, a humic gley soil of marine alluvium over fen peat.

It is characterised by deep, stoneless, clayey, slowly permeable humose soils, and some peat soils which are only calcareous in places. Similarly the land is flat, well drained and subject to wind erosion. This soil association covers most of the northern and eastern parts of the North Level area; its distribution approximately equates with that of the Barroway Drove Beds. This soil series has a land use capability class of 2.

The third association is the groundwater gley soil of river alluvium over peat of the Midelney Series. It is represented by stoneless, slowly permeable, seasonally wet, clay soils mostly overlying peat. It is characterised by high groundwater levels and a risk of localised flooding, despite being controlled by pumps and ditches. This river alluvium over peat is mainly found where the River Welland runs off the Welland First Terrace gravels and into the fen basin north and east of Peakirk, and along the northern side of the River Nene in the vicinity of Northey 'island'. This soil association has a land use capability class of 3 to 5, with the clayey surface and high ground-water levels having adverse effects on the soil.

The fourth association is the humic gley soil of river terrace drift of the Ireton Series. It is represented by permeable, humose, coarse and fine loamy soils, associated with humose, calcareous coarse loamy over sandy soils. The groundwater is controlled by ditches and pumps. An area characteristic of this soil type is the spine of March Gravels which runs northeastwards from Eye, more or less bisecting the peat basin. This soil series has a class 2 land capability; it is well drained and calcareous.

Soil erosion and peat wastage
Soil erosion and in particular peat wastage is continuing at an alarming rate in the fens, and has done so since drainage began in earnest in the mid 17th century. The pace of peat wastage has increased dramatically since World War II, initially as a result of the ploughing-up of pasture land during the 'Dig for Victory' campaign.

Peat wastage and drainage combine in an ever increasing, cycle of erosion: as the peat deflates and wastes, it blows away; as the level drops, drainage then deteriorates and the drainage dykes begin to 'silt-up' with wind-borne material, thus necessitating their deepening — which in turn leads to further wastage, and the start of another cycle. Peat wastage occurs because of desiccation and deflation, and coincident oxidation, with much increased bacterial action; the process is hastened by wind erosion (R. Evans 1981). Peaty and sandy soils, especially when they are exposed in the spring and early summer, are particularly susceptible to wind erosion (Davies *et al.* 1982; Hodge and Arden-Clarke 1986).

Rates of peat wastage are known (Hutchinson 1980; Richardson and Smith 1977; Seale 1975). Peat wastage following a new drainage scheme is extremely rapid, up to 220mm per year, but this slows to a longer term average of c.10–18mm per year over much of the fens. In general the level of peat in the Cambridgeshire fens has fallen by up to 4.6m in places since 1652. Indeed at the Holme Fen post, 3.9m of peat has wasted away between 1848 and 1950 (Hutchinson 1980). To take a more recent example, it is estimated that 55% of the Ely district has organic soils with a thickness greater than 0.3m, but at a wastage rate of c.18mm per year only c.20% of these soils will remain by c.2000–2010 AD (Seale 1975). In the Borough Fen area of the North Level, the thickness of the peat recorded in

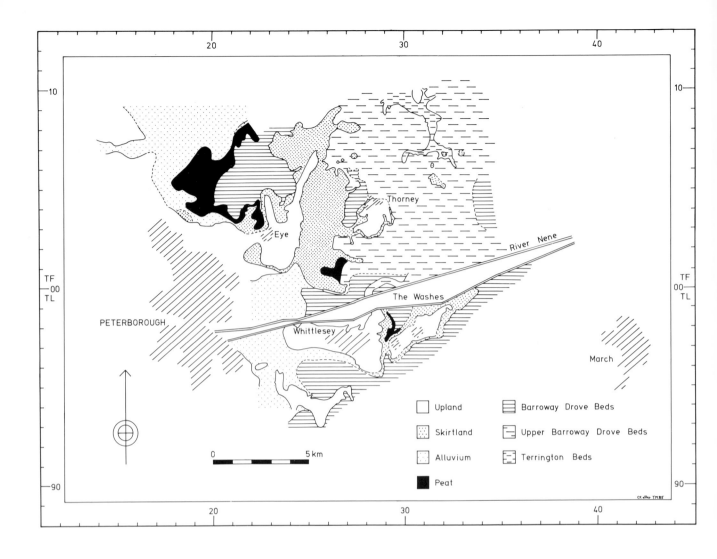

Figure 3 Flandrian geology of the North Level.

the British Geological Survey's borehole logs has declined in the ten years since the survey from an average depth of *c.*50–60cm to *c.*20–30cm. The latter figures have been observed and recorded consistently during the dyke survey in the past five years. This gives an approximate figure for peat wastage of *c.*20–30mm per year: if this continues, by the turn of the century much of the subsoil in Borough Fen will be brought to the surface by the plough, and the organic soils that now cover many fields will have gone. Indeed in some fields fen clay is already being ploughed up. However it should also be noted that once the clastic subsoil becomes mixed with the peat, the rate of peat wastage quickly diminishes.

The inherent qualities of peat which give it enormous agricultural value, also cause its susceptibility to degradation, instability and erosion. Soil organic matter has a strong positive effect on soil structure, stability and fertility. It is now recognised that reduced organic matter levels are a primary factor in the development of susceptibility to erosion (Hodge and Arden-Clarke 1986, 13; plus references). In the fenland, the switch to arable from pasture, over the past 40 or so years, has undoubtedly reduced soil organic matter levels drastically. Increased tillage leads to accelerated losses of organic matter by increased oxidation consequent upon the improved aeration of ploughed soils: for example, the organic matter content of pasture soils ranges between 5 and 10%,

whereas that of arable soils may be as low as 1–2% (Johnston 1973).

The effects of changes in organic matter content on the structural stability and susceptibility of soils to erosion have been demonstrated conclusively. Low (1972) found that old grassland soil had a structural stability of 73–78% whereas the same soil under old arable fields had a stability of 12–17%. The degree of cohesion of soil crumbs is also determined by soil organic matter content. For example, Dettman and Emerson (1959) reported that the cohesion of soil crumbs on unmanured arable land was 4% as compared to 50% on land which had been down to grass for four years. Indeed it has been shown that the critical level of organic matter content is 3.4%, below which soils were liable to structural instability (Greenland *et al.* 1975). Thus the addition of organic matter to the soil can only increase its capacity to absorb and retain water, as well as to increase the cohesion of the soil aggregates. Bearing these observations in mind, the intensively drained and cropped peaty soils of much of the East Anglian fenland are thus extremely susceptible to wind and water erosion, even without the effects of slope gradient.

Previous environmental studies
Many studies of sea level changes, stratigraphy and palynological sequences in the East Anglian fenland are to be found in the literature (*e.g.* Skertchly 1877; Miller and

12

Skertchley 1878; Godwin and Clifford 1938; Godwin 1941; Godwin and Willis 1961; Willis 1961; Clark and Godwin 1962; Jelgersma 1966; Phillips (ed.) 1970; Piggott 1972; Godwin and Vishnu-Mittre 1975; Godwin 1975 and 1978; Gallois 1979; Shennan 1980a, b, 1982a, b, 1986a, b). Professor Grahame Clark and his colleagues wrote a series of crucially important papers in which prehistoric settlement and the fen palaeoenvironment were successfully integrated; principal among these were the studies of Shippea Hill (Clark 1933; Clark and Clifford 1935; Clark and Godwin 1962; Clark *et al.* 1960).

Fenland successional sequences with an archaeological component have also been published on Woodwalton Fen (Godwin and Clifford 1938) and Whittlesey and Trundle Meres (Godwin and Vishnu-Mittre 1975). The important study (by the original Fenland Research Committee) of Roman settlement and land-use in the fens would undoubtedly have benefited from some of the recent environmental information being provided by the present Fenland Survey (Phillips 1970). Despite this activity, almost no work has been undertaken on the North Level area, apart from D.N. Hall's (1987) pioneering field survey. However, new results are now emerging, thanks to the integrated palaeoenvironmental analyses of the Fenland Project (in conjunction with the University of Cambridge radiocarbon laboratory) and Dr R.G. Scaife (of the University of Southampton), who is working on behalf of Fenland Archaeological Trust.

Before turning to site-specific and more general palynological and successional evidence, it is first necessary to examine the nature of sea level change in the fenland. There have been numerous studies, but little whole-hearted agreement: the following is an attempt to summarise a complex situation.

Sea level change

The Post-Glacial climatic amelioration caused water to be released from the Devensian ice-cap and sea levels rose sharply. The sea level curve for the Netherlands and the adjacent North Sea basin suggests that the North Sea may have been as low as *c.*37m below present day Ordnance Datum at about 10,000 BP (Jelgersma 1979; Godwin 1978). Thereafter the nature and timing of the sea level rise is a matter of academic debate.

Fairbridge (1961) has suggested that the sea level has been rising rapidly until the end of the Atlantic period when it stood about 3m above the present level, thereafter it fluctuated with an amplitude of up to 6m. Jelgersma (1966) believed that the rise was smooth and continuous, but slowing down after *c.*6000 BP. Other authors, such as Godwin *et al.*(1958) originally argued that the sea level rose steadily, reaching its present height at *c.*5000–3600 BP, with a standing sea level thereafter. Professor Godwin (1978) superseded this theory with the idea of an interrupted rise in sea level since *c.*4200 BP. Louwe Kooijmans (1974, 1980) suggested that the sea level rose continuously, but was subject to short term fluctuations or changes in rate, especially since *c.*6000 BP. These fluctuations are not fully understood, but may result from any combination of the subsidence of land masses, isostatic uplift (in marginal areas) and hydro-isostatic subsidence (in flooded areas) (Jelgersma 1966; Willis 1961). The East Anglian fenland has probably been characterised by subsidence since at least *c.*6500 BP (Shennan 1980a) with the mean

crustal subsidence rate calculated at *c.*0.9m per 1000 years (Shennan 1986b).

More recent work on the sea level curve for coastal Essex (Devoy 1980; Greensmith and Tucker 1973) shows a rapid rise of relative sea level until *c.*8000 BP at *c.*-9.0m OD. Then there was a slackening in sea level rise, which continued (with some possible marine retreats intervening), up to the present day, when the maximum height was reached. Understanding the process has undoubtedly been made more difficult by the realisation that southeastern England was gradually sinking (subsidence) whilst the sea level (eustatically) continued to rise (Godwin *et al.* 1958; Shennan 1986a).

The most recent studies of Flandrian sea level change in the fenland are by Shennan (1980a, b; 1982a, b; 1986a, b). Shennan's analysis of the physical evolution of the fens is characterised by eight positive tendencies and seven negative tendencies, based on over 100 radiocarbon dates. The positive (or transgressive) tendencies correspond to a rising sea level and landward movement of the coastline, with brackish/marine sediments tending to dominate; whereas the negative (or regressive) tendencies correspond to a reduced or negative rate of sea level rise, and a freshwater or terrestrial regime characterised by peat growth (Shennan 1980a; 1986a, b). As a result of this work, it is suggested that the rates of sea level change vary from approximately static on at least four occasions (lasting up to 300 years) to approximately 5mm/year (or 5m/1000 years) on a number of occasions prior to *c.*3000 BP. Since 3000 BP, the average rate of sea level change has slowed to *c.*1mm/year (or 1 metre per 1000 years).

This wealth of research does not explain much of the observed sedimentological record in the fens: in essence, although the nature of fenland sediments is relatively consistent, their formation and deposition were not synchronous events across the whole region. Indeed, the only synchroneity that can be observed occurs within very small topographical areas, largely confined to individual fens. The more new sedimentological studies that are carried out, the more they illustrate the wide variety of fen environments that must have existed at the same time, more or less side by side. Clarification must await the publication of the Fenland Project's environmental volume (Waller forthcoming).

Palynological record

Palynological and related stratigraphical investigations have been carried out at a number of locations near the present study area and these will be discussed below. Principal studies include the investigations at Holme Fen, Whittlesey and Trundle Meres (Godwin and Vishnu-Mittre 1975); more recent work to be noted is in progress, or just published, on the route of the A47 Wisbech bypass (Alderton 1984/5; Waller 1985/6), in Adventurer's Land (Shennan 1986a), at Farcet (Waller 1986/7) and at Flag Fen (Scaife in Pryor *et al.* 1986).

The stratigraphic sequence at Holme Fen and Whittlesey Mere in the Middle Level exhibits a basal wood peat or alder fen woods, followed by a eutrophic *Phragmites-Cladium* dominated fen, which was suceeded by a floating 'scraw bog' or *Sphagnum* ombrogeneous mire which developed into an oligotrophic, acidic raised bog dominated by *Sphagnum*, *Calluna* and *Eriophorum* which continued growing until after *c.*1850 AD (Godwin and Vishnu-Mittre 1975). Such acidic raised bogs are a very rare occurrence in fenland, with the only other known example observed in the upper peat at Wiggenhall St Giles (Waller pers. comm.).

At Holme Fen, the first temporary clearance and indications of agricultural activity occurred about (Q406) 4950 BP. It was indicated by the first decreases in elm and oak, and the first appearance of *Plantago lanceolata*, Chenopodiaceae, *Artemisia* and cereals, with a large peak of grass pollen, followed by one of alder. A second, more pronounced but short-lived clearance episode was recognised in the Holme Fen sequence and occurred about (Q403) 3400 BP or in the earlier Bronze Age. It was marked by a pronounced fall in lime pollen relative to that of oak and elm. There were also three peaks of the pollen of cereals, *Centaurea*, Chenopodiaceae, Compositae and Urticaceae. A similar clearance horizon occurred at Trundle Mere. Although the pollen rain may have collected from more distant sources, it had a larger element of pasture represented (Godwin and Vishnu-Mittre 1975).

The clearance episode was bracketed by two thin bands of clay. They were thought to represent freshwater flooding containing material that probably resulted from soil erosion of woodland soils exposed as a result of clearance on the upland to the northwest (Godwin and Vishnu-Mittre 1975). But recent work by Waller (1986/7) at Farcet, a few kilometres to the north suggests that the clay bands are likely to coincide with, and are therefore probably the result of, the fen clay marine incursion, although this does not prevent them from having been deposited in a freshwater environment.

The Late Bronze Age witnessed the largest yet scale of clearance and agriculture in the Holme Fen record at c.3000 BP. The fall in hazel and the large increase in bracken, with cereals over 10% and *Plantago* over 60% suggest both mixed agricultural practices and secondary forest growth being prevented, except for *Fagus*. The pollen record at Trundle Mere exhibits a similar extensive clearance slightly later around 2750 BP. The pollen sequence in the upper peats at Whittlesey Mere is similar to the other two sites with evidence of both Bronze Age clearance phases. The upper peat accumulated in shallow, open water, and contained much detritus derived from the surrounding *Sphagnum* bog and fen wood, possibly with floating matts of bryophyta (Godwin and Vishnu-Mittre 1975).

The clays and silts found in the northeastern part of Whittlesey Mere are also probably a western (landward) extension of the fen clay. The margin of the fen clay does not taper out, rather it was arrested by higher bog growth to the west and south in the Mere basin. Then the whole Mere area was overlain by shell marls of a freshwater lake, created by freshwater backing-up landward of an area of upper peat which may have begun in the pre-Roman Iron Age (Godwin and Vishnu-Mittre 1975; Waller forthcoming).

Pollen and diatom analyses (with associated radiocarbon dates) have recently been completed in Adventurer's Land in the southeastern part of the North Level (Shennan 1986a). The basal peat began to accumulate prior to (Hv10011) c.6575 ± 95 BP, as a result of a locally rising water table. Then the onset of marine conditions occurred, which is not dated directly because of the erosion of the upper surface of the peat. Peat growth resumed for a time slightly prior to (Hv10817) c.5840 ± 90 BP (4940–4510 Cal. BC), but nevertheless indicates an increasing marine

influence. Marine conditions prevailed again at (SRR1589) c.4180 ± 75 BP (2925–2540Cal. BC) and were interpreted as low energy, high salt marsh sediments. Peat growth resumed about (SRR1588) 1845 ± 50 BP (25–245 Cal. AD), but there was salt marsh in the close vicinity (Shennan 1986a).

Palynological analysis of an intercalated peat bed at c.0.5m OD, separating two marine/brackish deposits at six sites along the line of the A47 Wisbech bypass, has recently been completed and the following preliminary results are available (Alderton 1984/5; Waller 1985/6). Radiocarbon dates for the beginning of peat growth vary from 2720 ± 70 BP to 2430 ± 60 BP or within the earlier half of the 1st millennium BC. Dates for the end of the peat accumulation also vary, but there is some consistency around 2100 to 2010 ± 50 BP. The earlier dates at several sites may be attributable to the erosional truncation of the peat surface (Waller 1985/6).

Pollen analysis of the site at the Railway Crossing in the Wisbech sequence (TF452075) exhibits four local pollen assemblage zones (Waller 1985/6). The following results should not be used to make inferences about more distant and dry land results. First, salt marsh conditions pertain; non-arboreal pollen dominates with abundant Chenopodiaceae and high frequencies of Gramineae and Cyperaceae. The pollen assemblages prior to organic deposition herald the approach of freshwater conditions. In the second zone, the frequency of Chenopodiaceae declines while those indicative of reedswamp (Gramineae and *Typha augustifolia* type) and sedge fen (Cyperaceae) communities increase. In the third zone, fen carr species become established, first *Salix* and then *Alnus*, whilst Cyperaceae and especially Gramineae decline. There is then a sharp decline in *Alnus* and *Salix* with a rise in Gramineae, which indicate a return to reedswamp conditions between zones three and four. In the fourth zone there is a gradual return to brackish water conditions.

Correlation of this work with previous work in the fens is still difficult. Other peats at Manea (Hall and Switsur 1981), Saddlebow (Godwin, Willis and Switsur 1965) and Welney Wash (Churchill 1970) have been dated to within the period 3000–1900 BP, but the various relationships remain to be elucidated. Work in progress by M. Waller on the correlation of the Wisbech sites with other fenland sites may help to resolve some of these difficulties (Waller forthcoming).

The sequence at Clap Gate Farm, Farcet Fen (TL 2323 9212) on the southwestern fen margin, shows how the vegetation responded to the rising base water levels that accompanied the marine incursion. Pollen from the underlying buried soil suggests that lime was a major component of the forest canopy prior to the rise in groundwater levels, with high alder values suggesting the presence of waterlogged environments nearby. It is interesting to note that there is no evidence of anthropogenic interference with the vegetation. A reedswamp characterised by high grass values suequently became established as water levels rose. Peat formation occurred over a period of some 250 years, with the transgressive overlap (basal peat/fen clay contact) dated to (Q2552) 3700 ± 60 BP (2305–1900 Cal. BC). The final pollen zone probably reflects the regional pollen rain (high oak and hazel), plus some local elements (such as grasses and Chenopodiaceae), with the fen clay being deposited in a brackish, probably salt marsh, environment. Sequences similar to this have been identified elsewhere in the fens, irrespective of their age (Waller 1985/6).

Pollen analyses at Flag Fen, Peterborough, both of the Late Bronze Age platform site and its environs are at an early stage, but a few tentative results may be summarised here. Analysis of a profile through the upper peat about 2m outside and to the southeast of the platform suggests a predominantly open environment with much open, shallow water and grass or reed fen. A few shrub species such as alder were growing on the margins of the fen, on local 'islands' and along the terrace edge. There are also indications of larger hardwoods, such as oak, elm, lime and hazel, but they are probably growing on higher ground perhaps in the vicinity of modern Peterborough (Scaife in Pryor *et al.* 1986).

Diatom analysis of two profiles at Flag Fen, one *c.*100m to the south and one within the platform itself, have been completed (Juggins 1984; Juggins in Pryor *et al.* 1986). The diatoms indicate a slightly less open environment than the pollen evidence, with the platform initially being built in a sedge fen/alder carr environment. The surface of the peat stood above the water table for part of the year and the vegetation was rooted in annually standing water. At some point towards the end of the life of the monument (at *c.*0.45m OD) there was a marked change to a wetter, marginal, reed-swamp type of environment followed by a gradual transition to open water with the slight indications of a brackish element. This change in diatom evidence coincides with a distinct break in the peat stratigraphy which may well reflect the change in depositional conditions.

Together the pollen and diatom evidence at Flag Fen indicate at first a swampy carr environment, possibly transitional to alder carr in places around the margins of the small basin; towards the end of the lifetime of the site this then became a reed-swamp with much open water. The absence of evidence for a raised bog here in the earlier half of the 1st millennium BC and the topographically isolated nature of the site, within a small basin defined by the high ground of Northey 'island' and the Fengate First Terrace gravels, suggests that the area may have been cut- off from the major events occurring in the fen to the east during the Late Bronze Age. Peat within the small basin then received a succession of freshwater-borne alluvial silty clays derived from the higher ground of the hinterland to the west. The latter process continued throughout the next two and a half millennia.

Environmental evidence from neighbouring archaeological sites
A variety of environmental evidence has been obtained from sites just outside the North Level study area which is of general relevance. The main sites include Maxey, Etton Woodgate and Etton in the lower Welland valley/fen margin, Fengate in the lower Nene valley/fen edge and Stonea Grange on Stonea 'island' to the southeast of March.

There are three pollen analyses available from the Maxey area: from a late Bronze Age pit context at Tallington (French after Dimbleby in Pryor and French 1985, 89), a late Roman pit context at West Deeping (Dimbleby in Simpson 1966) and a Neolithic pit context at Maxey (Pilcher in Pryor and French 1985, 249, 251). These pollen analyses indicate that the area was largely open by the late Bronze Age, and by the Roman period was significantly open land. The composition of the tree cover had changed with a decrease in oak and hazel, no alder, and a slight increase in willow. Pasture and therefore livestock are important in the valley, although some cultivation was probably occurring in the vicinity, either upstream or on the higher ground to the west and southwest.

The recently excavated henge and barrow complex at Maxey was located on an 'island' composed of First Terrace gravels in the lower Welland valley (Pryor and French 1985). The site was not waterlogged, so the primary source of environmental evidence was the micromorphology of the preserved buried soils. Palaeosols were found preserved beneath a late Neolithic oval barrow within the entrance to the henge and beneath the contemporary round mound at the centre of the henge. They exhibited micromorphological evidence which suggested that by the late Neolithic the area had once been forested, then subject to clearance and a limited amount of agriculture (French in Pryor and French 1985, 205–216). The site does not seem to have been permanently settled until the Iron Age and Roman periods, when a series of farmsteads within rectilinear ditched field systems were constructed. The farmstead appears to have been located between the lower lying land which fringed the seasonally flooded meadows of the floodplain and the higher ground of the modern village. The mainstays of the economy were primarily sheep and some cattle, with the former kept mainly for meat (Halstead in Pryor and French 1985, 219-224). The botanical evidence suggests that the primary processing of crops was taking place away from the settlement areas, possibly on the higher ground to the north (Green in Pryor and French 1985, 224–232). The molluscs provide complementary evidence by indicating generally open surroundings with ditches containing temporary standing water (Evans 1972, 346–349; French in Pryor and French 1985, 216).

The earlier Neolithic site of Etton Woodgate was located about 0.5km east of the Maxey henge complex near the southeastern edge of the 'island', towards the contemporary fen-edge. Some 100m further east lies the Etton causewayed enclosure. The Etton Woodgate site consisted of a possible post-built structure on the higher ground within a large L-shaped ditch which marked the edge of the higher ground of Maxey 'island' to the northwest. Micromorphological analysis of the buried soil indicated that, as at Maxey, the area had been forested and cleared prior to occupation in the earlier Neolithic period. Subsequently the original soil (an argillic brown earth) became eroded and developed into a brown earth by the end of the prehistoric period, the lower part of which subsequently became gleyed due to a high local ground water table. This soil was subject to seasonal waterlogging throughout its development, and was built-up by the addition of colluvial and alluvial material. A meandering stream channel partially eroded the ditch during the later Neolithic period, before being infilled with eroded stream bed material and colluvium. The colluvium was probably derived from the high ground immediately to the west on Maxey 'island', perhaps as a result of clearance and agricultural disturbance.

The Etton causewayed enclosure's buried soil is well preserved with the lower A and B horizons of a relatively poorly developed argillic brown earth surviving. As at Maxey and Etton Woodgate, the soil was cleared prior to the site's use as a monument, sometime prior to the middle

Neolithic. Coincident with and subsequent to the middle Neolithic use of the site, the soil was subject to gleying, seasonal waterlogging and considerable additions of alluvial silty clays. The pollen evidence (Scaife in Pryor *et al.* 1985, 289–292), insect remains (M. Robinson pers. comm.) and the macro-botanical evidence (S. Nye pers. comm.) suggest the existence of shallow fen/semi-aquatic conditions in the enclosure ditch and the immediate vicinity during the middle Neolithic period. Neither Etton nor Etton Woodgate shows clear evidence for use after the Beaker period, so it must be assumed that this part of the lower Welland valley probably remained as freshwater fen or seasonally flooded meadowland until it was drained in 1953. Substantial alluvial deposition continued throughout the two millennia AD, and resulted in the laying-down of from *c.*50–130cm of silty clay alluvium over both sites.

Due east of Peterborough, the prehistoric and Romano-British sites at Fengate were located in a similar terrace gravel or fen-edge position, but in the lower Nene valley. The evidence from the 2nd millennium BC field system suggests an economy based on the keeping and rearing of cattle in which the fen-edge pastures were doubtless augmented by seasonal recourse to damper fenland meadows (Biddick in Pryor 1980a, 217–232; Pryor 1980b). Pasture and meadow predominated with little evidence of cereal crops or on-site processing, and there were suggestions of the growth of localised woods and hedges associated with the droveways (Wilson 1980, 1984). The molluscan evidence suggests that there was no significant scrub wood and regeneration after the abandonment of the ditch system; rather open, slightly unkempt conditions which were becoming damper. The indications of increasing wetness in this fen margin area may have culminated with the localised freshwater flooding horizon on the Fourth Drove subsite at about 1000 BC (French in Pryor 1980a, 210–212).

Somewhat later, at the Cat's Water subsite, Fengate, grassland continued to predominate throughout the Iron Age and Roman periods, although there was increasing evidence for arable land and waste ground (Wilson 1980, 1984). The molluscs suggest freshwater slum conditions pertained in the ditches, with the site becoming damper as the Late Iron Age progressed. In the early to mid 3rd century AD silty clay alluvium was deposited over most of the site; this was probably due to the backing up of freshwater on the landward side of the peat fen (French in Pryor 1984).

The only recent large-scale excavations in the fens that have produced abundant environmental evidence were at Stonea Grange, near March. The site was discovered by David Hall and seems to have been an early Roman failed town, situated on the southern edge of Stonea 'island' (Potter and Jackson forthcoming). The study of diatoms, pollen, macro-botany, molluscs and soil/sediments has produced a variety of new evidence for the on-site environment during the 2nd to 4th centuries AD. Remarkably, all types of evidence are more or less complementary. The diatoms, snails and macro-botanical records are indicative of a marginally wet, predominantly open environment. The diatoms suggest that the site was situated at the inland limit of brackish water influence (Alderton 1983/4), and there was a minor brackish water element to the molluscan assemblage (French in Potter and Jackson forthcoming). Analyses of both mollusc, pollen and plant remains, suggested that low-lying areas and features held standing water for at least part of the time, possibly seasonally, with marshy conditions in places (van der Veen in Potter and Jackson forthcoming). Both the molluscan and botanical studies also suggested a generally open landscape, but with a scattered woodland element — perhaps some old scrub or the existence of hedgerows in the immediate vicinity of the settlement. The soil micromorphological evidence suggested that the contemporary soil had been subject to the input of alluvial material, and must therefore have been occasionally (and seasonally) waterlogged (French in Potter and Jackson forthcoming).

The over-riding impression gained from the environmental studies carried out at these fen-edge and fen 'island' sites is one of predominantly open ground with localised shading by shrubs or hedgerows, coupled with a high ground water table for all, or part of the year. Settlements of all periods seem to be directly influenced by changes in the adjacent natural fen environment. This would suggest a close association between each settlement and its surroundings.

Chapter 2. Past and Present Archaeological Research

I. The archaeological background
by Charles French and Francis Pryor

The archaeological richness of the lower Nene and Welland valleys, and their adjacent fen-edge is well known. A number of recent publications have reviewed this evidence in some detail and it is not intended to repeat them here (*e.g.* Pryor 1984; Pryor and French 1985; Pryor and Palmer 1982; Pryor *et al.* 1985; RCHM 1960; Simpson *et al.* forthcoming). The true fen to the east, however, has received less attention from archaeologists, prior to recent research by the Fenland Survey (Coles and Hall 1983; Hall 1987), undertaken by David Hall — and briefly reviewed by him below. Most of the land in question comprises the North Level whose drainage is the responsibility of the Commissioners of the North Level Internal Drainage Board (henceforth referred to as the NLIDB).

We have not attempted an overall review of fenland research, as this has also been considered at some length in a number of recent publications (*e.g.* Godwin 1978; Hall 1987; Phillips 1970; Pryor 1984, 1986). Instead we will attempt a brief summary of the published archaeological evidence for the North Level and the surrounding region.

There are as yet no known early Post-Glacial sites in the region, but at least one flint collection from the 'Peterborough area' in Peterborough Museum, is Levalloisian in character (J.J. Wymer pers. comm.). Three possible Mesolithic sites were found on light, sandy soils on limestone uplands north of the Nene (Hall and Martin 1980); these sites are represented by surface scatters of numerous microliths. Three other possible late Mesolithic/early Neolithic sites were discovered during the survey discussed in this volume (Chapter 3:I; French 1988a, b). These sites are located on small gravel 'islands', or promontories, sealed by lower peat or fen clay.

The recently discovered site at Etton Woodgate I, on the lower Welland valley and fen-margin interface is the only other known (or probable) early Neolithic site in the area (this, however, is based on the evidence of plain Neolithic bowls whose dating is notoriously difficult to tie down with any precision; radiocarbon dates are awaited with interest) (Pryor *et al.* 1985). The site was excavated during gravel extraction and what survived is undoubtedly incomplete; principally it consisted of a large ditch about 150m in length which more or less followed the contours of the land and thereby appeared to define the extreme southeastern edge of the higher ground of Maxey 'island', at the point where it was cut off by the course of the relict stream channel that meandered past the north and west sides of the Etton causewayed enclosure. The ditch was broached by a single 'entranceway' within which was a scatter of pits and post-holes, possibly defining one or more rectilinear structures (Pryor *et al.* 1985, fig. 4). There is little doubt that this site was built in an already predomi-

nantly open landscape on the edge of the contemporary floodplain (French 1988a, b).

During the middle Neolithic period the causewayed enclosure at Etton was built about 100m to the southeast of Etton Woodgate I, probably on an 'island' created by former meanders of the river Welland. This site contained little convincing evidence of any contemporary settlement, only a multitude of small pits sometimes containing 'placed' artefact assemblages which presumably related to the ceremonial aspects of the site's use (Pryor 1987). Indeed, 'placed' and back-filled deposits were found in most segments of the enclosure ditch. Two other causewayed enclosures at nearby Barholme and Uffington in Lincolnshire are also known in the lower Welland; both on aerial photographic evidence alone appear to be located near meandering relict river channels (Palmer 1976). The Etton causewayed enclosure was built, like Etton Woodgate I, in an open, fen-edge type of environment (Scaife in Pryor *et al.* 1985) which was probably subject to seasonal flooding (French 1988a).

The land around Etton has been the subject of renewed research, specifically focused on the Neolithic and Bronze Age periods. The Etton Landscape Project is particularly concerned with buried sites and landscapes around the causewayed enclosure and is closely integrated with the larger southwest fen-edge (dyke) survey discussed in this volume. It may be seen as an intermediate step between site-specific projects at Etton, and larger surveys; as such, it combines elements of both: dyke survey and field-walking.

The Etton Landscape Project has revealed a number of important new sites, north and east of the causewayed enclosure, broadly speaking in the same relative position as Etton Woodgate I, but near the extreme south and east edge of Maxey 'island' (French and Pryor in preparation). These sites include two barrows (both of which lacked burials), a buried midden-like occupation site of later Bronze Age date, Grooved Ware pits, a remarkable and very complex Dorchester-style henge monument (Atkinson *et al.* 1951), which was succeeded by an adjacent, less complex henge with a circular central pit arrangement and a small Class II henge about 100m to the east. The Maxey cursus has been discussed at length (Pryor and French 1985) and was traced in 1982 below alluvium immediately west of the Etton causewayed enclosure. The Etton cursus was first recognised in 1986. Its southern ditch runs southeast from within the causewayed enclosure, where it terminates, on an alignment slightly different from that of the Maxey cursus. Its parallel northern ditch was traced in 1987, both to the north and south of the Maxey Cut.

The sites of the 'island' edge and fen margins are 'linked' to those of the 'island' proper by the Maxey cursus. These sites include the large, double-ditched Maxey henge complex (Pryor and French 1985) and the smaller henges dug in the early 1960s by Simpson (1967, 1981).

Apart from Etton Woodgate I and the sites discussed in this volume, excavated Neolithic settlements are rare. Excavations in advance of the A15 Glinton-Northborough Bypass in the summer of 1987, some 450m to the east of Etton, revealed extensive redeposited midden deposits of the later Neolithic period in a similar topographical position to Etton Woodgate I, following the contours of the land, and bordered and sealed by relict stream courses. These deposits may be the only tangible remains of the domestic component that complements the ceremonial aspect of the various henge monuments (French 1990). A possible Neolithic 'house' was excavated at the Padholme Road subsite, Fengate, and was described in the First Report (Pryor 1974). There are now grounds to suspect that even this hitherto securely 'domestic' site may have formed part of a series of mortuary monuments (Pryor forthcoming). It is close to, and aligned on, the rectangular ditched enclosure excavated in 1968 by Mahany (1969) and an association seems highly probable. The rectangular enclosure is now interpreted as a funerary enclosure, perhaps reminiscent of Rivenhall, Essex (Buckley et al. 1988). The rarity of earlier Neolithic settlement sites in the area has led one of the present authors (French 1990 and Pryor 1988) to suggest that the contemporary settlement and land-use pattern may have been far more mobile than had hitherto been supposed.

Palynological data provided by the Fenland Project palaeoenvironmentalist will help to establish the extent of tree cover in the fen and on its 'islands' and margins in the earlier Neolithic. Nevertheless a pattern is emerging in which initially small inroads are made into the forest, and these are followed by more substantial clearances. Field survey, for example, on the limestone upland in the Barnack/Wittering heath region, between the Nene and Welland valleys, has discovered concentrations of Neolithic material, mainly stone axe fragments (Hall and Martin 1980). Elsewhere in East Anglia at Broome Heath, Norfolk, it is suggested that primary forest clearances occurred around 5450 BP (Dimbleby and Evans in Wainwright 1972) and at Holme Fen, Cambridgeshire, about 4950 BP (Godwin and Vishnu-Mittre 1975). At Hockham Mere, Norfolk, the elm decline (whatever its cause) was associated with cereals and other indicators of human activity. This occurred over a period of c. 230 years after 4986 ± 115 BP (Sims 1973). Indeed the intensification of clearance, evidence of agriculture and increased human activity during the third millennium BC coincide with the construction and use of causewayed enclosures, the first non-funerary field monuments found in the region (Bradley 1978).

Forest clearance is by no means even partially complete in the mid-third millennium BC (Evans 1978; Thomas 1982; Thorley 1981), as some authors have supposed (Barker and Webley 1978). Spratt and Simmons (1976) have suggested that a feature of the later third millennium BC is the succession of small forest recessions prior to it, which are probably suggestive of Mesolithic and Neolithic inroads into the primary forest cover. A similar model, based on the use of gradually enlarging forest clearings by herding communities, has been suggested for the earlier Neolithic in lowland England in general, and in East Anglia in particular (Pryor 1988). The countryside around sites such as Etton and the Maxey

henge complex must have been substantially open (Pryor and French 1985; Scaife in Pryor et al. 1985), since monuments such as cursuses make little sense in the context of dense forest. Similarly, it has been suggested that Fengate might well have had an organised landscape whose alignment altered radically well prior to 2000 BC (Pryor forthcoming); again this landscape presupposes a fair degree of clearance. Nevertheless, it would still be very rash to assume that what applies to the fen-edge applies with equal force to the marshes and 'islands' of the fen proper. The two are very different landscapes.

Evidence for the organisation of the earlier Neolithic landscape is tantalisingly thin. We have referred to Fengate and the Etton landscape area, but might it not be suggested that the Maxey and Etton cursuses, which after all follow a closely similar alignment, are respecting the orientation of the (organised) landscape? Indeed the discovery of a substantial Neolithic ditch during the A15 Glinton Bypass excavations in 1987 could be significant; it was aligned approximately NNE-SSW and was positioned at an approximate right angle to the former stream courses and, most significantly, to the Etton cursus. One ditch and two cursus do not make an organised landscape, but neither do they disprove such a supposition. The evidence is fragmentary, but the period in question is remote, and what little data there is supports the hypothesis advanced here.

The archaeological evidence becomes less sparse by the onset of the 2nd millennium BC in the lower Nene valley and contiguous parts of the fen-edge. By contrast, in the lower Welland valley, direct evidence for land division is rare: here large tracts of the landscape have produced a thin 'background' scatter of Bronze Age flint implements and by-products (Taylor in Pryor and French 1985, 15–23). This scatter has tentatively been interpreted as the result of manuring. If this landscape was parcelled-up, the methods used have not left archaeologically identifiable traces — which may well be a post-depositional effect, perhaps reflecting the intensity of agriculture in the region. On the other hand, in the lower Nene valley the organisation of the landscape relied in large part upon ditches which defined a series of fields or paddocks, separated by droveways, and laid out at right-angles to the fen (Pryor 1980a). Elements of perhaps the same organised landscape have been traced to fen 'islands' nearby (Gurney 1980). The Fengate field system was abandoned by or around 1000 BC due to a combination of factors, of which increasing wetness was probably an important element; these wetter conditions are well attested by the freshwater flooding horizon which overlay both ditch and bank of the 2nd millennium BC field system in the Fourth Drove subsite (French in Pryor 1980, 190). The relationship of the timber platform site at Flag Fen to these events is not yet clear, but present indications suggest that the latter site was abandoned due to rising base water levels and an association seems, on the face of it, quite possible (Pryor et al. 1986).

Evidence for Early Iron Age settlement and land-use is thin. The best known material of this period from the area is that published by Hawkes and Fell (1945). Laying aside the inherent problems of dating Iron Age pottery, which the Fengate groups have been used to illustrate (Spratling 1974), there are now reasons to doubt whether the 'pits' contained closed groups at all (Pryor 1983a, 190). It can be argued that these pits are in fact small 'sock' wells (the term 'sock' refers to the ground water or sock level), and that the material in them accumulated over a considerable period of time.

Even given these problems, it seems reasonable to suppose that there were settlements in the area in Early Iron Age times, but their size, number and duration must remain unknown. A small, but long-lived settlement of this period is, however, known from the Vicarage Farm sub-site, Fengate (Pryor 1974, 1984). Iron Age settlement and land-use in the region is comprehensively reviewed in the Fourth Fengate Report (Pryor 1984) and the Lower Welland Valley volume (Pryor and French 1985). Recently Knight (1984) has published an account of contemporary settlement sites further up the river Nene.

The principal discovery of recent years in the area under review was the recognition that Scheduled Monument 222, known here as Borough Fen Site 7 (BoF 7) was not medieval, but rather a defended enclosure of Iron Age date, located at *c.* 3.0m OD (Pryor 1983b). The site is described in this report (Chapter 3:1), and its significance and setting are further discussed by French (1988a, b). It would not be appropriate to isolate all Iron Age features from the large quantities of aerial photographic evidence, but three possible Iron Age field and enclosure systems have recently been recognised by D.N. Hall on gravel soils west of Thorney (Hall 1987, sites Th30-32).

Many Romano-British settlements along the fen-edge have origins in the later Iron Age, as witnessed by Cat's Water, Fengate (Pryor 1984) and Maxey East Field (Pryor and French 1985); smaller settlements such as Werrington and Monument 97 often show a similar pattern of development (*e.g.* Mackreth and O'Neill 1980; Mackreth 1988; Dallas 1975). Romano-British settlement and land-use in and around the lower Nene valley has been reviewed by Wild (1974). For present purposes, one of the more significant events is the supposed widespread deposition of alluvium in the 3rd century AD. This is a problem that is discussed in full by Bromwich (1970); latterly it has been treated in the Fourth Fengate Report (Pryor 1984) and the Lower Welland Valley volumes (Pryor and French 1985). Flood silts attributable to this period have been recognised in our area at low-lying settlements (below the 10–15 foot contours) at, for example, Grandford, Flaggrass, Stonea, Upwell, Welney, Hockwold-cum-Wilton, Earith and Fengate (Potter 1981; Pryor 1984).

The precise causes of the 3rd century AD alluviation are likely to alter from one place to another, but simple, monocausal explanations are probably inappropriate. Although some authors attribute the flooding and deposition of alluvium to worsening climatic conditions (Potter 1976, 1981) and a breakdown in drainage systems (Bromwich 1970), it is more probable that they are manifestations of the intensification of land-use in the earlier Roman period (Jones 1981) — doubtless exacerbated by other, purely local, factors. The clearance and cultivation of a much greater range of soils and topographical areas inland probably created more soil water run-off; this consequently increased soil erosion. The eroded soil or colluvium then found its way into the river system. Once in the fenland, the poor river outfalls and peat growth caused physical obstacles to drainage which in turn led to freshwater back-up; as water ponded around areas of high ground, so silts and clays came out of suspension and alluvium was deposited.

Turning eastwards to the fens of the North Level, the distribution of Romano-British sites was discussed re-cently by Hall (1987), but general descriptions may also be found in Phillips (1970) and *The Victoria County History* (Wilkes and Elrington 1978). In this report we will be concerned particularly with Roman period occupation of Thorney and Eye 'islands'; we will also examine a small farmstead of mid-2nd to mid-3rd century AD date on the same spine of First Terrace deposits as the fortified enclosure (BoF 7), mentioned above.

The Romano-British settlement pattern in the March area is extensive. There are four large villages ranging in size from about 25 to 40 acres at Stonea (Potter 1975), Grandford (Potter and Potter 1982), Flaggrass and Coldham (Potter 1965), and a possible failed Roman town at Stonea Grange (Potter and Jackson forthcoming). There are also a number of smaller hamlets, varying in size from about 7 to 20 acres (*e.g.* Waldersea and Stags Holt) and numerous farmsteads. Most of the sites lie at the hub of a network of small ditched enclosures which are linked to the settlements by ditched droveways (Potter 1981).

The March area has the largest network (*c.* 150 acres) of undoubted Romano-British fields in the country (Hall 1987). The enclosures, droveways and vast empty areas of peat and silt fen are considered to be evidence for a largely pastoral-based economy, with wool a particularly important component (Potter 1981). However, the Maxey East Field excavations, although they produced a number of loomweights, showed also that sheep there were kept primarily for meat rather than wool (Halstead in Pryor and French 1985); similarly, C. Evans (pers. comm.), working at Haddenham in the southern fens, has shown that the economy of later Iron Age communities was probably based on mixed farming, with a very significant cereal component. It would appear that in Roman, just as in prehistoric times, it is very difficult to reconstruct fenland economies using broad brushstrokes. Doubtless this economic heterogeneity reflects in large part the region's size and ecological diversity; doubtless too we are also witnessing the results of many ancient and very dissimilar histories of social and economic development.

This report is mainly concerned with sites and deposits found in stratified contexts in dykes. Almost by definition this means that our attention has largely been confined to sites of the prehistoric and Roman periods. However, although wetter conditions prevailed in many parts of the Saxon and early medieval fen (Hall 1987), settlement and land-use continued seemingly unabated around the fen margins. Indeed, after the collapse of official Roman rule around AD 410, there is ample evidence to suggest a continuation and later expansion of the existing system of land-use. The sites appear to concentrate on gravel terraces; for example, in the lower Nene valley the later Romano-British farmstead at Orton Hall farm (Mackreth 1976) continues into the early Saxon period; there is also a very large Saxon settlement at Castor (Hall and Martin 1980), and another, smaller, settlement overlying the failed Roman town at Stonea Grange (Potter and Jackson forthcoming). Many sites of this period are also found in the lower Welland valley (Pryor and French 1985; Hall and Martin 1980; Simpson *et al.* forthcoming); perhaps the best known example is that at Maxey (Addyman and Fennell 1964).

Towards the end of the 1st millennium AD we see the establishment of the local fenland abbeys, at Peterborough (King 1973), Crowland and Thorney (Raban 1977). This, however, is not the place to discuss the intricacies of the medieval fenland economy (for which see Darby 1940a), as contemporary deposits occur rarely in stratified contexts along dykesides. By and large the medieval fen either escaped burial or has suffered severe erosion in the post-medieval period.

The 17th century and later drainage of the fenland has been comprehensively reviewed by Professor Darby (1940b). Some of the engineering problems encountered are also examined by Hills (1967). The reader's attention is specially drawn to the detailed drainage histories of various parts of the North Level which have been discussed with great expertise by P.R. Charnley, until recently Chief Engineer to the NLIDB (Charnley 1977, 1979, 1980, 1983). The latter detailed histories illustrate clearly the manner in which drainage has to take account of pre-existing landforms.

II. The fenland project survey, 1977-83
by D.N. Hall

Introduction
The Cambridgeshire part of the North Level was surveyed using archaeological fieldwork techniques between 1977 and 1983. The parishes of Borough Fen, Newborough, Eye and Thorney were visited in winter months when the ground was bare and weathered. Each field was searched by walking in transects 30 metres apart, which ensured that most exposed monuments and habitation sites were discovered. A summary of the chief findings is given below; for greater detail the reader is referred to Hall (1985, 1987).

In general, there were few remains of the early prehistoric period, partly because the greater part of the old ground surface was covered by fen deposits. On the 'islands' and fen-edge where the pre-Flandrian surface could be examined the lithology was mainly of various types of clay which were unfavoured by early prehistoric settlers.

Early prehistoric
Turning to the Mesolithic period, only perforated polished stones are known from Eye and Borough Fen, and a lithic site occurs on sand under Borough Fen at Crowtree Farm (see Chapter 3: I).

The Neolithic period is likewise rather sparsely represented. Axes have been recorded, but none of the finds spots proved to relate closely to any identified habitation or monument. A lithic scatter that probably does represent settlement occurs at the Singlesole part of Thorney. There were also a few background flints west of Thorney 'island'.

The main prehistoric remains are two large dispersed barrow fields, named the Borough Fen and Catswater fields. The latter group is now plough damaged; the monuments lie in a dispersed manner around the Bronze Age fen-edge. Three barrows were partially excavated at Eye in 1910–15 and completed in 1984 in a salvage operation before destruction by quarrying.

The Borough Fen barrow field contains twenty-five barrows which are quite well preserved. Several of the clusters within it lie in a northwest-southeast alignment. Two barrows have been cut by a modern dyke, and a section of one of them (BoF 10d) was obtained when the dyke was cleaned, proving that the mound was artificial (see Chapter 3: I). The best preserved barrow in Borough Fen is only just visible, being buried by peat. The importance of the group is that several barrows are in good condition and not likely to have been robbed in the Middle Ages or by later antiquarians. Most were built on dry land in the Early Bronze Age, and were only subsequently engulfed by fen. Some of them probably still retain wet deposits *in situ* which would be important sources of post-Early Bronze Age environmental information.

No settlement site of the Early Bronze Age has been identified, but there were a few 'background' flints on the gravels at Eye and Thorney. Sherds and other occupation remains of the Late Bronze Age were found at the western part of Eye.

Iron Age
The Iron Age is well represented, mainly at Thorney on the gravels at Willow Drove. Here there are the usual dark occupation areas with sherds and other debris, often associated with cropmarks of enclosures. The largest Iron Age monument is an earthwork in Borough Fen, which survives as a ringwork with ditch and inner rampart some 220m in diameter. There is a possible slight outer ditch forming a concentric circle 280m in diameter (see Chapter 3: I).

Roman
Many sites of the Roman period occur, both on the upland and on the silt-lands in the north of Thorney parish. Deposits of silt laid down in the fen during the Iron Age became dry and habitable in the Roman period, and from evidence elsewhere, supported a grazing and salt-making economy (Hall 1987, 42–3). Salt water came inland up the natural drainage channels; it was collected and evaporated using fen peat. The northern part of Thorney parish just reaches this extensive settlement that occurs on the silt fen around Wisbech and in Lincolnshire (Phillips 1970). The sites are associated with cropmarks interpreted as animal paddocks and linking droves.

An abundance of sites also occurs on the upland of Eye and Thorney, some continuing from the Iron Age. Several of them have earthwork areas, and where ploughed reveal the usual occupation debris with sherds and burnt stones from hearths. All of them appear to be agricultural without signs of any large buildings as would be expected from a villa. A partially excavated site at Eye yielded a stone coffin. The pottery used is almost exclusively from the nearby Nene valley kilns. The Car Dyke, a Roman catch-water drain running from the Nene north along the Lincolnshire fen-edge, cuts along the western part of the region.

Medieval
Saxon material is known only from Eye at an early cemetery found in 1908. Recently more early Saxon burials were discovered in Bronze Age barrow mounds, also at Eye.

Fenland settlement of the Middle Ages was largely associated with various monasteries founded in the Saxon period, notably Peterborough, dating from the 7th century. Eye became the property of the abbey, and was organised manorially not from the village itself, but from Eyebury, a separate moated site. There were three other small monastic settlements in the parish, Tanholt, Northolm and the hermitage of Singlesole. Thorney was originally an anchorite cell and later developed into an abbey.

No previously unknown medieval sites were discovered during the recent survey; a few sherds were recovered from near Singlesole. The upland was subjected to ridge-and-furrow ploughing, now largely erased except for light-and-dark marks and linear banks of the old field boundaries. The historical records of the abbeys offer much local and topographical detail for the region. Several copies of a map made in the 14th century survive, showing the state of Thorney Fen at that time.

III. Distribution and Significance of Bronze Age Metalwork in the North Level
by J. Downes

Introduction
(Fig. 4)
Of the many studies of Bronze Age metalwork undertaken, some concentrate on a particular period of the Bronze Age and study all types of artefacts, others take a particular type and trace its technological development, and there are those that apply these and other elements of research to specific regions. The framework of this study is very broad temporally and typologically, whereas spatially it is very narrow, being defined by the limits of the North Level survey area. The aim of this paper is to investigate the distribution of bronze objects in relation to the wider context of Bronze Age material culture located along the fen-edge. This will be undertaken with reference to the reconstruction of 2nd millennium BC topography provided by survey (Hall 1987; see Chaper 2:II above) and the evidence recovered through excavation.

There is a general tendency in the archaeological literature for bronze artefacts to be considered in isolation; originally, however, they formed just a single, albeit conspicuous, element in a wider range of Bronze Age material culture. Here it is suggested that they can only be understood in terms of their social context. Moreover, in examining distribution, only patterns of final deposition are visible: the broader social role of bronze work remains hidden. Those depositional practices that can be detected, and the changes which occur in them do, however, constitute forms of social transactions, which embody the reproduction of social relations, and therefore may be seen in conjunction with variation in other fields of material culture and depositional practice.

A primary task in assessing spatial distribution patterns involves recognising the potential biases of the data-base. Figure 4 shows that the recovery rate of bronze artefacts is by no means constant. There is a peak just before the turn of the century, after which the number of finds recovered falls away, before rising to the present day. This pattern is not restricted to the North Level area, but is a constant trend embracing adjacent areas of the fen-edge. Although the recovery rate of bronzes varies through time, it is important to discern the spatial characteristics of these finds, since it is essential to have a sufficiently representative sample to allow comparative analysis.

In the late 19th century there was a general increase in industrial activities around Peterborough, including gravel and clay quarrying, both of which often involved hand-digging. These different forms of extraction contributed strongly to the peak noted in recovery of bronze objects. Although quarrying still continues, modern mechanical methods of extraction make it less likely that objects will be observed; this is particularly true of single finds.

Accompanying the early quarrying was the extensive development of Peterborough city centre which lies on slightly higher ground. The increase in bronze objects recovered from wetter, low-lying areas partly coincides with the change from pasture to intensive arable cultivation which has occurred most extensively during the past forty years (see Chapter 1: IV). The ensuing effects of peat erosion, which has become more marked in recent years, are that more scatters of prehistoric material including bronze artefacts are now being ploughed to the surface. As a consequence of these and other activities, different topographic areas have been exploited in various ways, all of which have produced archaeological material. Thus, although a bias-free picture can never be expected, this particular area does provide the potential for a fairly balanced sample.

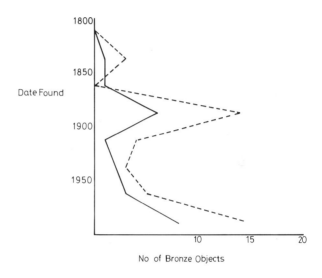

Figure 4 The recovery record of bronze artefacts from the North Level.

Earlier Bronze Age
(Fig. 5)
Surveys and excavations in the North Level area have provided a range of settlement and funerary data which is rich in comparison with other regions of Britain. For the earlier Bronze Age this evidence takes the form of settlement, field systems and burial mounds. Interestingly, metalwork from non-funerary contexts is unrepresented during the earliest phases of bronze working, with the possible exception of an awl from Fengate (Pryor 1980a, 130). This scarcity of earlier Bronze Age metalwork continues north, along the fen-edge, with no significant increase until the concentration occurs in the Trent valley in north Lincolnshire (Davey 1971, 1973; Rowlands 1976, 119). Similarly, to the south of the study area, the flat and flanged axes from Yaxley Fen and Whittlesey Mere (Evans 1881; Green 1977) represent the periphery of a concentration of earlier Bronze Age metalwork centred around Cambridge. Like the Trent valley, finds from the Cambridge area are so numerous that Rowlands (1976, 119) has termed it a 'metal working centre'.

The apparent peripheral nature of the study area is also revealed within the wider distribution of pottery. Whether or not Clarke's (1970) attribution of North and South types of beaker can be fully accepted (Lanting and van der Waals 1972), the local distribution of the two types does, none-

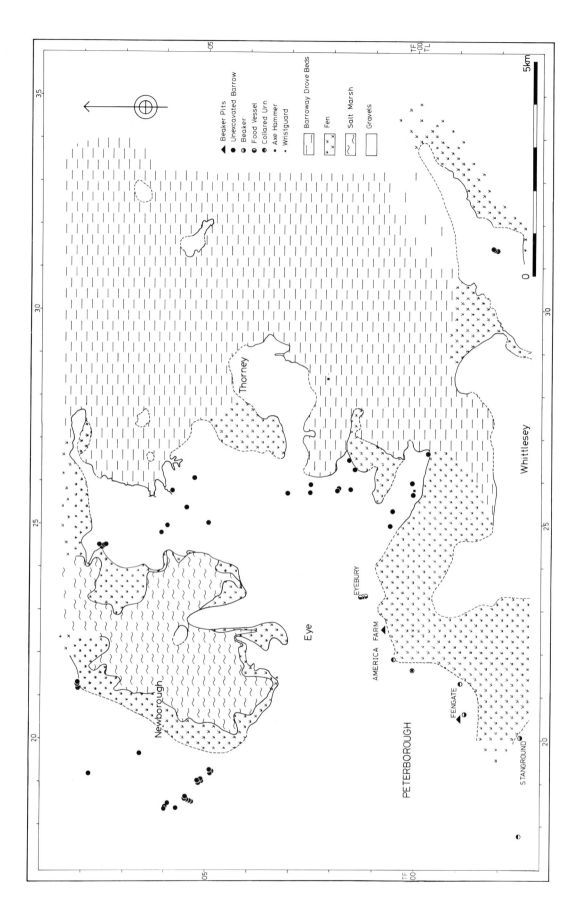

Figure 5 The distribution of contemporary sites and monuments in the North Level and immediate area.

theless, hint at a real 'boundary' or division. The presence of both Southern types of beaker (from Fengate and America Farm) and Northern British types (from Stanground) (Fig. 5) is of interest since the study area lies at the edge of the main concentration of Southern beaker types in East Anglia (Clarke 1970, 238–9) and below the concentration of Northern beakers, 94% of which are located above the Trent and Humber (Clarke 1970, 239–58). This trend is also recognisable in the distribution of food vessels, with the area constituting the interface of two recognised style zones (Megaw and Simpson 1979). As with the metalwork and northern beakers, Yorkshire food vessels concentrate to the north as opposed to the southern types which are found below the Severn-Wash line (Gibson 1986, 35). To the north of the study area, at Tallington, of two barrows excavated, the primary burial within the larger mound was associated with a Yorkshire food vessel (Simpson 1976), whilst another was found accompanying a secondary burial at Barnack (Donaldson 1977). However, a southern bipartite vessel together with two Yorkshire types were associated with inhumations in a group of three barrows excavated at Eyebury, to the south of Eye in the study area (Leeds 1912, 1915; M. Howe pers. comm.).

Although the distributions of metalwork and ceramics suggest a peripheral situation for the North Level area, it is perhaps significant that of the few barrows excavated in the lower Welland valley, close to the northwestern fen-edge, several contained rich burials. For instance, at Barnack, Cambridgeshire, a cemetery barrow contained a primary male inhumation accompanied by a tanged bronze dagger, a bone/ivory pendant, a greenstone wristguard trimmed with gold and a fine bell-beaker (Donaldson 1977). At Tallington, Lincolnshire, in the smaller of the two barrows excavated, there were four or five primary inhumations accompanied by a pair of bronze earrings and a long necked beaker (Simpson 1976). On the route of the Northborough A15 bypass, Cambridgeshire, a large multiple inhumation barrow contained ten burials, of which the earliest burial was associated with a long-necked beaker, and another burial was associated with a bronze dagger (French and Pryor in prep.).

These burials constitute a discrete group of some of the richest burials in the eastern region since 'grave goods associated with beakers in East Anglia are virtually non-existent' (Lawson 1984, 146). Yet, as we have seen, they occur in an area previously deemed peripheral under different criteria. This serves to highlight the problems associated with interpreting style zones and spatial concentrations of artefact types without understanding the underlying complexities of social organisation. In particular this brings the whole concept of 'core' areas (see papers in Barrett and Bradley 1980) into question.

Survey in the North Level region has greatly added to the number of recognised barrows in the area (Hall 1987). The main result of this increase in numbers is to highlight their spatial distribution which tends to favour the immediate contemporary fen-edge (Fig. 5) and the lower Welland valley in the vicinity of the monument complex around the Maxey henge and cursus. Whilst the distribution at Maxey may conform to the wider phenomenon of barrow cemeteries clustering around Neolithic monuments (Whittle 1981; Bradley 1984; Thorpe and Richards 1984), the positioning of barrows adjacent to the fen-edge requires further attention.

The 'marginal' situation of the barrows on the fen-edge should not be seen purely in economic terms. Barrett (1980, 81) stresses that the siting of barrows in places where they would be most visible could be more important than 'the need to avoid wasting utilised land'. This idea may be extended to include the positioning of barrows and, therefore the dead, in areas which are conceptually appropriate. In the landscape of the fen-edge the barrows doubtless would have been visible, not only to those living and working in fertile inland areas, but also to those who approached from the fen. Their situation, therefore, is not merely on marginal land but the meeting place of many 'worlds' (Barrett 1980, 81), or the all important liminal area (Leach 1977) which bounds all categories of distinction. The relationship between boundaries and the dead within a different form of discourse is revealed in the location of three earlier Bronze Age crouched inhumations interred in the ditches of the enclosure system at Fengate (Pryor 1980a, 174–5).

Although a small proportion of the recognised barrows has been excavated in this 'marginal' area, a beaker burial was excavated on the fen-edge at Fengate by Abbott (Leeds 1922, 235; Clarke 1970, 490). Moreover, in the same area a crouched inhumation was located in a sizeable pit which shared distinctive characteristics with 'many other' similar pits thought then to represent houses (Abbott 1910, 333). Abbott (1910, 333–34) notes 'the average example would be a circular excavation about 10–12 feet in diameter at the top, 3.5–4 feet deep, and saucer shaped', occasionally the larger pits were accompanied by smaller pits. The fill of the pits maintained a notable consistency with a basal layer containing 'remains of charred wood and many had burnt pot-boilers, flint flakes and scraps of animal bones'. They also contained an unusually high proportion of fine beaker pottery (Gibson 1980, 235). This pattern is continued in the discovery of two further pits, during more recent excavations at Fengate (Pryor 1974, 14). Similar pits were excavated further along the fen-edge at America Farm which also produced fine beaker pottery (Clarke 1970, 490). A crouched inhumation associated with beaker pottery and abundant charcoal was also found in a secondary context in a massive pit at Etton Woodgate, which may have been initially used as a quenching pit in the production of charcoal. This burial was situated in the midst of the second concentration of burial mounds at Maxey (Pryor et al. 1985, 302–3), and highlights the situation of these pits in areas of mortuary activity.

When the evidence is drawn together, we can identify particular areas in the landscape which were deemed appropriate for burial and, moreover suggest that these locations were most significant in the symbolic representation of the contemporary social landscape. Furthermore, the consistent association of fine beaker pottery and burnt material in pits which in some cases contained burials, within these areas provides ample evidence for the extensive ritual activity that must have surrounded the process of interment. The unweathered condition of the fine ware sherds leads Gibson (1980, 235) to suggest a ritual of which the breaking of vessels was a part. This would suggest a complex sequence of events involving rites of passage, elaborate practices of feasting and the destruction of various materials.

Whilst the majority of the beaker types found at Fengate and America Farm are Late Southern styles (Clarke 1970, 490; Gibson 1980, 235), the occurrence of All-over

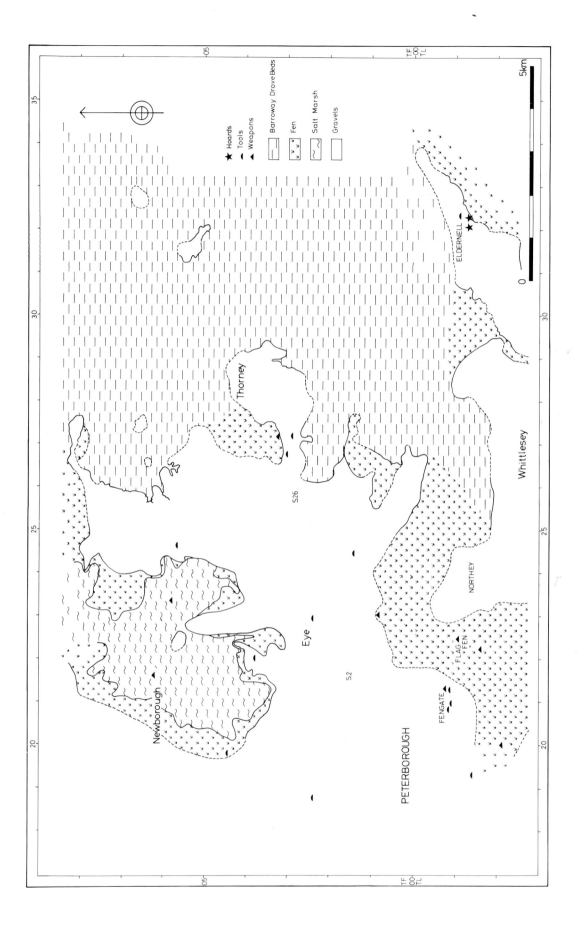

Figure 6 The distribution of metalwork recovered from the North Level.

Corded, Wessex-Middle Rhine and rusticated beaker (Clarke 1970, 490) would indicate a long period of activities — a minimum of two or three of Lanting and van der Waals' (1972) steps. It has not been possible to determine the definite association of beaker types within features, however it does seem likely that the majority of the Southern beakers were present in the 'ritual' pits (Clarke 1970, 490–1; Gibson 1980, 235). An extended beaker chronology is now well accepted for southern Britain, which necessarily involves an overlap of beakers, food vessels and collared urns. This is confirmed in the North Level and lower Welland valley, by association in the case of beakers and food vessels, and by radiocarbon dates for food vessels and collared urns. Although these relationships remain problematic, suffice it to say that all the earlier Bronze Age material located within the study area is peripheral to main concentrations both north and south, a condition which continues through the Middle-Late Bronze Age.

Middle and Later Bronze Age
(Figs 6–10)

There is no evidence yet to suggest that bronze casting was being undertaken in the early 2nd millennium BC within the study area, nor that metalwork was being deposited in non-funerary contexts. This picture changes fundamentally in the succeeding period where evidence is found both for metal production and for its widescale deposition.

The bulk of evidence for bronze working is derived from the Fengate area. Two scraps of cast bronze waste were found in a pit (Hawkes and Fell 1943, 192), and a 'runner' from a mould was discovered in a pot now assigned to the later Bronze Age (Champion 1975, 136; Pryor 1974, 31). Of particular significance is the reference to a 'small cup shaped hole, found in 1912, (which) had a lining of clay 4 inches thick' (Hawkes and Fell 1943, 194), which may now be re-interpreted as a bronze smelting furnace. Furthermore, analysis of the metallic composition of a spearhead fragment and a 'spill' of bronze, from the recent Fengate excavations, revealed them to be almost identical (Craddock 1980, 129). However, from this evidence alone it is difficult to establish the actual scale of production.

The general distribution of bronze objects recovered from the fen-edge shows that the North Level area is peripheral to a large concentration of metalwork further south towards Cambridge. The sheer volume of metalwork from the fen-edge, especially in southern Cambridgeshire, has long attracted attention, many authors regarding it as comparable with the Thames valley. Burgess (1974, 179) saw both areas as rising new centres at the beginning of the Middle Bronze Age, areas whose new wealth stemmed from the 'new water based religion'. In a somewhat different framework, Rowlands (1980, 34–5) views the apparent rise of the Thames valley and East Anglian fens as being due to the advantage of their situation as riverine (such as Fengate) and coastal settlements, whose natural resources provided them with the wealth and power to usurp the older centres of power. However, this correlation between concentrations of finds and centres of power is hardly straightforward since we have to distinguish between production and consumption in spatial and social terms. Moreover, it is of interest that the Cambridge area, a suggested production centre (Rowlands 1976, 118–9), has yielded no direct evidence

(moulds, furnace fragments *etc.*) for production of bronze implements (Lawson 1984, 161).

To date only single finds of Middle Bronze Age metalwork are known to have been recovered from the North Level. A similar situation existed for the Late Bronze Age metalwork until the recent discovery (in 1988) of a post-Wilburton hoard at Eldernell, near Whittlesey (Fig. 6). The hoard (Figs 8–10, catalogue numbers 1–20) consisted of twelve socketed axes, a peg socketed spearhead, a small socketed hammer, two lumps of bronze, part of a plano-convex ingot and a small fragment, probably from a socketed axe. A sherd of Late Bronze Age pottery found with the hoard suggests that the material had been deposited either with, or inside, a pottery vessel.

This collection of metalwork had a linear distribution of no more than 15m in extent, in a ploughed field, and had been brought to the surface as a result of ploughing. The first two socketed axes illustrated (Fig. 8, nos 1 and 2), however, were found some years previously to the larger hoard, and were discovered together with further samples which were unfortunately discarded. This earlier find was situated aprroximately 60–70m away from the main hoard, and it is highly probable that they were part of a single hoard deposit. In addition to these finds, a socketed axe was discovered in 1982 in a neighbouring field (Hall 1987, 49 and fig. 31). This is an example of a group of bronzework which, under traditional archaeological classification procedure, would be labelled a 'founders' hoard that comprises at least three separate deposits.

Given the accidental discovery and poor recording of so many bronzes, there is a tendency to presume that bronze artefacts found in fairly close proximity to each other are part of a single deposit or hoard. There are numerous instances of this, for example the material from Bullington and from West Halton in Lincolnshire (Davey 1973, 93 and 98), are but two examples. It is possible that some of these cases might have been more than one deposit. This point has been noted by Barrett and Gourlay (1984), and led them to suggest that many hoards could represent 'multiple rather than single deposits' (1984, 349). The identification of some hoards as multiple deposits not only questions the status of hoards as single events, but conversely goes some way to resolving difficulties in the interpretation of single finds.

Much work has been directed towards interpreting hoards, although single finds, especially in East Anglia, comprise the bulk of the finds (Burgess 1974, 198; Rowlands 1976, 118–119). Rowlands (1976, 99) stresses the importance of comparing the distribution of hoards with that of single finds in the same region. When the single finds from the North Level are plotted onto a map of the contemporary 2nd millennium BC topography (Fig. 6), it can be seen that weapons comprise the main proportion of metalwork deposited in 'wet' places (rivers, marshy areas and lagoons), whereas the majority of tools have been recovered from areas that would have been dry land (Fig. 7). Although the study area from which the sample is drawn is fairly small, when a larger area of the fen-edge is examined the trend remains the same.

To suggest that metalwork from 'wet' areas conforms to some sort of controlled depositional strategy would be considered acceptable; to suggest the same for the tools recovered from dry land one immediately encounters the problem of which finds are considered as 'stray finds' or

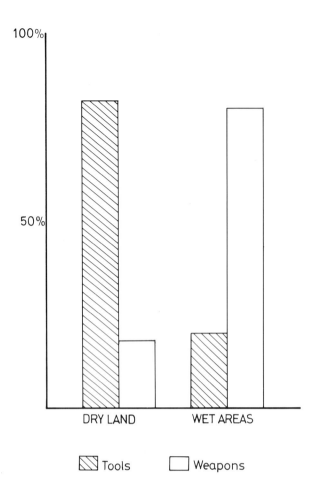

Figure 7 Histogram showing the ratios of different categories of single bronze objects in relation to wet and dry environments.

'chance losses'. That such finds are 'stray', or without a context, is a problem that also exists for many hoards, but is frequently ignored as each artefact provides a 'context' for the others. This can be very misleading due to the casual manner in which many hoards are recovered. With regard to the question of 'chance losses', in the North Level study area the distribution of single finds on dry land tends to be restricted, like the barrows, to the fen 'skirtlands', with a notable decrease westwards up to and on the limestone uplands. Thus tools are derived from areas with proven and presumed scant tree cover. That these tools were lost during extensive felling and clearing of the forest is unlikely. A contextual description for a single palstave located at Fletton, Peterborough, does indicate that these finds are more deliberate than 'chance losses'; the palstave was found 'four feet deep in a basin of gravel, with one face touching the Oxford Clay' (Peterborough Museum accessions list).

Single finds from rivers or areas that were previously wet or boggy are frequently termed votive offerings, the widespread phenomenon being displayed most remarkably in the material from the Thames (Needham and Burgess 1980). In the North Level, tools have also been identified as a discrete type of metalwork from a particular context and so, too, can be seen as purposeful deposits.

The occurrence of single finds forming part of multiple deposits is indicative that they are part of the same motivation that was behind the deposition of hoards. As Bradley (1982, 110) suggests, the deposition of metalwork from all the above mentioned classes of context 'may be variants of one underlying pattern.' As the practice of placing weapons in graves in southern Britain decreases, so the number of votive deposits of weapons increases (Bradley 1982, 113; 1984, 102) giving rise to the theory that such deposits took the place of grave goods. Although it would be an oversimplification to suggest *all* deposits of metalwork are deposited in the place of a grave, it should be observed that finds of Bronze Age metalwork, such as at Eldernell, are frequently in or with a pottery vessel, treatment similar to that accorded the cremated bones of the dead in this period; likewise multiple deposits of bronze work imitate the large cemeteries found from the later Bronze Age. At this point it is appropriate to examine the contemporary funerary evidence in the study area.

It is notable that the decline in single burial, in barrows, coincides with the dramatic increase in metalwork deposited in non-funerary contexts. Indeed, this period marks the introduction of large, apparently undifferentiated cremation cemeteries throughout southern Britain. An area of burials at Fengate described by Hawkes and Fell (1943, 190) can now be identified as an example of such a cemetery. Although the exact location of this feature is difficult to establish it appears to have been positioned about 150m to the west of a ditched enclosure (C. Taylor 1969, fig. 1). Thus, it was situated inland and to the northwest of the field systems as they faced out towards the fen. The cemetery consisted of 20 inhumations and 130 cremations deposited in and around a large oval ring ditch, *c.* 25 × 35m. The two different forms of burial showed no spatial distinction and one of the cremations, which are curiously described as being 'in little skin bags' (C. Taylor 1969, 7) was accompanied by fragments of a bucket urn. Hawkes and Fell (1943, 190) also record that 'at the east end of the oval was the contemporary crematorium'. This enclosed cemetery is unusual as it combines two burial rites and the crematorium or pyre area — a feature which makes it more akin to the continental urnfield tradition (Coles and Harding 1979, 361).

Although burial traditions alter through time, an examination of the character of settlement and land management along the fen-edge reveals a stable and largely unchanging economic base, revolving around livestock, mainly cattle, and possibly salt production (Gurney 1980; Pryor 1980, 18). Indeed, the high degree of structure in the cultural and physical landscape is the most striking feature of the North Level area. The extensive layout of field systems and enclosures which stretch along the fen-edge, taking in Fengate and Northey (see Chapter 3: IV; Gurney 1980) creates an impression of 'order and stability' (Pryor 1980, 188) within a regulated landscape, unlike the 'discontinuity and competition' (Bradley 1984, 114) postulated for the Thames valley.

The apparent continuity breaks down around 1000 BC, with increased flooding and raised groundwater levels which probably contributed to the demise of the ditched enclosures (Pryor 1980, 186-9). However, during this hiatus in the occupation of Fengate large scale land clearance is detectable nearby, at Holme Fen and Whittlesey Mere (see Chapter 1: IV; Godwin and Vishnu-Mittre

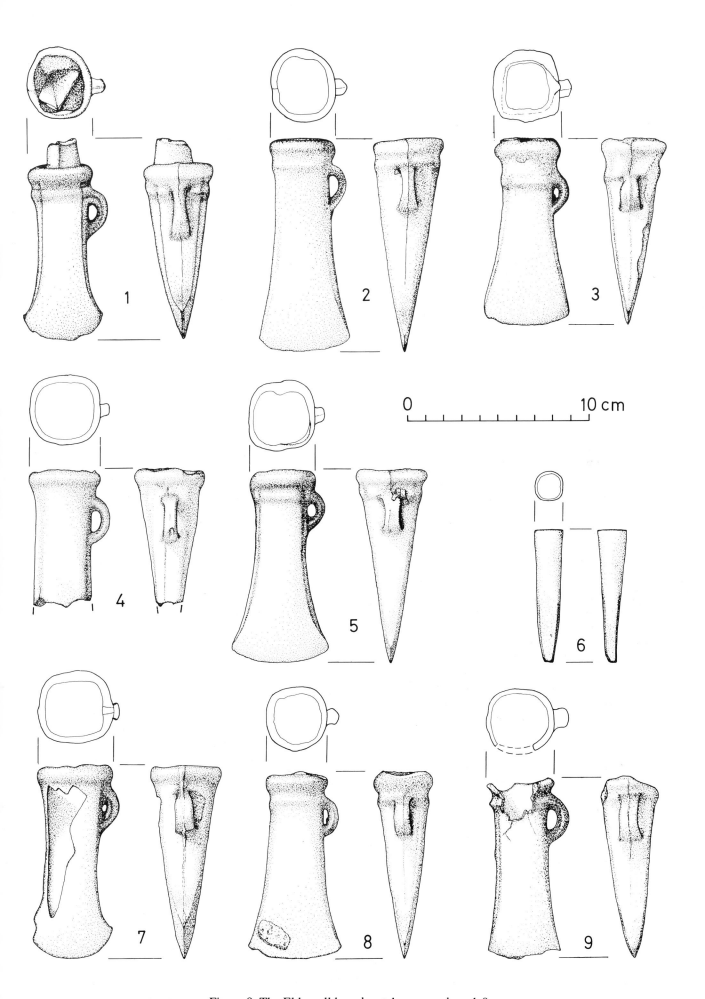

Figure 8 The Eldernell hoard, catalogue numbers 1-9.

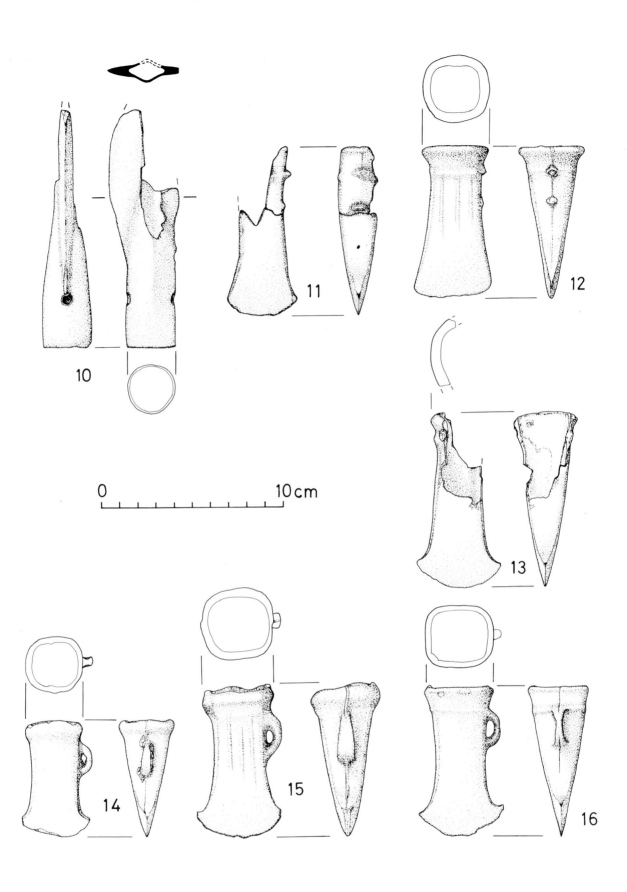

Figure 9 The Eldernell hoard, catalogue numbers 10-16.

0   10 cm

1975). Settlement shift may be witnessed in the construction of Flag Fen (Pryor *et al.* 1986), and two other occupation areas (Fig. 6) located by Hall (1987, 32, 49), one to the south of Eye (site 2) and the other to the southwest of Thorney (site 26). This evidence suggests a reorientation in economic practices as the fen-edge continues to be occupied. Ecomomic practices may have altered, but there is no apparent variation in the distribution pattern of metalwork in the region during the late Bronze Age period.

Conclusion

It has been possible, by examining a small area of fenland, to document both continuity and discontinuity in time and space, as demonstrated in different forms of material culture. Changes in the burial record appear to coincide with variation in the deposition of metalwork. However, the evidence of settlement and land use maintains a notable constancy and stability, particularly during the early and middle Bronze Age. This apparent dichotomy may originate in the distinction between the wet fen and the dry areas around it. Both the situation of burials in the Early Bronze Age and the differential deposition of metalwork in the later Bronze Age serve to define these two physically different areas. Embodied within these practices is a categorisation process which structured the physical and social landscapes. The changes noted in social practices are governed by the basic distinction between wetland and dryland. The apparent wet-dry distinction which influenced metalwork depositional practices would have been part of much broader and more elaborate classification schemes. This is revealed in the evidence of mortuary practices where the same topographical division assumes different meanings involving the place of the living and the place for the dead. Thus, in investigating metalwork deposition we are seeing more than a division of the landscape or selectivity of deposit; we are glimpsing a particular conception of the world and what to do in it.

Catalogue of illustrated metalwork from the Eldernell hoard (Figs 8-10)

(Note: all widths of axes were taken across the cutting edge.)

1. **Looped socketed axe** with piece of bronze scrap pushed into mouth of socket. Mouth sub-rectangular with one moulding; below, horizontal rib across faces and sides. Body hexagonal in section; traces of longitudinal casting seam along each side. Cutting edge blunted and corroded. Surfaces corroded in patches. Length (of axe): 9.3cm; width: 4.4cm.

2. **Looped socketed axe.** Mouth sub-rectangular with one moulding; below, horizontal rib across face and sides. Body sub-rectangular in section; traces of longitudinal casting seam along each side. Cutting edge well preserved; small hole under top of loop. Length: 11.3cm; width: 4.9cm.

3. **Looped socketed axe.** Mouth sub-rectangular with one moulding; below, horizontal rib across face and sides. Body sub-rectangular in section; traces of longitudinal casting seam along each side. Cutting edge blunt. Surfaces badly corroded. Length: 10.0cm; width: 4.7cm; weight: 316.8g.

4. **Looped socketed axe.** Mouth sub-rectangular with one moulding. Body sub-rectangular in section; traces of longitudinal casting seam along each side. Cutting edge broken off in antiquity. Surfaces smooth and fairly well preserved. Length: 7.4cm; weight: 119.8g.

5. **Looped socketed axe.** Mouth sub-rectangular with one moulding; below, horizontal rib across face and sides. Body sub-rectangular in section; slight traces of longitudinal casting seam along each side. Cutting edge sharpened. Surfaces fairly well preserved. Length: 10.3cm; width: 5.2cm; weight: 245.4g.

6. **Socketed hammer,** found inside no. 7. Mouth rounded in section; end squared; hollow socket. Surfaces fairly well preserved. Length: 7.1cm; width: 1.6cm; weight: 38.0g.

7. **Looped socketed axe.** Mouth sub-rectangular with one moulding. Body sub-rectangular in section; traces of longitudinal casting seam prominent along each side. Cutting edge now blunt and abraded on one side. Surfaces badly corroded including large hole in one face. Length: 10.3cm; width: 4.3cm; weight: 170.4g.

8. **Looped socketed axe.** Mouth sub-rectangular with one moulding; below, horizontal rib across face and sides. Body sub-rectangular in section; traces of longitudinal casting seam along each side. Cutting edge damaged. Surfaces badly corroded in places. Length: 9.9cm; width: 5.0cm; weight: 255.6g.

9. **Looped socketed axe.** Mouth sub-rectangular with one moulding; below, horizontal rib across face and sides. Body sub-rectangular in section; traces of longitudinal casting seam along each side. Cutting edge broken. Surfaces pitted, mouth broken. Length: 9.6cm; width: 4.0cm; weight: 178.7g.

10. **Leaf-shaped socketed spearhead.** Blade convex in outline, edges now blunted and corroded. Mid-rib angular in section, externally and internally. Two opposite peg-holes in socket. Surfaces rough; blade broken and corroded. Length: 12.6cm; width (max.): 3.8cm; weight: 103.4g.

11. **Looped socketed axe.** Single moulding. Body sub-rectangular in section with trace of longitudinal casting seam along side. Cutting edge corroded. Axe damaged and loop broken in antiquity. Length: 8.9cm; width: 3.9cm; weight: 96.6g.

12. **Looped socketed axe.** Mouth sub-rectangular with one moulding; below, horizontal rib across face and sides. Body sub-rectangular in section; three vertical ribs on each face; traces of longitudinal

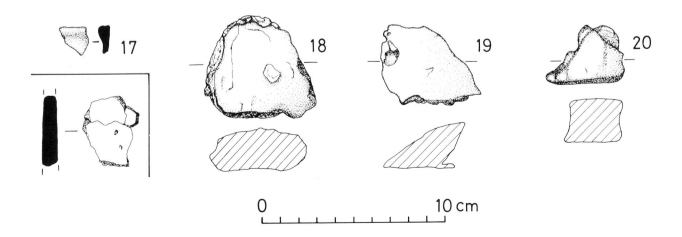

Figure 10 The Eldernell hoard, catalogue numbers 17-20, and the sherd of pottery.

casting seam along each side. Cutting edge now blunt and corroded. Surfaces fairly well preserved, loop broken off in antiquity. Length: 8.2cm; width: 4.2cm; weight: 193.2g.

13. **Socketed axe**. Mouth with one moulding broken; below, horizontal rib across face and sides. Body sub-rectangular in section. Cutting edge sharpened, now abraded. Axe badly damaged and partly corroded. Length: 9.3cm; width: 4.5cm; weight: 112.4g.

14. **Looped socketed axe**. Mouth sub-rectangular with one moulding. Body sub-rectangular in section; traces of longitudinal casting seam along each side. Cutting edge damaged. Surfaces fairly well preserved; casting fault around loop. Length: 6.2cm; width: 3.7cm; weight: 67.8g.

15. **Looped socketed axe**. Mouth sub-rectangular with one moulding; below, trace of horizontal rib on one face. Body sub-rectangular in section; three vertical ribs on each face; traces of casting seam prominent along each side. Cutting edge now blunt and corroded.

Surfaces fairly well preserved. Length: 8.1cm; width: 4.6cm; weight: 170.1g.

16. **Looped socketed axe.** Mouth nearly rectangular with one narrow moulding; below, horizontal ridge across faces and sides. Body oval in section; traces of longitudinal casting seam along each side. Cutting edge jagged. Some corrosion on surface. Length: 8.0cm; width: 4.6cm; weight: 132.3g.

17. **Rim fragment,** probably from a socketed axe. Length: 1.5cm; width: 1.5cm.

18. **Lump of bronze**. Length: 5.4cm; width: 6.0cm; weight: 260.1g.

19. **Part of plano-convex ingot**. Length: 4.2cm; width: 5.0cm; weight: 162.4g.

20. **Lump of bronze**. Length: 3.1cm; width: 5.0cm; weight: 112.9g.

(Present location of the artefacts: catalogue numbers 1 and 2 are in Whittlesey Museum; numbers 3-20 are in private hands.)

Chapter 3. The Dyke Survey
by Charles French

Introduction
(Figs 1 and 2; Table 1)

The dyke survey results are discussed by general archaeological period and within four main areas of the North Level: Borough and Newborough Fen, Morris Fen, Guy's Fen and Flag/North Fens (Figs 1 and 2). Dyke survey necessarily depends on the activities of drainage authorities and the grants made available to them; consequently the dykes surveyed comprise only a fraction of those actually available. The account of the survey that follows is necessarily patchy, both topographically and chronologically, and must be regarded as an initial statement of a continuing, long-term investigation.

Although some radiocarbon dates do exist for the North Level area (Appendix V; Table 1), they are too few and often poorly provenanced. Consequently the dating of the possible archaeological 'sites' is generally of an approximate and relative nature. Work in progress by the Fenland Project will hopefully enable more specific placing of these 'sites' within the fenland sedimentary sequence.

The reader should note that the present report is best read in conjunction with Hall's (1987) account of the surface survey for the parishes of Newborough, Eye, Thorney and Whittlesey.

To date some 28km of dyke have been surveyed in the North Level. From this survey seven 'new sites' have been discovered, and four known sites (discovered by D.N. Hall or previously known) investigated (Fig. 2). It is worth stressing that no trace of the seven new sites was evident either in Hall's surface survey (1987) nor by our own field walking of the same areas once the sites were identified by dyke survey.

I. Borough and Newborough Fens

Introduction
(Figs 1, 2, 11, 12, 24, 29, 33, 41)

Borough and Newborough Fens have witnessed more attention from the drainage authority (the NLIDB) in the past five years and consequently more sites have been discovered and investigated in this part of the North Level than anywhere else. The area is defined by the River Welland to the north, the Car Dyke to the west, the high ground of Werrington (Peterborough) and Eye to the south, and the Cat's Water to the east (Figs 1 and 11).

Two late Mesolithic/earlier Neolithic sites have been discovered at Crowtree and Oakhurst Farms; these are probably outliers of a very much larger buried Mesolithic/Neolithic landscape on the northwestern side of the Eye peninsula (Figs 2, 11, 12, 24, 29) (see below). Two barrow sites (Borough Fen sites BoF 3 and 10d) discovered by Hall (1987) were also investigated, as was the purported monastic site of St Pega's (BoF 7) and the possible Romano-British settlement site (BoF 1) (Figs 2, 11, 33, 41).

First a general account of the stratigraphic development of the Borough/Newborough Fen area will be given, followed by more specific descriptions of investigations at individual sites or landscapes as exemplified by various dyke profiles. Thicknesses of deposits and their heights above Ordnance Datum will be given to the nearest 5cm.

Stratigraphy
(Figs 3, 11, 14, 25, 26, 29, 34, 35, 42)

The Borough/Newborough Fen areas contain deposits representative of two distinct sedimentological sequences. The eastern half of this area is dominated by the fen clay and roddons (Hall 1987, figs 9 and 10); the western half is characterised by an absence of fen clay and the presence of a mixture of peat and alluvium (Fig. 3). Between the two areas is a transitional zone in the vicinity of the modern village of Newborough (Hall 1987, fig. 10).

The eastern half of Borough/Newborough Fen is approximately defined by the Crowland Washes to the north, Newborough village to the west, Eye to the south and the Cat's Water to the east (Fig. 3). It is characterised by the following sequence of deposits (Figs 14, 25, 26, 29) (Hall 1987, figs 9 and 10). The underlying geological substrate is Oxford Clay, which is overlain in places by Fen (March) gravels such as in the south where the land rises onto the Eye peninsula and in the west as the land rises onto the fen margin. The surface of the subsoil falls from c. +0.20m OD in the west to c. -1.40m OD in the east.

A buried soil tends to be developed on the subsoil where the ground rises onto the fen 'islands' or onto the fen margins to the south and west. It is composed of silty clay loam to sandy loam, varies in thickness from c. 10–80cm, and often exhibits an undulating surface.

A thin lower peat, c. 5–40cm thick, overlies the buried soil or subsoil. It thins landward to the south and west. The surface of the lower peat varies in height from c. +0.55cm to as low as c. -0.85m OD. It is suspected that the upper surface of the peat is generally truncated to some extent by the action of deposition of the overlying fen clay.

The overlying fen clay or Barroway Drove Beds is thick, and thins westwards to the west side of Newborough village and southwards to the Eye peninsula. It was drained by an extensive system of roddons (Hall 1987, fig. 9). Thin peat lenses are sometimes found within the fen clay (such as described in Chapter 1: III). The fen clay varies in thickness from 15 to 145cm; its upper surface varies in height from c. +0.75 to c. -1.05m OD.

The upper peat (Hall 1987, figs 10 and 12) is thin (c. 10–40cm) and extremely well humified, although it is sometimes mixed with silt loam alluvium. Its upper surface varies from c. 0.35 to c. 1.30m OD.

Dykes exhibiting this stratigraphic sequence include 1–4, 14 and 45–48 (see Appendix IV) (Figs 14, 25, 26, 29; M. Pls 1–4, 7–15).

The second sedimentological unit in the western half of the fen is less complex and more indicative of the fen margin or 'skirtland'. This area of fen is approximately

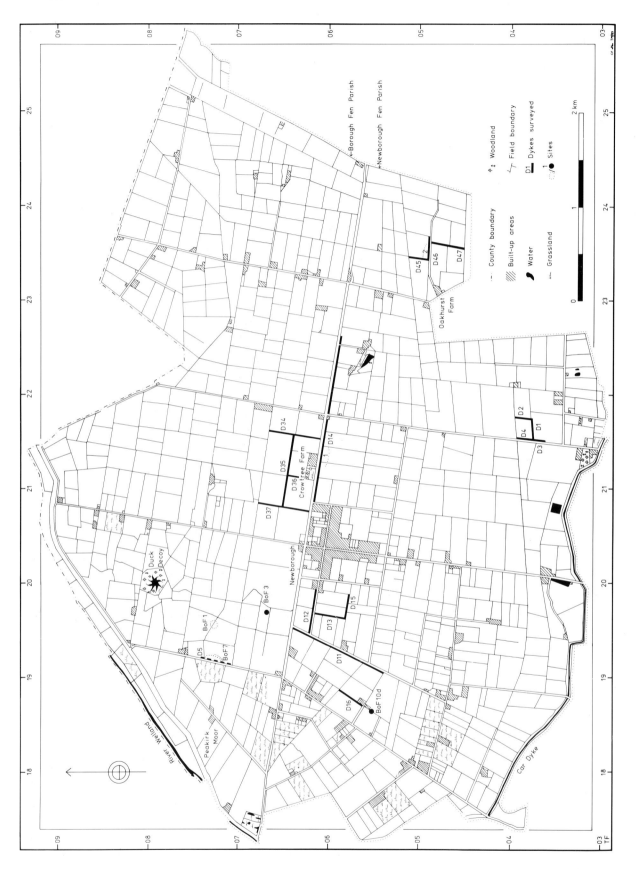

Figure 11 Modern landscape and topography, the dykes surveyed and sites discovered.

32

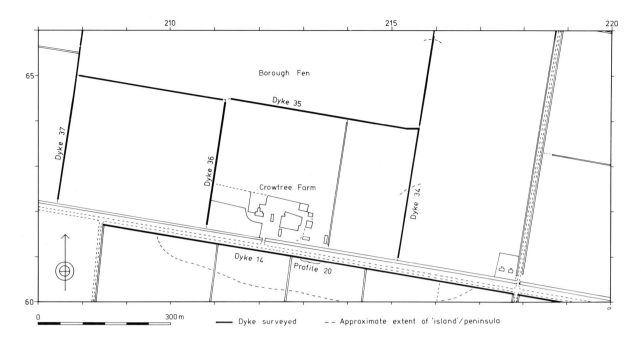

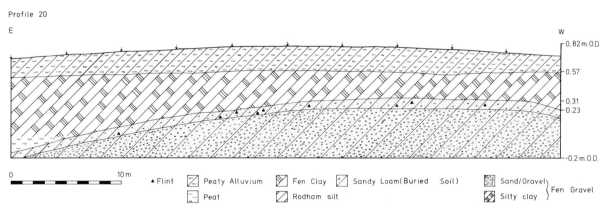

Profile 20

E
W

▲ Flint   ▨ Peaty Alluvium   ▨ Fen Clay   ▨ Sandy Loam (Buried Soil)   ▨ Sand/Gravel ⎫
⎬ Fen Gravel
▨ Peat   ▨ Rodham silt   ▨ Silty clay ⎭

Figure 12 Location and section of Crowtree Farm 'island'.

defined by the River Welland to the north, the Car Dyke to the west and south, and the western side of Newborough village to the east.

The underlying subsoil consists of Fen gravels/First Terrace deposits resting on Oxford Clay. The surface of the subsoil rises from c. +0.75 to c. +0.90m OD from east to west. The buried soil developed on this subsoil consists of a sandy or silt loam, from c. 10–28cm thick, with its surface at c. +0.90 to c. +1.25m OD. A mixture of peat and silt loam alluvium overlies the buried soil. It ranges in thickness from c. 60–150cm, with its upper surface at c. +1.55 to c. +2.0m OD (Fig. 34).

Dykes 5 (BoF 7) and 11 exhibit this stratigraphic sequence (see Appendix IV) (Figs 34, 42; M. Pls 18, 20, 21). The Borough Fen barrows also fit within this sequence.

The area of transition from one stratigraphic unit to the other occurs in the immediate vicinity of the modern village of Newborough (Fig. 11), as exemplified by Dykes 12, 13, 15 and 34–37 (see Appendix IV) (Fig. 35; M. Pls 5, 6, 16).

The Fen gravel subsoil rises gently from east (c. +0.20m OD) to west (c. +0.75m OD), as the lower peat thins westwards to a thickness of only 2 or 3cm, with its upper surface at c. +0.5 to 0.85m OD. Similarly the overlying fen clay thins westwards to a thickness of c. 5–20cm, with its upper surface at c. 0.75–0.90m OD.

The dykes and the possible 'sites' recognised during dyke survey will now be discussed in greater detail in approximate chronological order.

Archaeological Survey: Later Mesolithic/Earlier Neolithic

1. Crowtree Farm (TF 5213 3061) (Dykes 14, 34–37)

Survey and excavation
(Figs 11–14, 17, 70; Pls I and II)
Dyke 14 was first surveyed in the autumn of 1982, and the borehole survey and trial excavations took place in February 1985. Further survey to the north of Crowtree Farm took place in the autumn of 1987, and revealed the approximate area of dry land around the farm in Dykes 34–37 (Figs 11 and 12).

Dyke cleaning of c. 1.7km of dyke parallel to the Peakirk-Thorney road (B1443) immediately to the east of Newborough village revealed an elongated, c. 500 metre wide (west to east), peninsula composed mainly of sand and fine gravel just to the south of Crowtree Farm (Figs 11–14; Pl. I; M. Pls 1–4). This 'tongue' of land extends northeastwards from beneath the modern village of Newborough to the west; the site is now thought to be situated at the eastern extremity of a peninsula, of at least seasonally dry land, extending northeast out from the early

33

Plate I The buried peninsula at Crowtree Farm, Dyke 14 (Site 1).

Plate II The buried soil beneath the fen clay and peat at
Crowtree Farm, in trench 2.

prehistoric fen-edge (Fig. 70). Indeed the farm buildings on the north side of the road are built on the same peninsula; the northern part of the same peninsula may be seen in Dykes 34–37.

The upper surface of the buried soil that developed on the peninsula is at c. +0.20m OD at its highest point. Seven flints of the later Mesolithic/early Neolithic were recovered from the buried soil revealed in the dyke 14 section, and another six flints were recovered from the buried soil exposed in Dyke 34 (see Middleton below). This was overlain by a very thin and in places discontinuous lens of basal peat, which thickens eastwards as the fen dips seaward. A considerable thickness of fen clay and a thin upper peat complete the overlying stratigraphic sequence (Figs 11–14; Pls I and II).

The buried soil consists of an apedal, somewhat porous (10–30% total porosity), pinkish grey (5YR6/2) loamy sand, c.15cm thick, which is developed on a structureless yellow (10YR7/8) sand subsoil. There was no evident horizonisation of the buried soil either in the dykeside or in the excavation trial trenches (Pl. II). Stratigraphic and artefactual evidence suggest that the soil on this peninsula was available for man to frequent during the Mesolithic and earlier Neolithic periods.

On the basis of the dyke survey and the later borehole survey, two 2 metre-square trial trenches were excavated to reveal the buried soil in plan (Figs 17 and 18). Trench 1 was located on the eastern edge of the peninsula between boreholes 36 and 36A, and Trench 2 was approximately in the centre of the higher ground of the peninsula between boreholes 45 and 46 (Fig. 17).

Trench 1 revealed a thickening (eastwards) fen clay (c.115cm thick) overlying a thinning but waterlogged

Figure 13 Location of Dyke 14.

35

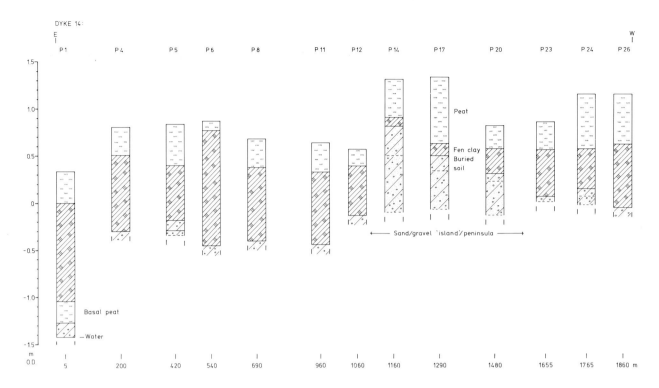

Figure 14 Dyke 14 profiles.

buried soil (*c.* 10cm thick). Wood was found on and in the buried soil, and it is possible that some of it was in fact axed (M. Taylor pers. comm.). A sample core for pollen analysis was taken from this trench (see Scaife below).

Trench 2 revealed a thicker (*c.* 15cm) buried soil beneath a lens (*c.* 4cm thick) of more organic soil, possibly the remains of a basal peat, and a thin layer of fen clay (*c.* 30cm thick) (Pl. II). Both the basal peat and the organic component of the upper 5cm of the buried soil were submitted for radiocarbon assay. The dates obtained from the basal peat were (Har–8513) 3660 ± 60 BP (2270–1890 Cal. BC) off the peninsula and (Har–8510) 3740 ± 100 BP (2460–1890 Cal. BC) on the peninsula in Trench 2. The radiocarbon date from the upper buried soil in Trench 2 was (Har–8913) 3190 ± 90 BP (1730–1230 Cal. BC) (see Appendix V.II).

The excavation of Trench 2 proceded as follows. First, the ploughsoil and fen clay were removed by hand. The organic lens and buried soil were then sampled for pollen before their removal (see Scaife below); next, the buried soil was removed and thoroughly wet-sieved through 4 and 2mm mesh sieves. It was found to contain charcoal and fifty-one flints including several flint debitage flakes, two bladelets and a micro-burin from the adjacent borehole 46 (see Middleton below). The relatively high density of artefacts in such a small volume of soil (*c.* 600,000cu. cm) suggests that the peninsula was indeed a 'site', and was utilised for at least part of the year.

The boreholes made for the geophysical survey also contained a small number (10) of flints from the buried soil, and they are described below.

The Flints from Crowtree Farm and its Region
by H.R. Middleton

Catalogue of illustrated flints
(Figs 15–17; Tables 2 and 3)

1. Crowtree Farm: **Core Type A2** with cortical striking platform. CTF 85 Archive No. 30. Surface find.
2. Crowtree Farm: **Core Type A2**. CTF 85 Archive No. 5. Trench 2, spit 2.
3. Crowtree Farm: **Micro-burin Butt Type notched RHS**. CTF 84 Archive No. 141. Borehole survey.
4. Crowtree Farm: **Edge Blunted Point** with ancillary retouch. CTF 85 Archive No. 123. Trench 2, spit 3.
5. Crowtree Farm: **Rod**. CTF 85 Archive No. 8. Trench 2, spit 2.
6. Crowtree Farm: **Denticulate** (note denticulations are not visible in top view). CTF 85 Archive No. 131. Trench 2, spit 3.
7. Crowtree Farm: **Utilised Flake**. Dyke 14, profile 20. Archive No. 83.
8. Crowtree Farm: **Retouched Flake**. Dyke 14, profile 20. Archive No. 76.

Introduction
(Figs 15 and 17; Tables 2 and 3)
A total of 111 flints were recovered from eleven locations in the North Level survey area between 1982 and 1986 (Table 3), with 74 of these coming from the survey and excavation undertaken at Crowtree Farm (Table 2).

With such a small number from each site (no more than 12: see Table 3) (except Crowtree Farm) no attempt has been made to quantify the attributes of each assemblage or to attempt detailed technological reconstructions. Instead the form (*i.e.* typology and technology) of the artefacts will be used to date the layers in which they were found.

General Description
(Table 2)
Seventy-four flints were recovered from Crowtree Farm, from dyke survey, the later small-scale excavations in Trench 2 and the borehole survey. The overall typology is given in Table 3. The assemblage from the buried land surface appears to be discrete and contrasts with the material from the dykeside exposures, which may be later in date (see below).

Context	D14/P20	D34/P3	D34/P4	Surface	T2/F1	T2/spit 1	T2/spit 2	T2/spit 3	T2/spit 4	Borehole survey	Totals
Type											
Waste flake (C)	4	2	-	-	-	5	7	1	4	3	26
Waste flake (NC)	-	-	1	-	2	3	3	8	9	2	28
Irregular workshop waste	-	1	-	-	-	-	-	-	-	-	1
Core Type A2	-	-	-	1	-	-	-	1	-	-	2
Core Type B1	-	-	-	-	-	-	1	-	-	-	1
Core Type E	-	1	-	-	-	-	-	-	-	-	1
Micro-burin	-	-	-	-	-	-	-	-	-	1	1
Utilised flake	1	-	-	-	-	-	-	-	-	-	1
Retouched flake	1	-	-	-	-	-	-	-	-	-	1
Rod	-	-	-	-	-	-	1	-	-	-	1
Edge blunted point (w/AR)	-	-	-	-	-	-	-	1	-	-	1
Denticulate	-	-	-	-	-	-	-	1	-	-	1
Burnt flint	1	-	-	-	-	-	3	1	-	4	9
Totals	7	4	1	1	2	8	15	13	13	10	74
Total weight (g)	35	76	2	15	1	10.5	22	151	10.5	5	328
% pieces under 1 g	14	25	-	-	100	75	73	71	87	100	54.5

Notes: C = cortex present; NC = no cortex; T2/spit 1 = Trench 2/spit 1; D14/P20 = Dyke 14/profile 20

Table 2. Typology of the flints from Crowtree Farm.

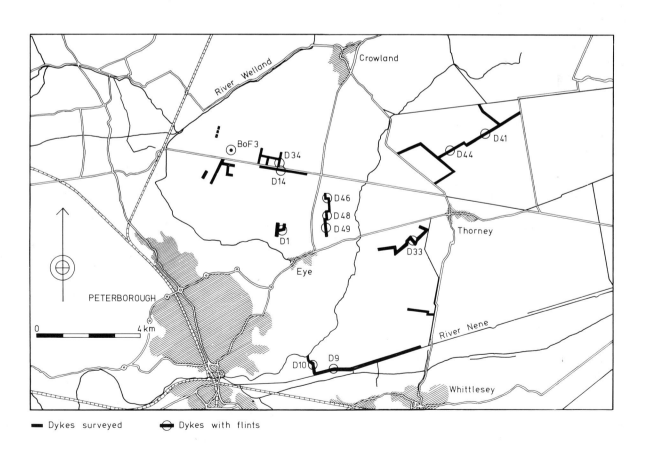

Figure 15 The occurrence of flints in the dykes surveyed.

Area: Borough Fen

Context	D1/P7	D46/P2	D48	D49	BoF 3
Waste flake (C)	-	1	-	-	1
Waste flake (NC)	-	2	-	-	-
Irregular workshop waste	-	-	-	1	-
Core Type A1	-	-	-	-	1
Core fragment	-	-	-	-	-
Core R/J flake	-	1	-	-	-
Utilised flake	1	-	?1	-	-
Truncated blade	-	-	-	-	-
Scraper Type A2	-	-	-	-	1
Burnt flint	-	-	-	-	1
Totals	1	4	1	1	4
Total weight (g)	7	26	30	11	119

Area:	Morris Fen		Guy's Fen	
Context	D41/P2	D44/P4	D33/P1/2	D33
Waste flakes (C)	1	2	-	1
Waste flakes (NC)	1	1	-	1
Irregular workshop waste	-	-	1	-
Core Type A1	-	-	-	-
Core fragment	1	-	1	-
Core R/J flake	-	-	-	-
Utilised flake	-	-	-	-
Truncated blade	1	-	-	-
Scraper Type A2	-	-	-	-
Burnt flint	-	-	-	-
Totals	4	3	2	2
Total weight (g)	16	17	154	32

Area: Northey

Context	D9	D10	Totals
Types			
Waste flake (C)	4	-	10
Waste flake (NC)	3	1	9
Irregular workshop waste	2	-	4
Core Type A1	-	1	2
Core fragment	-	-	2
Core R/J flake	-	-	1
Utilised flake	3	1	6
Truncated blade	-	-	1
Scraper Type A2	-	-	1
Burnt flint	-	-	1
Totals	12	3	37
Total weight (g)	78	43	533

Notes: C = cortex present; NC = no cortex; D1/P7 = Dyke 1/profile 7

Table 3. Typology of flints found in the dyke survey (excluding Crowtree Farm).

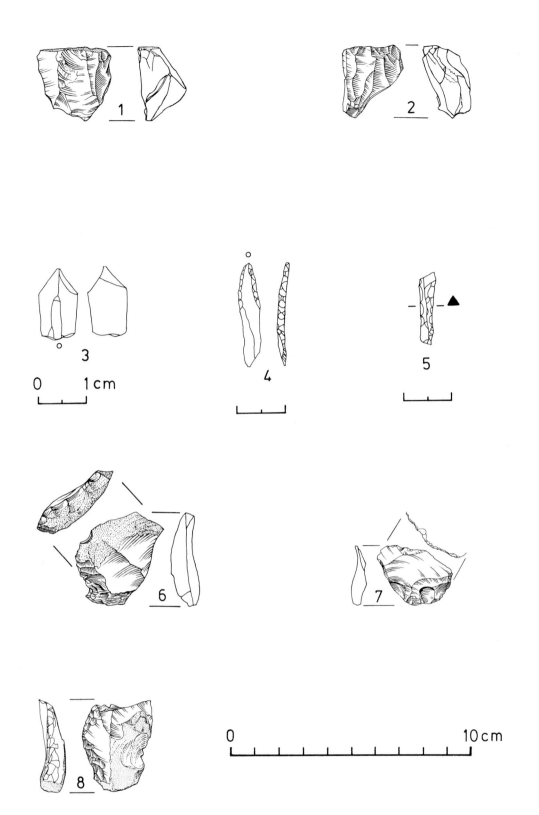

Figure 16 Flints from Dyke 14 and Crowtree Farm site.

There does not appear to have been appreciable movement of small (> 1g) flint chips through the profile of the buried soil; this suggests a lack of post-depositional distortion. Despite this, no spatial analysis was possible due to the small size of the sample. Nevertheless, the flints and other finds from the borehole survey are plotted together in Figs 12 and 17.

Technology
(Fig. 16)
The flints are made of good quality, dark brown or light grey flint with little evidence of frost-fracturing, or other flaws. Where present, the cortex on all of the pieces is thin and light brown, revealing the source of the material to be the local Welland valley gravels which can be found just to the northwest of the site itself. All of the pieces display a thin, white patina.

The technology appears to have been directed towards the production of small blades from well-prepared cores. Where present, the bulbs of percussion indicate an incipient 'bending fracture' (Coterell and Kamminga 1987), suggesting the use of soft hammers — possibly using an indirect percussor. The cores recovered from the site (e.g. Fig. 16, nos 1 and 2) have abraded platforms where irregularities were removed prior to striking, with the exception of one which has been struck from many directions, but was discarded before being fully worked — doubtless due to the poor quality of the flint involved (not illustrated). The other cores appear to have been worked until blades of adequate size could no longer be made and were then discarded.

The presence of a large number of small (defined as weighing > 1g) chips and waste flakes (64.5%) would indicate that knapping was undertaken *in situ*, although the sample is too small to say what stages of core production were involved.

The production of microliths is indicated by the presence of a single micro-burin in the palaeosol in borehole 46 (Fig. 16, no. 3).

Typology
(Table 2)
The overall composition of the assemblage is summarised in Table 2. Five implements were found, with three coming from an excavated context.

Microliths
(Fig. 16)
Two were recovered, one a rod (Fig. 16, no. 4), the other an edge blunted point with ancillary retouch (Fig. 16, no. 5). Both forms can be paralleled at other sites of late Mesolithic date in the east Midlands and northern East Anglia, such as at Shippea Hill (Clark 1955, fig. 2), Two Mile Bottom, Thetford (Jacobi 1984, fig. 4.7) and Honey Hill, Northamptonshire (Saville 1981, fig. 3).

Denticulate
(Fig. 16)
This example (Fig. 16, no. 6) fits well with a late Mesolithic date. Its careful manufacture contrasts strongly with later Neolithic and Bronze Age examples (e.g. Pryor 1985, figs 107–109).

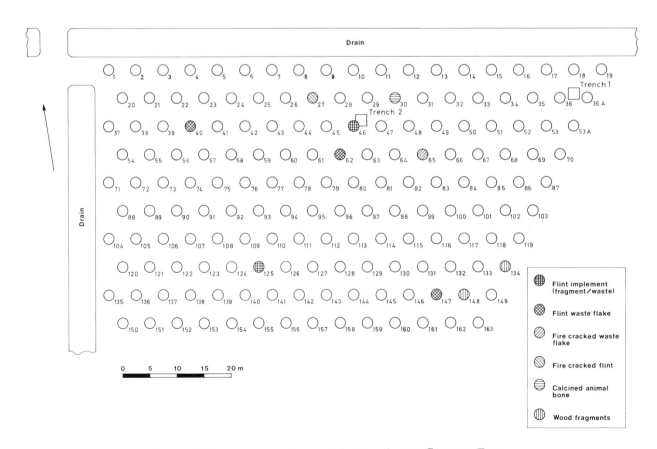

Figure 17 Borehole, trench and artefact locations at Crowtree Farm.

Other Implements
(Fig. 16)
One utilised flake (Fig. 16, no. 7) and one retouched flake (Fig. 16, no. 8) were recovered from dyke 14, profile 20. Both of these were unpatinated, in contrast to the rest of the assemblage. The material from Dyke 34, profiles 3 and 4, is in a similar condition and is the product of a slightly cruder technology, which is suggestive of a later use of the site, possibly in the Neolithic, although more precise dating is impossible.

The Magnetic Susceptibility Survey at Crowtree Farm
by A. Challands

Introduction
(Figs 12, 14, 20)
The magnetic susceptibility survey of Crowtree Farm was designed to test a technique which could be used to define the limits of sites revealed by dyke survey, or other methods, in parts of the fen where the depth of superficial deposits renders aerial photography and simple surface survey impossible.

The site in question was selected for trial survey because a well buried palaeosol containing flint artefacts in a discrete area had been observed in earlier dyke survey. The complete soil profile is described above and in Figs 12 and 14, and a cross-section profile was composed of the peninsula on which the site is situated, from the borehole logs (Fig. 20).

Methods
(Figs 17–19, 21, 22; Table 4)
The borehole survey was undertaken over a *c.* 45 by 79m area in order to measure the magnetic susceptibility of the buried soil with a field sensor (see Appendix III.2). Boreholes were augered at 5m intervals to an offset grid pattern in order to give maximum coverage (Fig. 17). Contour maps were made of the site for the present ground

surface (Fig. 18) and the old land surface (Fig. 19), using 0.05m contour intervals.

The results of the field measurements are presented in diagramatic and table form (Fig. 21; Table 4). All samples of the palaeosol were tested in the laboratory to compare the accuracy of the laboratory and field magnetic susceptibility values. A Bartington M.S.I. meter with a prototype borehole sensor was used in the field; in the laboratory this was linked to a coil sensor M.S.I.B. (Appendix III.2). The absolute readings are presented in diagramatic and table form (Fig. 22; Table 4).

A total of 165 boreholes were drilled for the Crowtree Farm survey. Three field measurements were taken on each layer within each borehole. The average of the three readings for each layer was calculated and multiplied by 1.26 to provide relative magnetic susceptibility values. The field sensor is not calibrated to provide absolute magnetic susceptibility values as the mass and volume of the soil at the point of measurement cannot be determined (Oldfield *et al.* 1984, 14). The laboratory absolute magnetic susceptibility readings were only carried out on the palaeosol samples.

The magnetic susceptibility data on the palaeosol, derived from both the fieldwork and laboratory testing, have been presented using symbols of different sizes (Figs 21 and 22: circles = laboratory; triangles = field). The mean and the standard deviation were calculated for both field and laboratory readings. Each magnetic susceptibility value which is higher than the n-1 standard deviation added to the mean, is shown shaded on the symbols (Figs 21 and 22).

Field magnetic susceptibility readings were also taken on the layers above and below the buried soil to determine the range of values for each layer. Although the palaeosol was buried below peat and fen clay, magnetic enhancement could have taken place due to the disturbance of the layers by agricultural processes. Likewise the magnetically enhanced minerals such as maghaemite may have been leached out of the palaeosol into the underlying

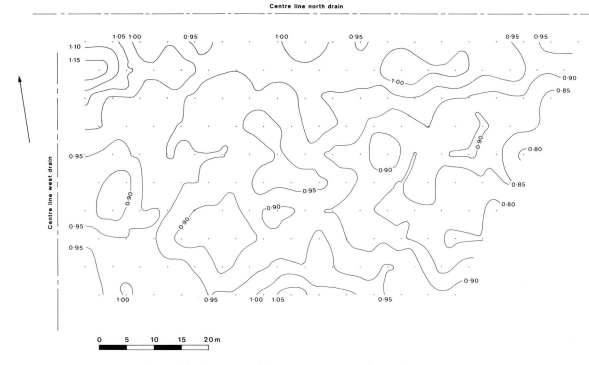

Figure 18 Contours of the present land surface at Crowtree Farm.

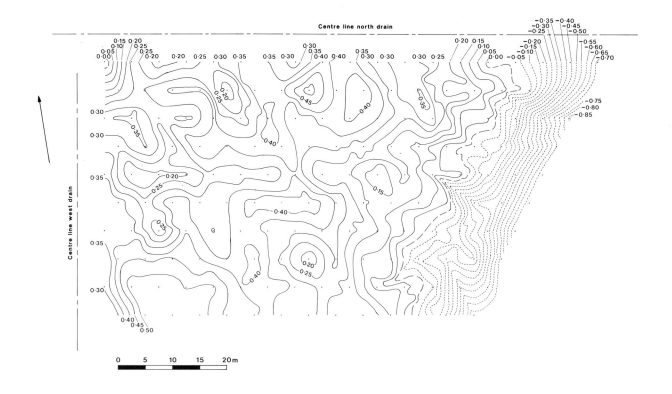

Figure 19 Contours of the buried land surface at Crowtree Farm.

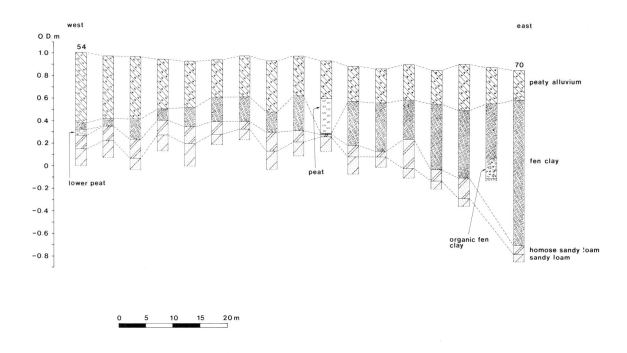

Figure 20 Schematic section through the peninsula, boreholes 54 to 70.

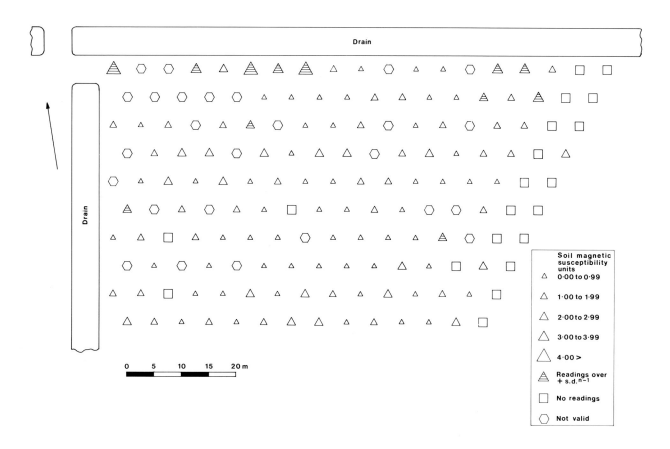

Figure 21 Field magnetic susceptibility at Crowtree Farm.

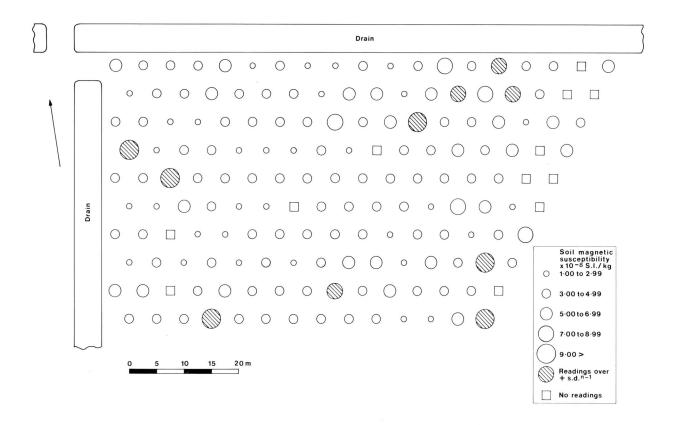

Figure 22 Laboratory magnetic susceptibility at Crowtree Farm.

Borehole number	(A)	(B)	(C)	Possible contamination	Borehole number	(A)	(B)	(C)	Possible contamination
1	7.98	5.20	*		51	1.68	6.72		basal peat and marling trench
2	NV	3.21			52	1.68	2.55		basal peat and marling trench
3	NV	4.14			53	none	5.21		
4	3.36	3.23	*	basal peat	53A	none	4.68		
5	2.10	5.83			54	NV	9.52	+	basal peat
6	5.46	2.58	*	basal peat	55	1.26	1.28		
7	3.36	3.21	*	basal peat	56	2.10	3.19		
8	5.04	2.60	*	basal peat	57	2.10	3.23		
9	1.68	2.56			58	NV	2.56		
10	0.84	3.26			59	2.10	1.92		
11	NV	2.59			60	0	2.59		
12	0.84	4.52			61	2.10	3.86		
13	0.84	8.64			62	2.10	2.57		
14	NV	3.86			63	NV	none		marling trench
15	3.36	8.98	*/+		64	1.68	3.85		
16	3.36	3.67	*		65	2.52	4.44		
17	1.68	4.51			66	0.84	6.45		
18	none	none		no palaeosol	67	1.68	3.89		
19	none	5.77			68	1.68	5.10		
20	NV	2.58			69	none	none		fen clay disturbed by subsoiling; borehole stopped by wood
21	NV	3.22			70	2.10	5.17		
22	NV	3.19			71	NV	3.87		
23	NV	5.80		basal peat	72	0.84	3.89		
24	NV	3.18			73	2.52	14.82	+	
25	0.42	4.47		basal peat	74	0.84	3.83		
26	0.42	3.21		marling trench; no fen clay	75	2.10	3.79		
27	0.42	2.58		basal peat	76	0.42	3.19		
28	0.42	5.74			77	1.68	3.23		
29	1.68	5.76		marling trench; thin fen clay	78	0.42	3.19		basal peat
30	1.68	1.72		basal peat	79	0.84	3.22		
31	0.84	5.09		basal peat	80	1.26	3.85		
32	0.84	8.84	+	basal peat	81	1.68	4.57		
33	2.94	8.18	*	trace of basal peat	82	0.84	4.51		basal peat
34	1.68	8.98	+		83	0.84	4.40		basal peat
35	3.36	8.60	*	marling trench	84	0.42	3.95		
36	none	3.19		no palaeosol	85	0	3.26		marling trench
36A	none	none		wood on subsoil	86	none	none		borehole stopped in fen clay by wood
37	1.68	3.0		basal peat and marling trench?	87	none	none		
38	0.42	3.24		basal peat	88	2.94	1.97	*	traces of subsoiling in fen clay
39	1.68	1.91		marling trench; no fen clay	89	NV	2.62		traces of subsoiling in fen clay
40	NV	2.55		basal peat and possible marling trench	90	1.26	5.91		
41	1.68	3.87		basal peat and possible marling trench	91	NV	4.63		
42	2.94	3.93	*		92	1.26	2.60		traces of subsoiling in fen clay
43	NV	3.87			93	0.42	2.59		
44	0.84	3.21			94	none	none		marling trench; palaeosol mixed with peat
45	0.42	7.66			95	0.42	3.27		
46	1.68	4.47			96	0	4.61		
47	NV	5.08		basal peat and wood					
48	0.42	9.97	+	marling trench; no fen clay					
49	1.68	4.56							
50	NV	3.22							

Borehole number	(A)	(B)	(C)	Possible contamination	Borehole number	(A)	(B)	(C)	Possible contamination
97	1.26	3.24		marling trench; no fen clay	131	0.84	5.39		
98	0	3.93		basal peat	132	none	3.19		traces of subsoiling in fen clay
99	NV	2.81		basal peat					
100	NV	7.14		traces of subsoiling in fen clay	133	2.52	19.80	+	traces of subsoiling in fen clay
101	1.68	5.63			134	none	4.75		
102	none	2.66			135	1.68	6.06		
103	none	none			136	1.26	5.52		traces of subsoiling in fen clay
104	0.84	4.43							
105	1.26	3.35			137	none	none		marling trench; palaeosol removed
106	none	none		marling trench; disturbed palaeosol	138	0.42	3.16		basal peat
107	1.26	2.14			139	0.42	5.20		basal peat
108	0.42	2.64			140	2.52	3.83		basal peat
109	0.84	4.03			141	0	3.25		basal peat
110	0.84	3.99			142	2.52	3.83		basal peat
111	NV	3.34			143	1.26	8.95	+	subsoiling; fen clay mixed
112	0.42	3.22		basal peat	144	0.42	3.37		
113	0.84	4.78			145	2.10	5.74		traces of subsoiling in fen clay
114	0.84	2.73							
115	0.84	4.64		marling trench	146	0.42	3.18		
116	2.94	4.11	*	traces of subsoiling in fen clay	147	1.26	3.17		
					148	0.42	3.91		
117	NV	2.61			149	none	none		wood; could not drill into palaeosol
118	none	3.21		marling trench	150	2.10	3.15		basal peat
119	none	8.0			151	1.68	3.88		
120	NV	2.71			152	0.42	4.42		basal peat
121	0.42	3.21			153	1.68	28.14		basal peat
122	NV	2.71		traces of subsoiling in fen clay	154	0.42	3.89		
123	0.42	4.08			155	1.68	3.19		
124	NV	2.57		basal peat	156	2.52	4.58		marling trench; top of palaeosol disturbed
125	0.42	3.26			157	2.10	4.69		
126	0.42	2.72		marling trench; palaeosol disturbed	158	0.42	4.24		
127	0.42	4.06			159	1.26	3.26		marling trench
128	0.84	5.09		traces of subsoiling in fen clay	160	0	1.94		basal peat
129	0.42	5.89		marling trench; palaeosol disturbed	161	0.84	1.47		
					162	2.10	5.86		
130	2.10	2.73			163	none	36.19	+	

Key : (A) = field measurements in magnetic susceptibility units; (B) = laboratory measurements in x 10 to the -8 SI/kg; (C) = significant values above mean and standard deviation to the n-1; * = field significant values; + = laboratory significant values; NV = not valid; none = no magnetic susceptibility measurement taken

Table 4. Field and laboratory magnetic susceptibility results for Crowtree Farm, set against possible sources of contamination.

layers. If the range of readings for either of the two layers above the buried soil had been lower than the range for the buried soil, then contamination would have been unlikely; in the event, readings from the fen clay varied very little from the palaeosol, so significant contamination of the palaeosol by the clay is unlikely. The range of readings from the topsoil was significantly higher than the average readings of the palaeosol, so the topsoil could possibly contaminate the palaeosol.

Validity of the Field Data
(Figs 21 and 22)
A comparison of the field (Fig. 21) and laboratory (Fig. 22) magnetic susceptibility measurements, shows that the two sets of data rarely correspond: in fact, there is only one borehole, number 15, where the significant readings (*i.e.* those above the mean plus the standard deviation) correspond on both field and laboratory magnetic susceptibility measurements. Since the lower values (*i.e.* those below 0.99 for the field readings and 2.99 for the laboratory readings) dominated, they were used to check the correspondance of units and values. Only 14.6%, or 8 out of 55, of these low readings from the field magnetic susceptibility testing correspond with the low laboratory magnetic susceptibility values. It must therefore be assumed the field magnetic susceptibility units obtained from the buried soil are unreliable. The reason for this may be that the very low magnetic susceptibility units from the palaeosol are too low for effective measurement with the prototype borehole sensor.

Field magnetic susceptibility units obtained on the sandy loam subsoil underlying the palaeosol were generally lower than those obtained from the palaeosol itself, and formed no coherent pattern with the field or laboratory values.

Tite (1972, 14) quotes substantially larger magnetic susceptibility values for six other archaeological sites. However, the figures which he quotes are from Iron Age and later sites which were probably occupied intensively over a longer period of time than the probable late Mesolithic/early Neolithic site at Crowtree Farm. High magnetic susceptibility values are generally a function of the intensity and length of human occupation on a site — but on sites where iron concentrations are high the occupation need not necessarily be so intense (Tite and Mullins 1971, 219).

Possible Contamination
(Table 4)
Magnetic susceptibility readings taken with the field sensor on the peaty alluvium topsoil proved to be very high when compared with values recorded from other layers. The relative magnetic susceptibility unit of the topsoil ranged from 22 to 42 units, compared to the fen clay where the field sensor values ranged from 0 to 2.94 units, and the palaeosol where field sensor measurements ranged from 0 to 7.98 units.

Peat is normally of zero or very low magnetic susceptibility, so the high magnetic susceptibility units for the peaty topsoil is probably due to magnetic enhancement caused by persistent stubble burning.

Conclusions
(Figs 16 and 17; Table 2)
Is there a future for field magnetic susceptibility reconnaissance on areas below the peats and sediments of the fenland? On the basis of the survey results from Crowtree Farm, the answer would appear to be no. However, the time-saving advantages of field as opposed to laboratory testing are considerable, and with improvements in the technique, it may prove viable.

There are many other questions which this survey has posed: the question of the effects of mineral movement occurring on sandy soils, for example (Graham 1976, 63). Soil micromorphological analysis of the buried soil at Crowtree Farm (see French below) has revealed much movement and deposition of iron oxides and hydroxides throughout the post-depositional life of the palaeosol as well as hydromorphism or gleying. There is also the problem of defining and distinguishing between higher magnetic susceptibilities, brought about by decaying natural vegetation or anthropogenic factors, such as fires and occupation debris (Tite 1972). Indeed the soil micromorphological analysis has revealed that the palaeosol was much affected by secondary rooting of fen plants as well as the possible anthropogenic disturbance of the soil (see French below). Despite these observations, there is no direct way of correlating or discerning the potential effects of these soil processes on the observed magnetic susceptibility values.

Soil micromorphology
by Charles French
(Pls II and III)
The buried soil profile exposed in Trench 2 was sampled in two intact blocks for thin sectioning (after Bullock *et al.* 1985a, b) (see Appendix I). The detailed micromorphological descriptions are found in Appendix VI.

As will become apparent from the micromorphological analyses of the other two buried 'island' sites of Oakhurst Farm (see 3.I.2) and Morris Fen (see 3.II.1), and of the Eye peninsula (see 3.I.3), the details of the soil micromorphology are remarkably similar. Consequently, the following interpretation of the results also applies to the other three micromorphological analyses.

The surviving buried soil profile at Crowtree Farm (Pls II and III, M. Pl. 59) is an illuvial argillic or Bt horizon of an argillic brown earth (Avery 1980; McKeague 1983). This horizon becomes better developed and more pronounced in the lower half of the buried soil, in terms of the increased abundance of clay coatings. An argillic brown earth (or *sols lessivé*) is created by the process of clay translocation known as lessivage. Clay particles are moved or translocated down the profile (or eluviated) and re-deposited (or illuviated) in a textural B horizon as clay coatings on the surface of the voids and within the fine soil fabric (Bullock and Murphy 1979; Fisher 1982; McKeague 1983). The illuviated horizon is called a Bt horizon (Fisher 1982; Limbrey 1975).

Three possible phases of clay illuviation have been identified. In the first phase, rare moderately birefringent limpid and laminated dusty clay coatings are found on grains, in the void space and in the groundmass. The relative scarcity of limpid clay, which is normally associated with an undisturbed woodland cover (Fisher 1982; Macphail 1985a; Slager and van de Wetering 1977) suggests that relatively little clay translocation had occurred before interference by man in the later Mesolithic/early Neolithic. It is generally thought that the major periods of clay translocation in the Flandrian occurred in the Atlantic (Fedoroff 1969; Keeley 1982) and the sub-Boreal periods

(Keeley 1982; Kwaad and Mücher 1977). Some clay illuviation may also have occurred previously in the late Devensian and early Flandrian (*c.*10,000 to 7,000 BP) (Bullock and Murphy 1979). In all these periods, seasonally dry periods alternating with moist periods would have provided optimum conditions for clay translocation (Bullock and Murphy 1979).

In the second phase, there are many non-laminated, weakly speckled dusty clay coatings on grains and in the groundmass. Soil disturbance such as caused by the clearance of trees damages the soil peds, thus causing the mobilisation of 'coarse' material (Macphail 1985a, 1986). The coarse material, such as poorly sorted charcoal, fine organic matter and silt, gives the coating its 'dirty' appearance (Macphail 1987). Thus the predominance of these dusty clay coatings is probably indicative of forest clearance at Crowtree Farm.

There are a variety of other pedological features that are also indicative of soil disturbance associated with probable tree clearance. Very fine sand size, sub-angular fragments of limpid and dusty clay occur rarely and randomly within the groundmass and void space. Thus clay coatings appear to have broken up as a result of soil disturbance. Also, loose aggregates of fine sand are occasionally found as channel infills. This is also suggestive of soil disturbance. In addition, one channel in the upper half of the Bt horizon contains a succession of 'crescentic-shaped' infills of dusty clay. This could possibly indicate successive phases of soil disturbance, but more probably suggests that there was variation in the intensity and amount of clay translocation within one disturbance episode.

In the third phase, many laminated and especially non-laminated dusty clay coatings in the groundmass and void space appear to contain amorphous organic matter which gives them a 'dirty' appearance. This type of 'coarse' illuviation does not normally occur under stable forest (or grassland) conditions (Imeson and Jungerius 1974). It is probable that the translocation of clay with organic matter may be associated with further disturbance of the prehistoric soil. This later 'coarse' illuviation may well be associated with soil disturbance caused by tree clearance, and in particular with tree-throw as interpreted at Hazelton long cairn (Macphail 1985b).

The palaeosol at Crowtree Farm then suffered severe soil truncation and erosion: both A and Eb horizons have been truncated. Certainly once this unconsolidated sand peninsula had been cleared of substantial vegetational cover the soil had been subjected to considerable disturbance, and would have been very susceptible to erosion. Such extensive soil erosion was probably coincident with either freshwater flooding associated with the growth of the lower peat, or more probably the subsequent marine transgression which led to the deposition of the fen clay. Indeed the few 'papule-like', sub-rounded aggregates of silt, clay and amorphous organic matter found within the groundmass of the Bt horizon are suggestive of water-eroded and -transported soil material being incorporated within the cleared and disturbed soil.

Both the upper and lower halves of the buried soil exhibit a few sesquioxide-impregnated, non-laminated, weakly birefringent dusty/dirty clay coating pseudomorphs of roots or stems. They may either reflect the rooting of fen and salt marsh plants in the truncated soil, or possibly be relics of previous vegetation growing *in situ*

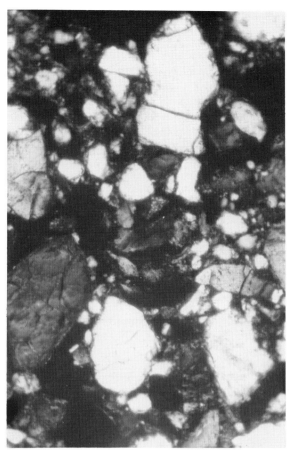

Plate III A photomicrograph of the Bt horizon fabric at Crowtree Farm in Trench 2 (PPL; frame = 2mm).

before the flooding and coincident soil truncation occurred.

Much of the soil fabric and pre-existing clay coatings have become impregnated by sesquioxides. Many dusty coatings in the Bt horizon have become impregnated with iron oxides and hydroxides. The soil fabric also exhibits zones of sesquioxides impregnation (from *c.* 30–75% of the groundmass). This hydromorphic effect (Duchaufour 1982) is probably indicative of alternating wet and dry conditions (Limbrey 1975), which undoubtedly reflects flooding, fluctuating water tables and seasonal waterlogging throughout the life of the buried soil.

Thus five phases of pedogenesis are discernible in the Bt horizon:

1. First, the rare oriented limpid and dusty clay coatings suggest a relatively short period of 'pure' clay illuviation under a presumed Boreal/Atlantic forest. The relative scarcity of oriented clay may also suggest that the forest cover was neither dense nor well developed, nor perhaps long-lived.

2. Second, the predominance of unoriented dusty clay coatings or 'impure' clay translocation is probably related to the opening-up of the forest cover. This was probably associated with the use of this peninsula by Mesolithic and early Neolithic man. The peninsula would have been an area of dry ground above the influence of the encroaching, growing freshwater wood/reed fen (or the basal peat).

3. There is considerable evidence for soil disturbance and possibly tree-throw associated with the clearance process. This is exemplified by the 'coarse' illuviation of impure clay and organic matter, and charcoal infills of fine sand size material. There is some slight evidence for successive

phases or variation in the process of 'impure/coarse' clay illuviation.

4. The buried soil was then severely truncated. It is possible that the soil disturbance feature of fine sand size channel infills is associated with the process of soil truncation. This was probably caused by the subsequent freshwater flooding and marine incursion episodes which occurred later in the Neolithic period.

5. The sesquioxide impregnation or waterlogging of the buried soil is a later, secondary process probably associated with the growth of the basal peat, and subsequently the deposition of the fen clay.

Pollen Analysis at Crowtree Farm
by R.G. Scaife
(Fig. 23)

Introduction
Samples for pollen analysis were obtained directly from open sections. Standard techniques were used for extracting the sub- fossil pollen and spores (Moore and Webb 1978). A micro-mesh (10μm) sieve was, however, used to remove the fine clay fraction which remained even after hydrofluoric acid treatment for the digestion of silica. The extract was stained with safranin and mounted in glycerol jelly. Pollen counts of between 300 and 600 grains were made (excluding spores). The pollen sums have been calcuated as a percentage of total pollen and extant spores as a percentage of the taxon plus the total pollen sum (thus making all pollen percentages d%). Similar procedures were used for the Oakhurst Farm material (see Scaife, below).

Both the lower part of the overlying fen clay and the buried soil were sampled in trial trenches 1 and 2. However, the pollen obtained from Trench 1 was badly degraded and sparse. This may be due to oxidation caused by the relatively recent drying-out of the fen. However, the pollen recovered from Trench 2 was better preserved and allowed a full analysis to be carried out. The results are presented diagramatically in Fig. 23.

Results
Three pollen assemblage zones have been recognised and are described from the base (0.21m OD) upwards. Pollen was absent below 0.21m OD, that is, at the transition from the lower-most buried soil and the top of the subsoil.

Pollen Zone I (0.21m–0.28m OD) comprises the lower half of the buried soil. It is characterised by high *Tilia* (lime) values with some *Quercus* (oak), *Alnus* (alder) and *Corylus* (hazel) type. Herb pollen is dominated by *Chenopodium* (oraches and glassworts), *Plantago lanceolata* (ribwort plantain), Gramineae (grasses) and Cyperaceae (sedges). A substantial number of unidentifiable (degraded) pollen grains from this basal zone strongly indicate that differential preservation took place. Pre-Quaternary (Upper Jurassic) spores and pollen grains were also present and are undoubtedly derived from the basal Oxford Clay lithology.

Pollen Zone II (0.28–0.37m OD) comprises the upper part of the truncated Bt horizon profile (see French, above). *Tilia* declines from the previous zone, but *Quercus* and *Corylus* remain important and *Alnus* expands. *Plantago lanceolata* declines. Herbs are dominated by *Bidens* type and Gramineae. A greater diversity of herbs is also

noted with peaks in *Chenopodium* type, *Filipendula* (meadow sweet), *Rumex* (docks), *Artemesia* (mugworts) and *Taraxacum* type (dandelion group).

Pollen Zone III (0.37–0.44m OD) consists of the basal part of the overlying fen clay (Barroway Drove Beds). This zone is characterised by increasing percentages of Cruciferae (Charlocks — *Sinapsis* type and *Hornungia* type) and *Chenopodium* type. Tree pollens are dominated by *Quercus* with some *Alnus* and *Corylus*. Pre- Quaternary spores also expand in this zone.

Discussion
The pollen sequence at Crowtree Farm, like that at Oakhurst Farm (below) comes from a truncated soil profile; it, too, is therefore truncated. Thus only a basal sequence is present, and not that representing the period immediately prior to marine inundation. It is likely, therefore, that the major phase of anthropogenic activity on the site is not represented in the pollen spectra. This, however, is not surprising since it is probable that such intense anthropogenic activity might itself have resulted in the subsequent soil truncation (see French, above). Nevertheless, it does appear that, unlike Oakhurst Farm, there is some evidence for the opening-up of the vegetation which is perhaps due to human activity. The vegetation of Zone I was dominant *Tilia* woodland; some *Quercus*, *Corylus* and *Alnus* may also have been present in the region. The latter was growing in damper and more marshy areas in the vicinity, forming fen carr woodland. Higher values of Cyperaceae also attest to areas of marsh or fen vegetation. This pollen zone may have occurred during the Atlantic and Sub-Boreal periods. This view is commensurate with the character of the woodland which the pollen evidence shows was growing on this sand peninsula.

It is notable that *Tilia* does decline from the base of Zone I into Zone II. This occurrence and the substantial presence of ruderals (*Plantago lanceolata*, *Chenopodium* type [non-halopytes] and the lesser presence of *Plantago major* type and Compositae spp.) and Gramineae also indicate some degree of disturbance and alteration of the woodland. Such disturbance may be the result of periodic encampment by Mesolithic communties at this site. In pollen Zone II, Gramineae and Compositae spp. increase sharply, whilst *Tilia* continues to decline. This zone may represent continued pressure on the soil, with the demise of *Tilia* woodland through clearance or through increased soil degradation. Little evidence for arable activity was found, and although early cereal types had poor pollen dispersion characteristics, it seems likely that cereal cultivation was not being carried out at this time. This may also indicate that the dating of this profile falls within the later Mesolithic (or later Atlantic period).

Pollen Zone II illustrates the effects of the marine transgression, with fine-grained sediments being deposited directly on the truncated old land surface. The pollen spectra reflect this, with increased in halophytic vegetation which include *Chenopodium* type (oraches and glassworts) and Cruficers typical of saltmarsh communities (*e.g. Beta, Crambe etc.*). As was noted at Oakhurst Farm, pre-Quaternary (Upper Jurassic) spores became more frequent. These are derived from the underlying Oxford Clay, transported fluvially and deposited along with allochthonous sediments. At least one phase of drying out of this salt marsh vegetation is indicated at

CROWT

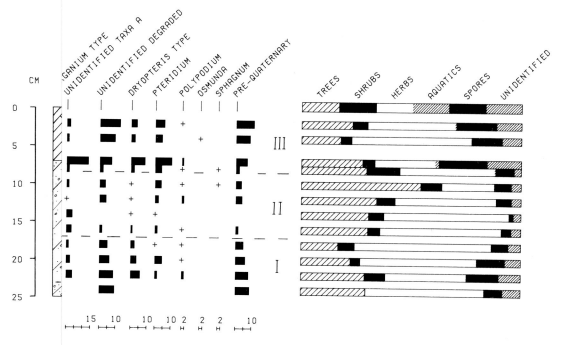

Figure 23

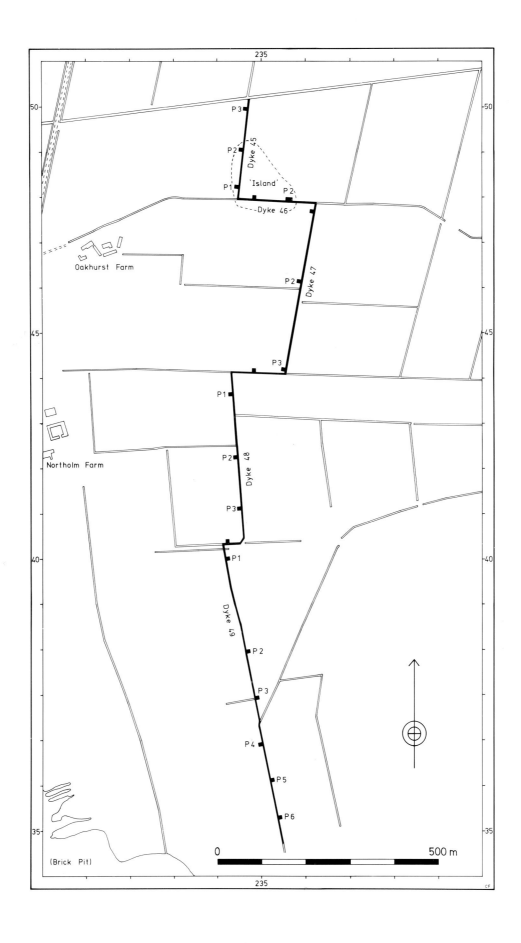

Figure 24 Location of Dykes 45-49 and Oakhurst Farm site.

4–5cm where pollen was absent or very badly preserved. Fungal spores were, however, abundant at this level. As at Oakhurst Farm, with the onset of the fen clay dating to *c.* 3650–3500 BP, the regional vegetation contained *Quercus* and *Corylus*. It is probable that some components of the vegetation may not be represented, due to the differential transport of taxa. *Quercus* and *Corylus* are high pollen producers and are thus well-represented, whereas, for example, *Fraxinus* (ash), *Acer campestre* (field maple) and *Tilia* are less likely to be present.

Further discussion of these results follows in the report on Oakhurst Farm (below).

2. Oakhurst Farm (TF 5235 3049) (Dyke 46)

The Survey
(Figs 2, 3, 24–26; Pl. IV)
Dykes 45–49 were surveyed in the spring of 1985 in the vicinity of Oakhurst and Northolm Farms. Mechanical widening of a *c.* 1.75km length of dyke running approximately north to south *c.* 0.5km to the east of, and parallel to, the A1073 road from Eye to Crowland revealed a small, *c.* 100m wide (west to east) fen 'island' in Dykes 45 and 46 (Figs 24 and 25; M. Pls 7–9). The surface of the buried 'island' is at *c.* -0.20m OD. This 'island' is situated *c.* 2km to the east of the Crowtree Farm site (Fig. 2), and *c.* 0.75km

to the north of the March Gravels which compose the Eye peninsula (Fig. 3).

The buried soil consists of an apedal, relatively non-porous (< 5% total porosity), light yellowish brown (10YR6/6) sandy loam with a few scattered gravel pebbles, *c.* 8–15cm thick. This soil was developed on a structureless, brownish yellow (10YR6/8) sand and fine gravel subsoil. There was no horizonisation of the soil evident in the dykeside. The artefactual and stratigraphic records suggest that man probably frequented this 'island' during the later Mesolithic and earlier Neolithic periods. The soil is overlain by a thin lens of lower peat, *c.* 40cm of fen clay and *c.* 30cm of upper peat (Appendix VI; Fig. 25; Pl. IV). A large roddon delimits the eastern edge of the 'island'.

In Dyke 45 immediately to the north, the northward extent of the 'island' was evident. The 'island' continued for *c.* 125m before dipping away steeply (Figs 24 and 25). As the 'island' does not continue in Dyke 47 to the south, it may be assumed that the exposure in Dyke 46 represents its southern extremity. In Dyke 47, the subsoil dips by about one metre in depth, and there is a considerable thickness of basal peat and fen clay evident. Continuing southwards towards the high ground of the Eye peninsula, the subsoil gradually rises and the lower peat and fen clay thin out in Dykes 48 and 49 (Figs 25 and 26; M. Pls 10–12).

Plate IV The buried 'island' at Oakhurst Farm, Dyke 46 (Site 2).

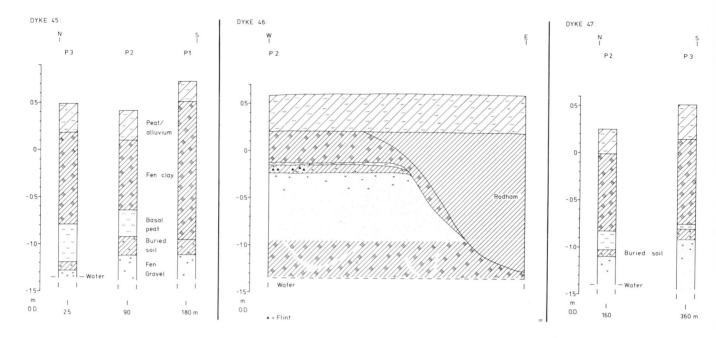

Figure 25 Dykes 45-47 profiles.

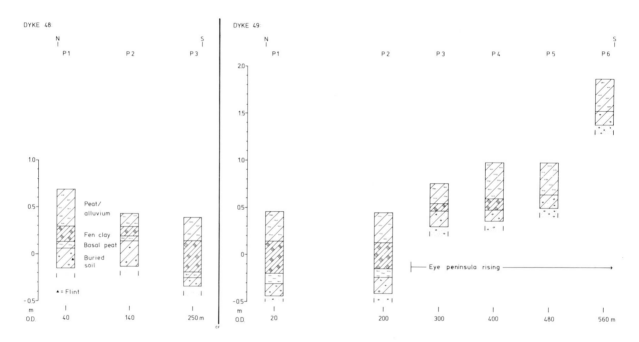

Figure 26 Dykes 48 and 49 profiles.

The Flints from Oakhurst Farm
by H.R. Middleton

Dyke 46, profile 2
(Fig. 27; Table 3)
Four flints were recovered from this site, all being debitage (Table 3). They were made from good quality dark brown flint with a thin, brown cortex indicating a gravel origin.

Due to the small size of the individual pieces it is difficult to determine the technological strategy that was employed, with the exception of one large core rejuvenation flake (Fig. 27, no. 11). This was struck to remove a large flaw on a core that was for both blade and flakes and

had abraded platforms to remove overhangs prior to striking. This may suggest a Neolithic date.

Dyke 48
One small blade of dark brown, good quality flint with small light grey inclusions was found. The severely abraded lateral edges combined with the fact that both ends are missing, may indicate a degree of post-depositional disturbance. This blade is possibly utilised.

Dyke 49
This findspot (*c.* 37m south of the northern end of the dyke) produced one piece of irregular workshop waste made of dark grey gravel flint with a thin grey cortex.

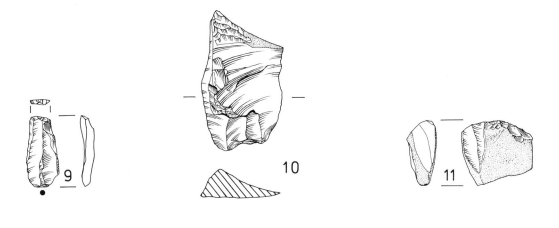

0   10 cm

Figure 27 Dykes 41 (nos 9 and 10), 46 (no. 11) and Site BoF 3 barrow flints (nos 12 and 13).

Catalogue of illustrated flints
(Fig. 27)
11.   Oakhurst Farm: Core rejeuvenation flake. Dyke 46, profile 2.

Soil micromorphology at Oakhurst Farm
by Charles French
(Fig. 25; Pl. IV)

The buried soil exposed in Dyke 46 was sampled at profile 2 in two intact blocks for thin sectioning (after Bullock *et*

al. 1985a, b; (Appendix I; Fig. 25; Pl. IV). The detailed micromorphological descriptions are found in Appendix VI.

The upper half of this sample is probably the base of an eluvial Eb horizon of an argillic brown earth (Avery 1980; Limbrey 1975; McKeague 1983). This eluvial horizon is characterised by: a very dense fabric composed mainly of medium, fine and very fine sand size quartz grains; very little organic matter in the groundmass; and rare to occasional (*c.* 1–5%) limpid and dusty clay coatings.

The lower half of this sample is probably the upper part of a B horizon. Although the fabric and fabric density remain as above, the increasing amount of dusty clay coatings towards the lower half of the slide suggests that this is a zone of illuviation, and it may therefore represent the uppermost part of the argillic or Bt horizon. This conclusion is supported by the following discussion of the micro-pedofeatures of the lower half of the buried soil.

The lower half of the buried soil (M. Pl. 60) is an illuvial argillic or Bt horizon of an argillic brown earth (Avery 1980; McKeague 1983). As at Crowtree Farm, this horizon becomes better developed and more pronounced in terms of the increased abundance of clay coatings towards the base of the horizon. Similarly, there are three possible phases of clay illuviation. First, there are very small amounts of limpid and laminated dusty clay. In particular, the relative scarcity of limpid clay which is normally associated with an undisturbed woodland cover (Fisher 1982; Macphail 1985a; Slager and van de Wetering 1977) suggests that little clay translocation had occurred prior to interference by man in the later Mesolithic/earlier Neolithic. Second, there are many non-laminated dusty clay coatings. The translocation of this 'coarse' material is a result of soil disturbance, most probably caused by tree clearance (Macphail 1985a, 1986). Third, the many 'dirty' clay coatings are indicative of the mobilisation of further 'coarse' material, associated with continued soil disturbance caused by tree clearance and possibly tree-throw (see French in 3:I.1 above) (Macphail 1985a).

There are several other pedological features evident in this Bt horizon that are also indicative of soil disturbance, probably associated with tree clearance. First, there are occasional, successive void infills of red/black dusty and 'dirty' non- laminated clay which give a 'layered' appearance. Second, one large void is infilled with three 'crescentic-shaped' infills of dusty clay. These 'layered' infills might suggest successive phases of soil disturbance, but more probably indicate variations in the intensity and amount of clay translocation after one disturbance event (Macphail pers. comm.).

This evidence for probable tree clearance at both the Crowtree and Oakhurst Farm sand peninsula/'island' (respectively) sites may be associated with their use by man in the later Mesolithic/earlier Neolithic period. Similar micromorphological evidence was found in Mesolithic soils at Selmeston (Macphail in Rudling 1985; Scaife and Macphail 1983) and High Rocks in Sussex (Macphail *et al.* 1987). These sites showed little limpid clay translocation, under a presumed Atlantic forest, prior to Mesolithic interference, followed by lengthy minor clearance and burning associated with the development of dusty argillans (Slager and van de Wetering 1977; Courty and Fedoroff 1982). At both sites it is suggested that the later 'coarse grained' illuvial phase was related to Mesolithic activity. This may have involved the opening-up of the forest canopy, which caused increased windshake of the trees, or some other form of anthropogenic action (Courty and Fedoroff 1982; Macphail *et al.* 1987; Slager and van de Wetering 1977).

Subsequent to the clay illuviation phases, the soil then suffered erosion, as at Crowtree Farm. The A horizon and possibly the upper part of the Eb horizon was truncated. This relatively severe soil erosion was probably coincident with either the freshwater flooding associated with the growth of the lower peat or the subsequent marine inundation which led to the deposition of the fen clay.

Much of the soil fabric and pre-existing clay coatings have become impregnated with sesqioxides as at Crowtree Farm. This indicates that the post-burial soil has been affected by alternating wet and dry conditions (Duchaufour 1982; Limbrey 1975). Flooding, seasonal waterlogging and a fluctuating water table were probably responsible for these conditions.

Finally, it is interesting to note that the same five phases of pedogenesis are evident at Oakhurst Farm that were previously observed at Crowtree Farm (French, above).

Pollen analysis at Oakhurst Farm
by R.G. Scaife
(Fig. 28)

Introduction

Using similar procedures to those employed for the Crowtree Farm analysis (Scaife, above), one profile was subject to pollen analysis on the eastern edge of the Oakhurst Farm 'island'. A well defined buried soil was present across the 'island', and was sampled at a depth of *c.* -0.08 to -0.20m OD. Micromorphological analysis of this soil (French, above) has shown that it is a truncated argillic brown earth which was subject to three phases of illuviation and subsequent soil erosion, all prior to the later Neolithic period. This had the effect of removing the A horizon and possibly the upper part of the Eb horizon. This of course means that any pollen investigation of the soil profile would also give an incomplete picture of vegetation development, with a major unconformity between the top of the soil profile and the overlying peat. It was hoped that pollen analysis of the buried soil might provide evidence for the vegetation of the sand 'island' prior to forest clearance, and to assess the nature and extent of prehistoric clearance. The former of these postulates has at least been achieved in the analyses of both the Oakhurst and Crowtree Farm soil profiles. The buried soil at Oakhurst Farm is overlain by a thin lens of basal peat as the surface of the 'island' dips eastwards, and by fen clay (or Barroway Drove Bed). Pollen analyses were carried out on each of these three stratigraphic units, and the results are presented diagramatically in Figure 28.

Results

Pollen zone I (-0.20 to -0.08m OD) comprises the buried soil profile, or Eb and upper Bt horizons. This is represented in the pollen record by relatively poorly preserved pollen. Pollen sampling was carried out to a much greater depth but plant microfossils were absent below -0.20m OD. The spectra are characterised by dominant *Quercus*, *Tilia* and *Corylus* type. Some *Alnus* is also present. Herb pollen are few with only Gramineae (grasses) and Cyperaceae (sedges) consistently present. Spores are numerous (*Dryopteris* type, *Polypodium* and *Pteridium*), and which with the substantial numbers of unidentifiable (degraded) pollen are indicative of strong differential preservation.

Pollen zone II (-0.08 to 0.01m OD) comprises the basal peat lens. This fen peat is a humified detrital monocotyledonous peat with little visible structure apart from root debris. The peat grades into the overlying fen clay, but rests cleanly on the truncated old land surface. Palynologically the zone is characterised by the dominance of tree

OAKHU...

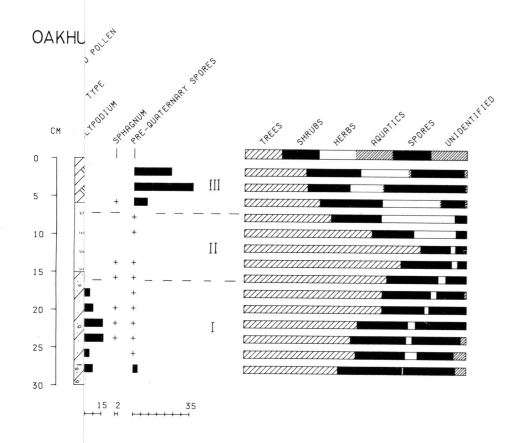

pollen. *Quercus* and *Alnus* are dominant, the latter increasing to 20% of total pollen in this zone. *Corylus* type remains important. Few herbs are present although *Chenopodium* type becomes important in the upper levels of this zone.

Pollen zone III (0.01 to 0.07m OD) comprises the lower part of the overlying fen clay. The zone is delimited stratigraphically and palynologically by the dominance of *Chenopodium* type (goosefoots and oraches), increasing percentages of Gramineae and *Bidens* type (daisy types). Pre-Quaternary (Upper Jurassic) spores are frequent and correlate clearly with the change from peat to marine/brackish water sediments (fen clay series). Tree and shrub pollen are dominated by *Quercus* (oak), *Alnus* (alder) and *Corylus* type (hazel but which may also include sweet gale). Small numbers of *Ulmus* (elm), *Tilia* (lime), *Betula* (birch) and *Fraxinus* (ash) are also present.

Discussion

It is clear that three major phases are present with pollen being deposited in widely different environments. Unfortunately the buried soil is truncated with the uppermost A horizon being absent. This means therefore that it is not possible to ascertain the character of the vegetation immediately prior to formation of the basal peat. Furthermore, it is not possible at present to provide an accurate date for the pollen represented in pollen zone I. However, information can be provided on the nature of the dominant woodland growing on the sand 'island' prior to forest clearance. This therefore complements the information obtained from the soil micromorphological studies. From the high values of *Tilia* which are recorded it is clear that lime was the dominant woodland element growing on the 'island'. As *Tilia* is entomophilous (insect pollinated), it produces relatively few pollen grains which are not widely dispersed. Thus, this taxon is usually under-represented in pollen spectra and where found in high frequencies such as are recorded here, indicates its 'on- site' dominance. This in itself is not unusual in southern and eastern England where its middle to later Flandrian dominance has been widely demonstrated (*e.g.* Baker *et al.* 1979; Scaife 1980, 1987; Grieg 1982). Locally its importance has also been demonstrated by Godwin and Vishnu-Mittre (1975) and recently by Waller (1986–7). *Quercus* and *Corylus* were also dominant elements in the landscape. It is difficult to ascertain whether these elements formed part of a community dominated by *Tilia* or were growing in different areas. It is probable that *Tilia* was growing on the well drained sandy soils which it favours, whereas *Quercus* with a *Corylus* understory were important on the thicker and moister soils fringing this 'island' and on larger areas of land at some distance away. Herb pollen is notably sparse in pollen zone I and there is little evidence therefore for any major anthropogenic impact from this phase of pollen deposition. This is not suprising since the evidence of soil erosion/truncation, perhaps resulting from anthropogenic activity, has removed the upper levels of the soil and soil pollen profile. Because of this, it is not clear what date can be placed on this *Tilia* dominated woodland. A late Atlantic (Godwin's pollen zone VIIa) or early Sub-Boreal (Godwin's pollen zone VIIb) date would seem appropriate. This is perhaps substantiated by the relatively low values of *Ulmus* present, indicating a post-*Ulmus* decline date. Artefactual evidence (Middleton, above) also suggests a pre-later Neolithic date by implication.

The subsequent pollen zone II rests directly on the truncated old land surface. Stratigraphically zone II represents the thin basal peat sequence which tapers in thickness westwards and peters out over the highest parts of the 'island'. This formation represents the first indication of waterlogging of the area by 'ponding back' due to rising sea and/or base levels. This waterlogging is illustrated by the increasing importance of *Alnus*. Whilst *Quercus* and *Corylus* remain important, *Tilia* declines sharply indicating the inability of lime to grow in waterlogged situations. Whilst *Tilia* remained important on the remaining areas of the sand 'island', it was undoubtedly forced away from areas fringing the 'island' where it had been previously dominant. The poor transport mechanisms of *Tilia* pollen would also result in such a dramatic decline as its nearest growth became farther away.

The imminent encroachment of marine/brackish water influence is indicated in the upper levels of pollen zone II by the rapid increase in percentages of *Chenopodium* type pollen. This taxon is highly characteristic of saline environments where halophytic elements of the Chenopodiaceae thrive (*e.g.* the oraches and glassworts – *Salicornia* sp.). The final inundation of marine or brackish water is seen in pollen zone III. In this zone, peat deposits give way to fine grained sediments which are again dominated by Chenopodiaceae. The high percentages of Jurassic spores are derived from the Oxford Clay, and were eroded from this basement lithology, transported in the fluvial system and redeposited in this near-shore marine environment. This is, however, interesting because it illustrates that a substantial degree of erosion of the adjacent land was taking place and that the sediments derived from not only marine transport but from the local river basins. The incursion of the fen clay in this area is dated to *c.* 1800–1650 BC (Chapter 1: IV).

The regional vegetation of this period is also represented. The dry land, less than half a kilometre to the south on the Eye peninsula, was dominated by oak and hazel with alder being important and growing in the wetter areas fringing the peninsula and the 'island'.

Comparison of results

The two pollen sequences analysed from Oakhurst and Crowtree Farms are broadly similar, being truncated soils of late Atlantic/early Sub-Boreal date. These profiles are separated geographically by *c.* 2km and are on the same substrate. Consequently, it is not suprising that the natural vegetation of these sites prior to extensive anthropogenic impact should have been similar. This was shown to be one of dominant lime woodland with evidence for oak/hazel woodland also in the region. The stronger archaeological evidence for occupation at Crowtree Farm is perhaps indicated in the pollen record with greater quantities and diversity of herbs present. These include ruderals such as *Plantago lanceolata*, but there is little evidence of cereal cutivation.

At both sites, it is unfortunate that the A horizon of the buried soil has been truncated in antiquity with the consequence that later evidence for anthropogenic (possibly early Neolithic) activity may be missing from both pollen records. However, it is plausible that a cause and effect situation may be in operation with such activities in themselves being responsible for soil depletion.

Also at both sites, the fen clay (or Barroway Drove Bed) sequence represents marine inundation. At Oakhurst

Farm, the thin basal peat sequence illustrates the 'ponding back effect' of the marine transgression giving rise to waterlogging and the accretion of fen peats. At Crowtree Farm, the marine sequence rests directly upon the soil of the sand 'peninsula', effectively sealing this surface, although basal peat encroaches upon the eastern fringe of this peninsula prior to the deposition of the fen clay. The implication of this is that the Crowtree Farm land surface remained available for human use for a longer time than the land surface at Oakhurst Farm.

Both pollen profiles from the fen clay show that the allochthonous sediments were derived not only from distant sources but also from the local river catchments which provided sediments and derived palynomorphs from the Jurassic Oxford Clay geology.

3. Dykes 1–4

The Survey
(Figs 2, 11, 29, 70–73; Pls V and VI; Table 3)
A series of four short dykes (centred on TF 5216 3038) were re-cut and cleaned out by the tenant farmer Mr P. Williamson immediately to the northwest of Eye on the northwestern side of the Eye peninsula. This peninsula of land is composed of Fen (March) gravels, and drops away

steeply to the northeast into Newborough Fen. The approximate landward edge of the fen is delimited by the Roman Car Dyke (Figs 2 and 11).

The dyke profiles examined exhibit relatively uniform stratigraphy at the extreme southernmost influence of the lower peat and fen clay (Fig. 29; Pl. V; M. Pls 13–15). The buried soil is *c.* 10–14cm thick, with its surface varying in height from *c.* +0.60 to *c.* +0.20m OD. It is composed of two horizons which were evident in the field. The upper horizon is an apedal, slightly porous (*c.* 5–10%), reddish grey (5YR5/2), gravel-free (sandy) loam with scattered flecks of charcoal, *c.* 6–8cm thick. The lower horizon is an apedal, somewhat porous (*c.* 20%), pinkish grey (7.5YR6/2) sandy (clay) loam, with *c.* 20% fine gravel content and numerous charcoal flecks, *c.* 4cm thick. This buried soil is cut by numerous archaeological features, as is the underlying Fen gravel deposits of very pale (yellowish) brown (10YR7/4) silty clay, sand and fine gravel (Fig. 29; Pl. V). At least three of the features, probably small pits, were infilled with lower peat material. One utilised flint blade characteristic of the Neolithic period was found in the buried soil as exposed in Dyke 1 (see Middleton below) (Table 3).

The buried soil is overlain by a thin deposit of lower peat (*c.* 7–15cm thick), a thin (*c.* 15–20cm) deposit of fen clay and upper peat (*c.* 25–40cm thick). The lower peat

Plate V The buried soil on the northern dip slope of the Eye peninsula in Dyke 3.

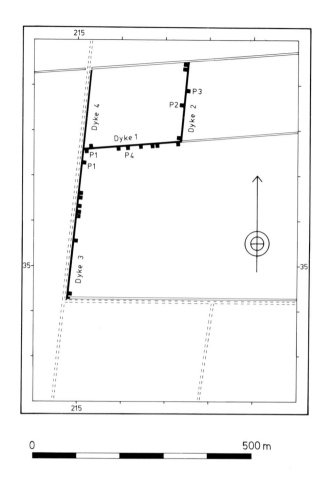

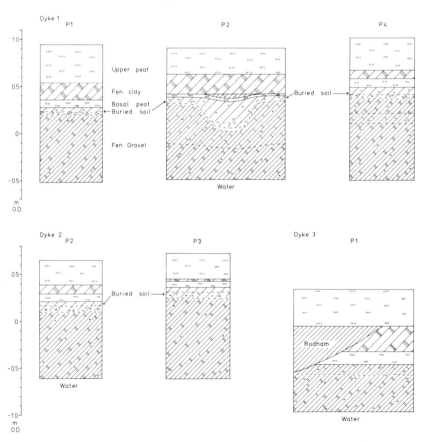

Figure 29 Location and profiles of Dykes 1-4.

and fen clay are at their southernmost extent in this part of Newborough Fen.

It is suggested that the buried soil probably extends over many hectares of land in this area of fen-edge created by the high ground of the Eye peninsula dipping northwards into Newborough Fen. The frequency of archaeological features in Dyke 1 suggests that the area was used by man. The relatively steeply rising ground to the south on the Eye peninsula would provide year-round dry ground, well above the influence of the encroaching fen. Thus it is probable that this part of the fen margin as represented in Dykes 1–4 would have been available for exploitation by man at least on a seasonal basis during the Mesolithic and earlier Neolithic periods, with the higher ground of the peninsula available for use throughout prehistoric and historic times (Figs 70–73).

The Flint from Dykes 1–4
by H.R. Middleton
(Table 3)

Dyke 1, profile 2
This dyke produced one large blade with a natural, distal truncation. It is of good quality, dark brown flint with a thin, white patina. Snap fractures are present on the dorsal right side; there is no cortex present.

Soil pH, Phosphate and Magnetic Susceptibility Surveys of Dykes 1 and 2
by D.A. Gurney
(Figs 30–32; Table 5)

Dyke 1: pH results
(Table 5)
The subsoil was neutral; the buried soil very slightly acid; and the ploughsoil alkaline along the length of the dyke.

Dyke 1: Phosphate results
(Fig. 30)
Samples for laboratory analysis were taken from the buried soil and subsoil at 23 profiles at *c.* 10m intervals from west to east along the Dyke 1 section. The results show a remarkably close correlation between the two soil horizons, with a distinct peak at profile 11. In general the buried soil appears leached (see soil micromorphology report below), and the phosphates have relocated in the uppermost zone of the subsoil (or at the lower Bt/upper B/C horizon).

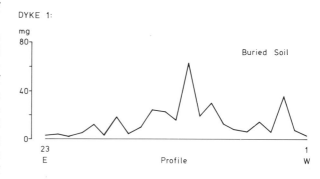

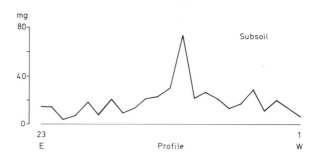

Figure 30 Dyke 1 phosphate results.

Dyke 1: Magnetic susceptibility results
(Fig. 31)
The buried soil was tested by both sensors along the whole length of the dyke from west to east. All results are very low, less than 15 SI. Sensor A (above) generally provided a higher reading than sensor B, but peaks located by both sensors were generally coincident.

Dyke 2: pH results
The pH results are comparable to those from Dyke 1 (above).

Dyke 2: Phosphate results
(Fig. 32)
Samples for laboratory analysis were taken from the buried soil and subsoil at 17 profiles at *c.* 10m intervals from south to north along the Dyke 2 section. The results are similar to those from Dyke 1; and there is a distinct peak at profiles 9–10.

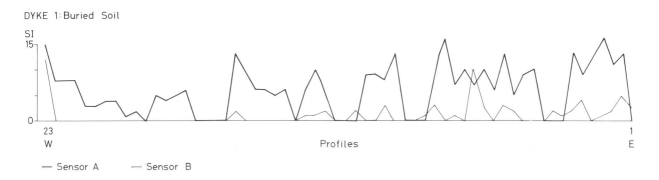

Figure 31 Dyke 1 magnetic susceptibility results.

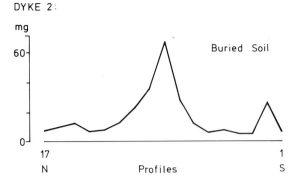

DYKE 2:

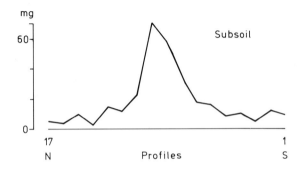

Figure 32 Dyke 2 phosphate results.

Soil micromorphology of Dykes 1–4
by Charles French
(Fig. 29; Pls V and VI; M. Pls 56–58; Table 5)

All the buried land surfaces visible in Dykes 1–4 have a remarkable visual similarity (Fig. 29). The upper horizon is organic-stained by the humic acids leaching out from the overlying peat, and the lower horizon is a bleached pinkish grey colour with an indistinct and undulating lower boundary with the subsoil. The buried soils tend to be neutral to slightly acidic, the subsoil is neutral, and the overlying peat is alkaline (Table 5).

The buried soil was sampled for micromorphological analysis at profile 4 in Dyke 1 (Fig. 29). The detailed micromorphological descriptions are found in Appendix VI.

The upper horizon of the buried soil (M. Pl. 56) is probably an eluvial Eb horizon of an argillic brown earth as at the Oakhurst Farm site (Avery 1980; Limbrey 1975; McKeague 1983). This eluvial horizon is characterised by: a relatively dense fabric composed mainly of very fine (*c.* 40%), fine (*c.* 25%) and medium (*c.* 18%) sand size quartz grains; very little organic matter in the groundmass; and very rare dusty clay coatings. In contrast to the Eb horizon at Oakhurst Farm, the small fragments of dusty clay in this horizon suggest that the soil has suffered some disturbance. Although there is a greater organic content than in the Eb horizon at Oakhurst Farm, it is mainly composed of abundant modern roots of plants previously growing on the dyke edge, whereas the fine fabric is generally depleted of organic matter.

The lower horizon of the buried soil (Pl. VI; M. Pls 57 and 58) is an illuvial argillic or Bt horizon of an argillic brown earth (Avery 1980; McKeague 1983). As at the Crowtree and Oakhurst Farm sites, there are three possible phases of clay illuviation. First, the rare limpid clay coatings and the occasional laminated dusty clay coatings in

Site/sample	pH (field)	pH (laboratory)
BoF 7:		
ploughsoil	alkaline	
buried soil	alkaline	
B/C	alkaline	
BoF 10d:		
ploughsoil		7.5-8.3
barrow ditch(upper)		5.4; 6.2; 6.4
barrow ditch(lower)		7.8
B/C		7.6
Dyke 1:		
ploughsoil	alkaline	
buried soil	slightly acid	
B/C	neutral	
Dyke 9:		
ploughsoil	alkaline	
buried soil	neutral	
B/C	neutral	
Dyke 10:		
ploughsoil	alkaline	
buried soil	acidic	
B/C	moderately acid	
BoF 1: 12		
0 -10		8.0
10-20		8.4
20-30		7.7
30-40		7.5
40-50		8.5
50-60		7.5
60-70		7.6
70-80		7.6

Table 5 pH values for various sites in the North Level.

the groundmass suggest that only a limited amount of clay translocations had occurred prior to the influence of man in the Neolithic or earlier. Nevertheless, slightly more clay translocation occurred here under the presumed Atlantic forest than at either of the other two sites.

Second, the relative abundance of non-laminated dusty coatings suggests that some soil disturbance occurred. Tree clearance, which disturbs and damages the soil peds and causes the mobilisation of 'coarse' material, is probably responsible (Macphail 1985a, 1986, 1987).

Third, many of the dusty clay coatings appear to contain amorphous organic matter which gives them a 'dirty' appearance. It is probable that further 'coarse' illuviation of clay with organic matter has occurred because of continued disturbance of the palaeosol. The most probable cause is tree clearance activities, and possibly tree-throw (Macphail 1985a).

There are several other features which additionally suggest further soil disturbance. There are infills of silt and fine sand size material in a few channels as well as in a few dusty coatings. Also fragments of limpid clay present in the groundmass suggest that these oriented coatings have been broken up since their translocation. Moreover, some of the laminated coatings appear to have been tipped sideways and changed their orientation abruptly. Although

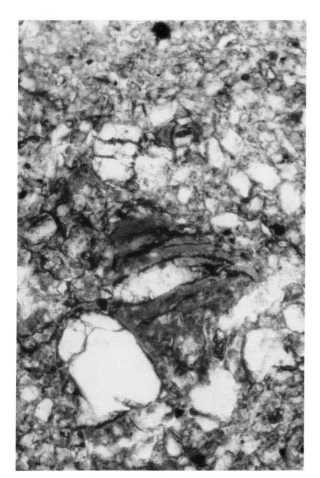

Plate VI A photomicrograph of the Bt fabric of the buried soil in Dyke 1 (PPL; frame = 2mm).

subsequent erosion and truncation of the uppermost part of the soil profile may have also caused these features, there was undoubtedly further soil disturbance, probably as a result of the continuing opening up of the forest cover by man, and possibly by tree-throw, during the later Mesolithic and earlier Neolithic periods.

The episode of probable clearance is followed by one in which the palaeosol suffered soil erosion and truncation, as at Crowtree and Oakhurst Farms; probably only the A and possibly the upper part of the Eb horizons have been truncated here (as at Oakhurst Farm). This event was probably associated with either freshwater flooding and the growth of the basal peat, or the subsequent marine transgression and the deposition of fen clay. Indeed the large nodule of silt and clay in the Bt horizon may have become incorporated in the palaeosol as a result of this soil erosion and disturbance.

Many of the clay coatings and zones of the soil fabric have become impregnated with sesquioxides. This feature is indicative of alternating wet and dry conditions (Duchaufour 1982; Limbrey 1975), since tree clearance and soil truncation occurred.

Thus similar sequences of pedogenesis are exhibited in the buried soils at Dyke 1, Crowtree and Oakhurst Farm sites. All three profiles exhibit remarkable uniformity, with only a few minor details of difference. There appears to have been lengthy episodes of minor clearance in each of these areas of higher ground prior to the Neolithic period, and also prior to their subsequent flooding or inundation.

Archaeological Survey: Later Neolithic/Early Bronze Age

1. Dykes 11–13 and 15

The Survey
(Figs 2, 11, 33–35, 70–72)
These four dykes are situated immediately to the west of Newborough village, and they exhibit stratigraphy which is transitional between the full fenland basin sequence to the east and the fen 'skirtland' to the west (Figs 2, 11, 33–35; M. Pls 16–18).

Dyke 15 and the eastern half of Dyke 12 exhibit the basal peat/fen clay/upper peat sequence, but at its westernmost extent. The underlying subsoil is composed of alluvial fan/Fen gravel sand and gravel deposits, probably of Second Terrace age. A thin sandy loam soil with scattered gravel pebbles has developed on the subsoil, with its upper surface rising from *c.* 0.35 to *c.* 0.90m OD from east to west. Although no micromorphological analysis of the palaeosol has been undertaken, the soil is visually similar to that observed *c.* 1km to the east at Crowtree Farm, and there is every probability that this soil is also a partially truncated argillic brown earth.

The buried soil is overlain by an organic (peaty) lens which thins and disappears westwards above *c.* 0.5 to 0.7m OD. This lens probably represents the landward (or western) limit of the growth of the lower peat. Similarly the overlying fen clay thins and disappears westwards above *c.* 0.8 to 0.9m OD. Neither the lower peat nor the fen clay deposits are visible in the western half of Dyke 12, the northern three-quarters of Dyke 13 and along the complete length of Dyke 11.

By implication this area of land to the west of Newborough village was probably the fen-edge of the later Neolithic/earlier Bronze Age periods. Freshwater flooding and marine inundation possibly would have played a less disruptive role, perhaps for a shorter period of time. As this area of the western fen-edge did not become permanently waterlogged until later in the Bronze Age at the earliest, it would have been a potential area of earlier prehistoric settlement (Figs 70–72). Radiocarbon dates from nearby (Newborough: TF 1953 0524) suggest peat growth in the Early/Middle Bronze Age ((SRR–1768) 3390 ± 40 BP or 1835–1555 Cal. BC) and in the earlier Iron Age ((SRR–1767) 2220 ± 50 BP or 410–160 Cal. BC). Nevertheless, settlements of the period have not yet been found, except for one possibility represented by cropmarks: Hall's site 4 (Hall 1987, fig. 10).

2. Borough Fen Barrow Sites BoF 3 and 10d

Survey and Excavation
(Figs 2, 11, 33, 36, 37; Pl. VII; Tables 5–8)
The principal monuments of the Bronze Age in Borough Fen are barrows; twenty-five have so far been discovered, of which thirteen are new discoveries by Hall (1987). Of these only two have been examined in any detail: sites 3 and 10d (Figs 2, 11, 33). Site 10d is one of a group of six barrows (TF 5186 3056), and site 3 is a single isolated barrow about 1.3km to the north (TF 5196 3066) (Fig. 33; Pl. VII). The former barrow was examined by cleaning

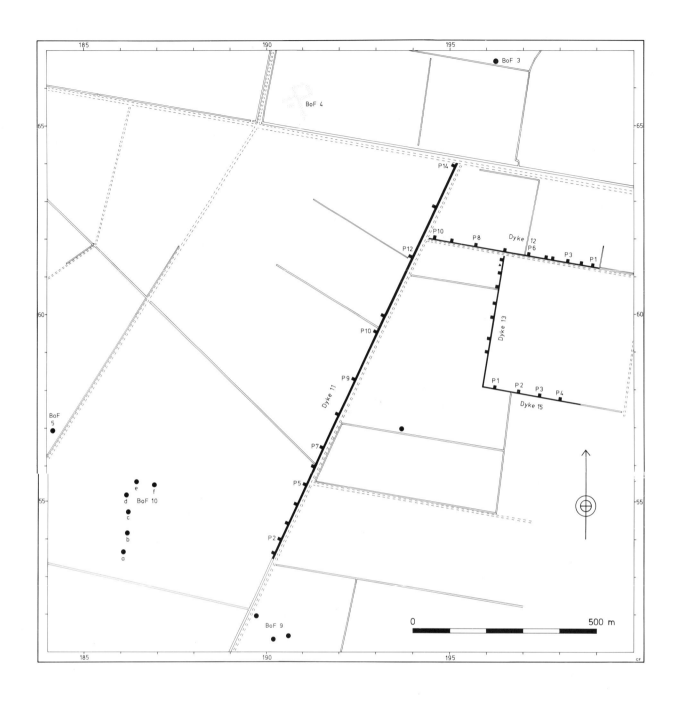

Figure 33 Location of Dykes 11–13 and 15, BOF Sites 3, 4, 5, 9 and 10.

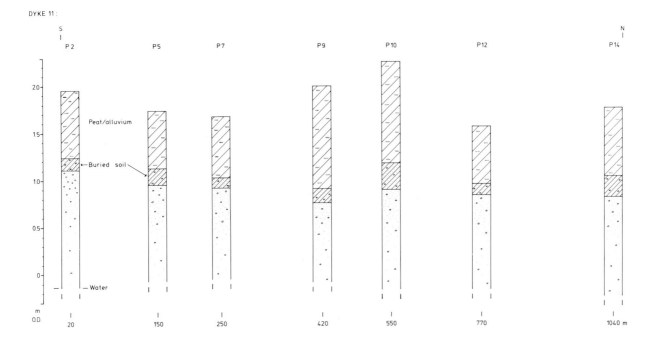

Figure 34 Dyke 11 profiles.

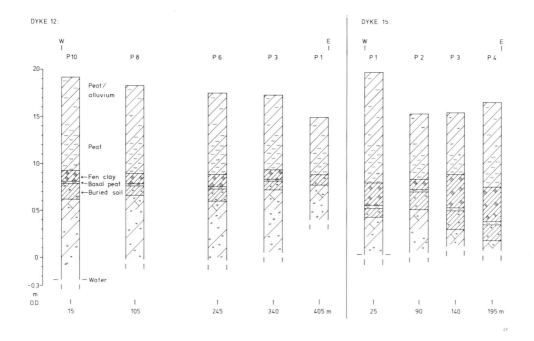

Figure 35 Dykes 12 and 15 profiles.

Plate VII North-south section through the Borough Fen Site 10d barrow.

down an existing dyke section which runs approximately north to south through the centre of the barrow (Pl. VII), and the latter was examined using a hand auger with boreholes made at 2, 3 and 5m intervals. Soil analyses were only performed on the barrow site 10d (Tables 5–8) comments on barrow site 3 are made from field observations obtained from the augering survey.

The former barrow group rests on river terrace/Fen gravel deposits of sand and gravel, and is partially buried by alluvium and peat (Fig. 33; Pl. VII). The latter single barrow is situated on the southern edge of a small 'outcrop' or knoll of river terrace drift deposits of First Terrace origin and is partially covered by peaty alluvium (Fig. 37). Both areas are subject to severe drainage, and the consequent shrinkage and wastage of the peat component of the overlying and surrounding soils has led to the exposure of the upper third of the barrow mounds. Barrows 10d and 10e were sufficiently upstanding obstacles to modern machinery that in 1986 their tops were bulldozed flat. Barrow 3 has probably once suffered a similar fate, as the mound make-up only survives to a height of c. 30cm.

Barrow 10d has a mound surviving c. 1.2m above the surface of the buried soil, c. 22m in diameter. The barrow ditch was c. 1.5m wide at the old ground surface and was c. 0.5m deep.

Barrow 10d exhibited the following stratigraphy (Table 6; Fig. 36; Pl. VII):

Sample (the top of the barrow is at c. 2.5m OD)
1   Sandy clay loam with scattered gravel pebbles. 10YR3/2. This is the present day ploughsoil.
2. Peaty loamy sand (33% organic matter content by weight). 10YR2.5/1.
3&7 Sandy loam and gravel. 10YR6/8. Together these deposits form the main secondary part of the mound and its revetment.

4   Sandy loam with some gravel and oxidation mottling. 10YR5/4. This may be a turf revetment around the secondary mound.
6   Sandy loam with some gravel and oxidation mottling. 10YR5/4. This probably forms the turf and topsoil dump core of the primary barrow mound.
5   Sand and gravel (34%). 10YR6/8. This forms the revetment to the primary mound.
B/C Sand and gravel (73%). 10YR6/8.

The stratigraphy of this barrow suggests the following history of construction. A wide, relatively shallow ditch and berm surrounds a primary, gravel-revetted mound of turves and topsoil. The whole mound was then covered by a secondary mound of sandy loam and gravel. This enlarged mound was revetted with turves and topsoil, which left no berm. This sequence of construction is reminiscent of the sequence of barrow construction of the central mound within the henge at Maxey (Pryor and French 1985). Despite severe leaching since the construction of the barrow, the monument is situated on a thin (c. 15cm) sand/gravel buried soil. This is probably the lower B and B/C horizons of the pre-monument buried soil which has been truncated to provide constructional material with which to build the mound.

Barrow 3 displayed the following stratigraphy after an augering survey was undertaken (Fig. 37):

Barrow Ditch: Depth below 1.6m OD
0–30   Peat and peaty alluvium. 10YR2.5/1; 10YR3/2.
30–50   Well humified peat with charcoal fragments. 10YR2.5/1.
50–85   Reduced sandy loam with charcoal fragments. 10YR5/2. This is the tertiary fill of the barrow ditch and the post-barrow and pre- peat land surface.
85–100   Oxidised sand and fine gravel. 10YR5/6. This is the secondary and primary ditch fill.
100+   Waterlogged sand and gravel subsoil. 10YR6/8.

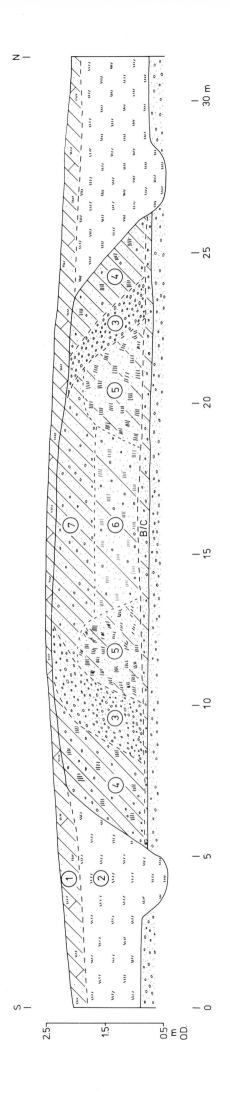

Figure 36 Section through barrow 10d.

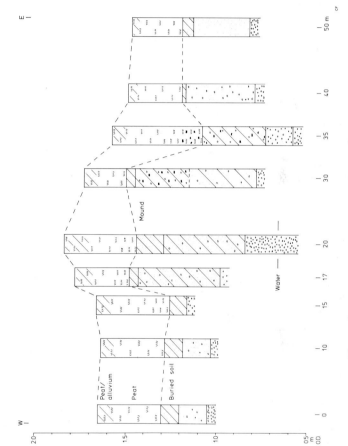

Figure 37 Auger survey profiles through barrow 3.

Sample	% clay	% silt	% sand	% gravel
BoF 7:				
Upper buried soil	26.25	13.75	60.0	1.5
Lower buried soil	17.50	22.50	60.0	0.9
F2	17.50	26.25	56.25	0.8
F3	27.5	27.5	45.0	0.8
BoF 10d:				
1	20.0	17.5	62.5	13.3
2	8.75	6.25	85.0	1.8
3	13.75	18.75	67.50	59.8
4	15.0	15.0	70.0	17.4
5	6.25	3.75	90.0	34.1
6	15.0	17.50	67.50	9.2
7	18.75	16.25	65.0	23.9
B/C	9.75	5.25	85.0	73.0
Dyke 1:				
Upper buried soil	12.5	47.50	40.0	0.7
Lower buried soil	28.75	26.25	45.0	20.8
Dyke 8:				
Upper buried soil	35.0	31.25	33.75	2.1
Lower buried soil	15.0	42.50	42.50	3.2
B/C	16.25	11.25	72.50	9.2
Dyke 9:				
Lens	8.50	38.0	53.5	-
Buried soil	30.0	36.25	33.75	10.2

Table 6. Percentages of clay, silt, sand and gravel of soils and features at various sites in the North Level.

Barrow Mound: Depth below 1.8m OD

0–30	Peat and peaty alluvium. 10YR2.5/1; 10YR3/2.
30–40	Humified peat with charcoal fragments. 10YR2.5/1.
40–55	This is the pre-peat soil which developed over the barrow mound.
55–100	Oxidised sandy loam and fine gravel. 10YR5/6. 5YR5/6. This is the barrow mound material.
100+	Waterlogged sand and gravel subsoil. 10YR6/8.
0.84m OD	Water table on 26/10/1982.

This barrow appears to be of simpler construction than barrow 10d. It is composed of an upcast mound of subsoil material probably generated by the digging of the surrounding ditch. There is a relatively high water-table, and considerable leaching of the profile. No turves or a pre-barrow land surface were recognisable. But the complete absence of a buried land surface is suspicious, and suggests that the area of the barrow was indeed stripped of turf and topsoil, which may now be unrecognisable in the mound material.

The post-barrow soil still survives, and indeed must have had sufficient time to develop prior to peat growth. This soil presumably became reduced as a result of freshwater inundation and the subsequent growth of an upper peat.

It is evident that these barrow sites and probably many more in this northwestern corner of the North Level are essentially dry land sites — both when they were built and since the Second World War. This area of Borough Fen is *c.* 0.25–0.5km beyond the known extent of the lower peat and fen clay. The barrows also appear to align approximately northwest to southeast, or at a right angle to the late Neolithic/earlier Bronze Age fen-edge (Hall 1987, fig. 10). The land must have been at least seasonally dry to

Sample	Mz	σ	Sk	KG
BoF 7:				
Upper buried soil	2.01	0.18	-0.09	0.98
Lower buried soil	2.35	0.27	0.03	0.9
F2	1.96	0.11	-0.06	0.96
F3	1.88	0.05	-0.08	1.03
BoF 10d:				
1	1.63	-9.84	-0.05	1.22
2	1.56	9.84	-0.08	1.17
3	1.75	0.08	-0.13	1.28
4	1.65	0.08	-0.08	1.37
5	0.6	-0.53	0.24	0.97
6	1.63	-0.02	-0.02	1.5
7	1.58	0.06	-0.06	1.47
B/C	0.75	-0.46	0.275	1.12
Dyke 1:				
Upper buried soil	2.21	0.26	-0.09	0.88
Lower buried soil	2.03	0.11	-0.07	1.0
Dyke 8:				
Upper buried soil	2.0	0.17	-0.14	0.99
Lower buried soil	2.2	0.18	-0.05	0.94
B/C	2.18	0.19	0.02	0.97
Dyke 9:				
Lens	2.95	0.56	-0.09	0.71
Buried soil	2.05	0.16	-0.05	1.04

Table 7. The four statistical measures for the sand fraction of samples from soils and features at various sites in the North Level (all as phi values).

Sample	Mz	σ	Sk	KG
BoF 7:				
Upper buried soil	5.41	1.12	-0.21	0.64
Lower buried soil	5.68	1.39	-0.16	1.31
F2	6.41	1.13	-0.19	0.84
F3	6.43	1.14	-0.1	0.83
BoF 10d:				
1	6.45	1.29	-0.06	0.97
2	5.96	1.12	0.23	0.66
3	6.16	1.21	-2.07	0.94
4	6.11	1.43	0.16	1.2
5	-	-	-	-
6	5.76	1.25	6.85	0.84
7	6.28	1.15	-0.1	0.73
B/C	5.33	1.13	-0.31	0.72
Dyke 1:				
Upper buried soil	6.21	1.43	-0.45	1.11
Lower buried soil	5.81	1.38	-0.16	1.17
Dyke 8:				
Upper buried soil	5.88	1.18	-0.23	0.94
Lower buried soil	5.7	1.34	-0.22	1.24
B/C	5.5	1.25	9.8	1.16
Dyke 9:				
Lens	5.76	1.32	-0.19	1.03
Buried soil	5.8	1.26	-0.26	1.15

Table 8. The four statistical measures for the silt fraction of soils and features from various sites in the North Level (all as phi values).

allow their construction, and was therefore potentially available as pasture or hay for communities based further 'inland', to the west.

Intensive leaching and very effective recent drainage have probably had a detrimental effect on the preservation of botanical evidence. Only the bases of the barrow ditches may remain waterlogged, and the upper peat and barrow deposits are mainly alkaline. Moreover the barrow mounds themselves are now subject to mechanical destruction by ploughing and bulldozing. Thus the archaeological and environmental potential of these sites is rapidly diminishing.

Soil pH and Phosphate Results from Barrow 10d
by D.A. Gurney
(Figs 38–40; Table 5)

The top of the barrow mound is emerging from the peat and is visible as a circular gravel patch, while the barrow itself is sectioned by a modern dyke. The western side of this dyke was cleaned and sampled at seven locations at 5m intervals (A–B on Fig. 38). This was a rapid exercise, and the sampling here is not as detailed as that done at BoF site 1 (see below).

Soil pH Results
(Fig. 39; Table 5)
Twenty-one samples were analysed for pH, sampling the ploughsoil, barrow ditch, barrow mound and subsoil. The results are illustrated in Figure 39, where profile 1 is marked A and profile 7, B. The ploughsoil samples all fall within the alkaline range 7.5–8.3, the upper fill of the ditch

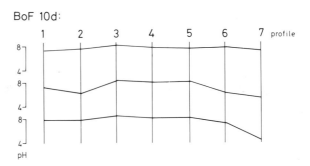

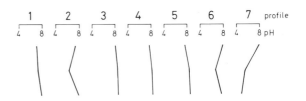

Figure 39 pH horizontal and vertical variation through barrow 10d.

has values of 5.4, 6.2 and 6.4 (slightly acid) and the lower ditch fill has a value of 7.8 (alkaline).

Phosphate Results
(Figs 38 and 40)
Three series of samples for laboratory analysis were taken from each of the seven profiles at 5m intervals through the barrow mound section from A to B (Figs 38 and 40). Results from the ploughsoil vary between 79 and 94mg,

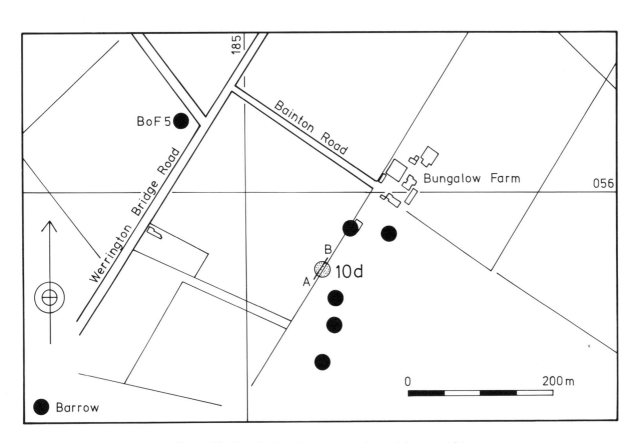

Figure 38 Sample location transect through barrow 10d.

and results from the subsoil vary between 31 and 91mg. Values from the barrow ditch and mound were generally low, and no meaningful patterning was apparent. There is no indication from the phosphate evidence that the Romano-British utilisation of the mound was anything other than occasional activity on the top of an 'island' in the peat created by the barrow mound.

BoF 10d:

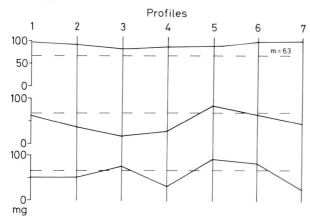

Figure 40 Phosphate horizontal variation through barrow 10d.

Flints from the BoF 3 Barrow
by H.R. Middleton
(Fig. 27; Table 3)
Field-walking of this ploughed out barrow produced three pieces of worked flint and one large burnt pebble fragment (Table 3).

All the flints were of dark brown, good quality flint with large light grey inclusions of a coarser grain than the surrounding matrix.

A rather simple technology is indicated with the three pieces, displaying the use of hard hammers and lack of core preparation. This is best shown by the large attempted core (Fig. 27, no. 13), with numerous impact fractures on its ventral surface.

This simple flint-working technology would tend to suggest a date contemporary with, or slightly later than the barrow. This hypothesis finds typological support from the scraper (Fig. 27, no. 12) whose form can be parallelled readily at other fenland Early Bronze Age sites, such as at Plantation Farm, Shippea Hill (Clark 1933, fig. 3).

Catalogue of illustrated flints
(Fig. 27)
12. BoF 3 barrow: Surface: **Scraper** Type A2.
13. BoF 3 barrow: Surface: **Core** Type A1.

Romano-British pottery from Barrow 10d
by D.A. Gurney
(Figs 11 and 47)

Three sherds were found in the uppermost fill of the barrow ditch, just below the junction of the ditch fill with the ploughsoil. The sherds are of a jar in a pale brown fabric with a dark grey external surface and a light grey internal surface, of late 1st to early 2nd century AD (finds nos 182–184) (Fig. 47).

It seems probable that these sherds were deposited in the upper fill of the ditch (which would have appeared as a slight hollow in the Roman period) doubtless from casual activity. There is no evidence of Roman settlement in the immediate vicinity, the nearest substantial occupation being Borough Fen site 1, *c.* 2km to the north (Chapter 3.I; Fig. 11). The presence of these sherds towards the top of the tertiary fill suggests that peat formation had long been underway on the landward margin of Borough Fen by the Roman period.

Romano-British Pottery Catalogue
(Fig. 47)
1. **Jar**. Light brown, with reddish brown margins and dark grey surfaces. Burnished decoration on the neck. Two joining sherds. Late 1st or early 2nd Century AD. From the upper ditch fill on the south side of the barrow.
2. Not illustrated. Two joining body sherds, probably from a large **jar**. Gritty dark grey fabric with brown surfaces. From the upper ditch fill on the north side of the barrow.

Archaeological Survey: Iron Age

1. Borough Fen Site 7/Dyke 5

The Survey
(Figs 41 and 42; Pl. VIII)
This earthwork site is situated on a spine of Welland First Terrace river gravels in the northwestern corner of Borough Fen (TF 5192 3074). The western two-thirds of the site is under pasture and is a Scheduled Monument (SAM number 222). The principal rampart is upstanding to a height of *c.* 1.5m, and encloses a roughly circular area of *c.* 3.8 hectares with an approximate diameter of *c.* 220m, and is broken by two possible entranceways. There are slight indications of a second outer ditch forming a concentric circle of *c.* 280m in diameter. The eastern one-third of the monument is under arable cultivation and is not scheduled. Here the single bank and external ditch are clearly visible as soil marks (Fig. 41) (Hall 1987, fig. 11 and pl. V).

Until the present investigation of the site took place, the monument was considered to be of probable medieval date. Pottery found within the occupation horizon and underlying features suggests a Middle Iron Age date of the 3rd/2nd centuries BC, and radiocarbon assay of charcoal obtained from the ploughsoil/occupation deposit gave a date of (Har–8512) 2090 ± 0 BP (380 Cal. BC to Cal. AD 80).

Although the interior of this earthwork site is now upstanding by about 1m above the surface of the surrounding peat and alluvium, prior to drainage, peat shrinkage and wastage, it was probably beneath the surface of the surrounding fen. The monument is not indicated on a map of AD 1637 (LRRO 1/301), which suggests that peat and alluvium completely obscured the earthworks at that time.

The site may have been chosen as it was a firm area of ground relative to the surrounding, growing peat fen. The massive (*c.* 4–6m wide and 2–3m deep) principal external ditch probably served a dual purpose for defence and drainage.

The stratigraphy of this monument was revealed using a combination of a north-south augering transect at 5 and 10 metre intervals across the monument, and the cleaning down of four selected sections of the modern dyke (Dyke 5) which cuts through the site from south to north (Fig. 42; Pl. VIII; M. Pls 20 and 21).

Figure 41 Location of BoF Sites 1, 2 and 7, and Dyke 5.

69

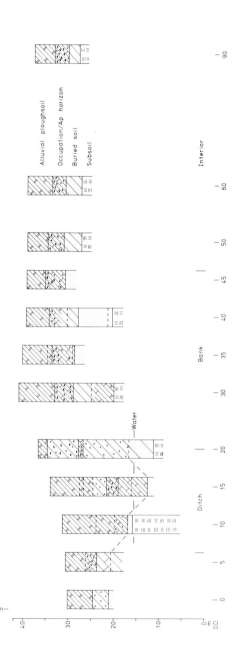

Figure 42 Auger survey profiles through BoF Site 7.

70

Plate VIII The ploughsoil/occupation horizon/buried soil in the interior of the Borough Fen ringwork Site, Dyke 5.

The interior of the monument revealed the following stratigraphic sequence (Fig. 42; Pl. VIII):

Depth in m OD

3.8–3.3	Peaty alluvium or a humose loam which becomes more loamy and oxidised with depth. 10YR4/2. Sharply defined boundary.
3.3–3.2	Organic sandy clay loam with abundant charcoal fragments. 10YR2.5/1. Merging boundary.
3.2–2.8	Organic loam with many charcoal fragments. 10YR3/1. These two layers together comprise a buried soil/occupation horizon. Narrow boundary.
(2.8–2.55)	(Features 2 and 3 are at this level)
2.8–2.7	Bleached and leached sandy loam. 10YR7/2. Narrow boundary.
2.7–1.8	Oxidised sandy loam to sand. 5YR4/6. Undulating, merging boundary.
1.8+	Reduced clay of First Terrace deposits. 10YR6/2; 5Y5/1.
-1.7	Oxford Clay.

The external ditch revealed the following stratigraphy:

Depth in m OD

3.0–2.7	Peaty alluvium. 10YR4/2. Merging boundary.
2.7–2.0	Loam. 10YR4/3. Merging boundary.
2.0–1.6	Loam with a weakly developed, fine blocky ped structure which may represent a standstill horizon or a former Ah/1 profile. 10YR4/3. Narrow boundary.
1.6+	Ditch (not bottomed) fill of sandy loam. 10YR5/4.
1.55	Water level: November, 1982.

The internal bank exhibited the following stratigraphy:

Depth in m OD

4.1–3.5	Peaty alluvium. 10YR4/2. Merging boundary.
3.5–3.3	Silt loam. 10YR3/2. Sharply defined boundary.
3.3–2.9	Loam with abundant charcoal fragments, which may be a buried soil. 10YR2.5/1. Sharply defined boundary.
2.9–1.6	Oxidised sandy loam and gravel. 5YR6/6.
1.6–1.1	Oxidised sand. 5YR4/6.
1.1+	Reduced clay. 10YR6/2; 5Y5/1.

Two internal features, probably small pits were revealed in the dykeside within the interior of the monument. The fill of feature 2 was a sandy loam to sandy clay loam (10YR4/3) with a few scattered gravel pebbles; feature 3 was infilled with a sandy clay loam (10YR4/3) with a few scattered gravel pebbles. Both features contained molluscan assemlages which are discussed below.

The features and overlying occupation horizon contained numerous sherds of middle Iron Age pottery as well as a small collection of animal bone, both of which are reported on below.

The Pottery from Site BoF 7
by F.M.M. Pryor
(Fig. 43)

The assemblage weighs 280g and comprises some 35 sherds, plus crumbs. The fabrics are tempered with crushed (probably fossil) shell, but are not especially coarse; they would approximate to Fengate fabrics 1b and 1c (Williams in Pryor 1984a, 134). There is also some evidence for the admixture of crushed flint, but the hard, sand-tempered, fabric (2) that characterised Iron Age wheel-made pottery at Fengate and East Field, Maxey is absent (Pryor and French 1985, 120).

Catalogue of Illustrated pottery
(Fig. 43)

1. Simple **rimsherd** of small jar. Hard oxidised fabric with finely crushed shell and (?) sand (Fengate/Maxey fabric 1C). Rimtop irregularly flattened; slight, smoothed, 'scoring' on ext., below rim. From occupation deposit, profile 2. Archive: BoF 176.
2. Simple **rimsherd** of small jar. Hard oxidised fabric with crushed shell (Fengate/Maxey Fabric 1B). From occupation deposit, profile 2. Archive: BoF 177.
3. Simple **rimsherd** of small jar. Hard oxidised fabric with crushed shell (Fengate/Maxey Fabric 1B). From occupation deposit, profile 4. Archive: BoF 180.
4. Simple **rimsherd** of small jar. Hard, reduced fabric without shell; well divided sub-angular dark inclusions. Unstratified. Archive: SW 205.

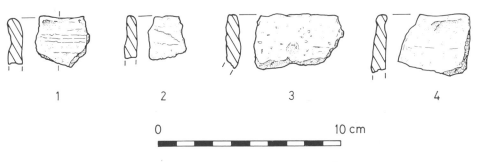

0   10 cm

Figure 43 BoF Site 7 pottery.

Discussion

For the small surface area of occupation deposit exposed, it was very rich in pottery. The assemblage was generally fresh and in good condition, although some of the smaller sherds are well abraded. The surface appearance of the various sherds is quite diverse and it is doubtful whether many derive from the same vessel. Most sherds seem to come from small or medium-sized bowls or jars: there are no cups, handles or storage vessels represented. At first glance this group probably originated from standard settlement contexts.

Dating is made problematical by the scarcity of diagnostic pieces. The 'scoring' of no. 1, hints at a Middle Iron Age date, but the fabrics are by and large hard and well-fired, suggesting, perhaps a slightly later date. One body sherd, from the shoulder of a plain small jar, is in the distinctive 'smooth dark' ware (fabric 1B) that is generally thought to be characteristic of the Middle Iron Age in the Nene valley (*cf.* Pryor 1974, fig. 21, 1).

Taken together the assemblage is undoubtedly Iron Age in style, but it lacks distinctively early (*i.e.* West Harling or Fengate, Vicarage Farm) or late (wheel-thrown or copies thereof) forms. Given that this is a very small sample from a particularly large site, a date perhaps somewhere between the 3rd and later 1st century BC seems appropriate.

The Animal Bone from Site BoF 7
by Miranda Armour-Chelu
(Table 9)

The bones were collected from the cleaning of Dyke 5, profiles 2, 3, 4 and 5, which cut from south to north through the ringwork. The preservation of the material was good, although the bones were very fragmented, suggesting that they were derived from domestic food refuse. The small sample size limits any further interpretation of these remains which are set out in Table 9 along with details of their age, butchery and preservation.

Identification	Element	Notes
Profile 2:		
Ox	scapula fragment	chopped
	right P4	in wear
Sheep/goat	upper molar	slightly worn
	left metatarsal	distal epiphysis not fused
	cervical vertebra	cutmarks on ventral side
Pig	mandible fragment	
Large ungulate	fragment	
	fragment	
	fragment	
Small ungulate	limb bone shaft fragment	
	limb bone shaft fragment	
	lumbar vertebra	immature
	rib	
	rib	
	rib	

Identification	Element	Notes
Profile 3:		
Ox	innominate fragment	cutmarks on the shaft of ilium
	right tibia fragment	canid gnawing on proximal end
Sheep/goat	lower molar	slightly worn
Large ungulate	rib fragment	chopped
Small ungulate	limb bone shaft fragment	
	limb bone shaft fragment	
Feature 1:		
Ox	scapula fragment	chopped
Small ungulate	limb bone shaft fragment	
	limb bone shaft fragment	
	fragment	
	fragment	
	fragment	
Feature 2:		
Pig	femur distal shaft fragment	
Small ungulate	limb bone shaft fragment	
	limb bone shaft fragment	
	limb bone shaft fragment	
	limb bone shaft fragment	
	rib fragment	
Profile 4:		
Ox	left upper molar	in wear
Sheep/goat	left upper molar	in wear
Profile 4: Ap/occupation horizon		
Large ungulate	scapula	
Profile 5:		
Sheep/goat	ulna fragment	
Large ungulate	lumbar vertebra	
	fragment	
	fragment	
	fragment	
	fragment	
	fragment	
Small ungulate	rib fragment	
	rib fragment	
	rib fragment	
	limb bone shaft fragment	
	limb bone shaft fragment	
	limb bone shaft fragment	
	fragment	
	fragment	
Profile 5: Ap/occupation horizon		
Horse	left metacarpal	distal epiphysis fused, weathered

Table 9. Animal bone from Dyke 5, Borough Fen site 7.

Soil pH, Phosphate and Magnetic Susceptibility Surveys
by D.A. Gurney

Soil pH
(Table 5)
The ploughsoil, occupation deposit and subsoil are all alkaline.

Soil Phosphate Analysis
(Fig. 42)
The occupation deposit was sampled at three profiles (2, 3, 4), and two features (F2 and F3) were also sampled (Fig. 42). The results (not illustrated) were obtained by spot test and laboratory analysis. In the laboratory, all five samples provided identical results of 360mg, while the spot test results varied from weak (profile 4) through positive (profiles 4 and 3: features 2 and 3) to strong (profile 2).

Magnetic Susceptibility
The same contexts were tested in the laboratory for magnetic susceptibility, and values ranged from 17 to 29 SI. The low magnetic susceptibility results contrast strongly with the high phosphate determinations. This suggests that the occupation deposit and features exhibit no signs of *in situ* burning.

Site BoF7: Soils and their Micromorphology
by Charles French
(Figs 3, 42; Pl. VIII; Tables 5–8)

The Soils: Formation and Preservation
This Middle Iron Age ringwork is situated on a humic gley soil of the Ireton Series, which has developed on a short ridge of Welland First Terrace deposits (Figs 3, 42; Pl. VIII). The probable Romano-British farmstead (site BoF 1) is similarly situated about 300m to the northeast (see below).

The humic gley ploughsoil is essentially an alluvial deposit which is resting on a *c.* 40–50cm thick buried soil/occupation horizon within the interior of the monument. This consists of an organic loam. It overlies occupation features. The ploughsoil, buried soil and subsoil are all alkaline (Table 5).

The buried soil has a relatively high clay content which suggests some degree of alluvial influence (Table 6). However, the absence of extreme values for the degree of sorting, skewness and kurtosis (Tables 7, 8) indicates that the soil has undergone few radical transformations since its formation. The dominance of the sand fraction (Table 6), and principally the medium sand fraction, betrays the origins of the soil as being a sandy loam that developed on a river terrace subsoil.

The augering transect (Fig. 42) indicates that this buried soil does survive outside the confines of the monument, but it is much thinner. The area of the monument is higher than the surrounding fen at present because of peat shrinkage around an area of higher First Terrace gravels, thus accentuating the actually low height of the remaining enclosure bank. The site has been subjected to the same land use both within and outside the monument since the Second World War, with pasture on the western two-thirds and intensive arable on the eastern one-third of the monument (S. Whitsed pers. comm.).

The Iron Age was a wet period of fenland prehistory and for this monument to have been built in the middle/later Iron Age, it must have been situated on dry land, at least seasonally. Doubtless the surrounding area must have been subject to increasing wetness, and with it peat growth, throughout the later Iron Age, the Roman period and into medieval times. The continued growth of the upper peat about 1km to the east, in the area to the north of Thorney, probably acted as a barrier to water movement and may well have caused freshwater back-up in this area. This is also suggested by the soils to the west of BoF 7, between the present River Welland and the Peakirk-Newborough road which are groundwater humic gleys of the Ireton and Midelney Series. There is also evidence for a former braided river channel system northeast of Peakirk (R. Evans pers. comm.). In effect, the ridge of gravels on which this site and the nearby Romano-British site (BoF 1) are situated is acting as a small peninsula. The combination of higher ground and relatively good drainage of the terrace deposits made this area tenable for settlement, at least during the Iron Age and earlier Roman period.

It is evident that the whole area became subject to extensive alluviation some time after the end of the Iron Age. The alluvium even covered the highest ground (up to *c.* 4.4m OD) on the ridge of the terrace deposits. This was intermixed with thin peat growth (*c.* 30cm) (R. Evans pers. comm.). It would seem then that the area must have been very wet at least periodically throughout the year in post-Roman times, but may have continued to provide seasonal pasture until the mid 17th century drainage of the area made arable agriculture more possible.

Soil micromorphology
(Pls IX and X; M. Pls 47–52)
Samples for thin sectioning were taken through the buried soil deposits underlying the alluvium at Profile 2. One sample was taken from the approximate middle of the *c.* 20–30cm thick 'occupation horizon', an organic sandy loam with abundant charcoal fragments (10YR3/1); and two samples were taken from the *c.* 40–80cm thick buried soil beneath. In the field the buried soil had two evident horizons. The upper horizon was a thin (*c.* 10cm thick) bleached sandy loam (10YR7/2), and the thicker (*c.* 30–70cm thick) lower horizon was an oxidised sandy loam to sand (5YR4/6). The detailed micromorphological descriptions are found in Appendix VI.

The 'occupation horizon' within the ringfort (Pls IX and X; M. Pls 47–50) is composed of a heterogeneous mixture of two main fabrics. Fabric (1) dominates the horizon and is composed of zones of very fine quartz sand, silt and fine charcoal, and zones composed solely of very fine quartz sand and fine charcoal. This fabric also contains a few very leached and small fragments of bone, and a few phytoliths. Thus this fabric is composed mainly of wood ash and other, probably dumped, occupation debris.

Fabric (2) is a dense fine material composed mainly of silt with much amorphous organic matter and numerous fine flecks of charcoal. It also contains occasional, fine sand-size, rolled clay aggregates and sesquioxide nodules. This fine, dense, organic fabric is characteristic of Ap or ploughsoil material (Bouma 1969; Jongerius 1970; Slager and van de Wetering 1977; Macphail pers. comm.). A similar ploughsoil fabric has been observed in thin section at Dyke 9/profile 2 on the southwestern edge of Northey 'island' (Chapter 3: IV).

The heterogeneous mixture of these two fabrics suggests that the horizon was subject to mechanical

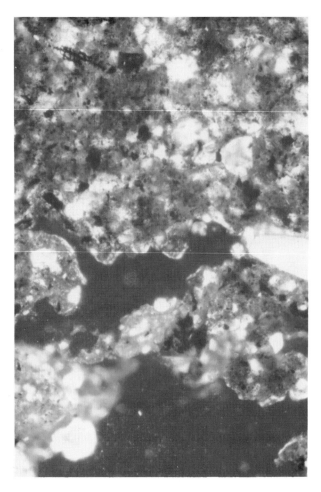

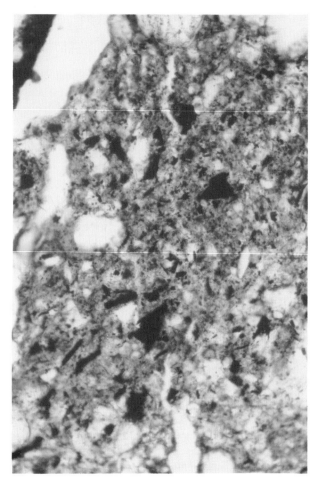

Plate IX A photomicrograph of fabric 1 in the Ap/occupation horizon at the Borough Fen ringwork (PPL; frame = 2mm).

Plate X A photomicrograph of fabric 2 in the Ap/occupation horizon at the Borough Fen ringwork (PPL; frame = 2mm).

disturbance, most probably ploughing. It is also possible that the dumping and incorporation of the ashy occupation debris was intentional, and was serving as a form of fertiliser.

The presence of occasional rolled clay aggregates in fabric (2) suggests that there was a slight alluvial component to the ploughsoil. Indeed, after the use of the ringwork, the whole northwest corner of Borough Fen became subject to considerable alluvial aggradation. Other evidence of post-depositional freshwater flooding occurs in the form of large zones of amorphous sesquioxide impregnation, particularly of the ploughsoil fabric (2), as well as the few amorphous iron infills of voids. The presence of vivianite is also suggestive of anaerobic conditions: it is a hydrated iron phosphate, which mainly occurs in waterlogged flood loams (Limbrey 1975) and wet, peaty soils (Bullock et al. 1985).

The results of the analysis of both underlying buried soil samples will be discussed together below.

The fabrics of both horizons of buried soil within the ringfort (M. Pls 51 and 52) are similar, and are essentially apedal, homogeneous, very fine sandy loams. Very fine quartz sand and silt predominate. The upper horizon is more organic than the lower horizon, but relative to the overlying ploughsoil there is very little organic matter in these horizons. There are few to occasional fine flecks of charcoal in both, and some amorphous organic matter in the upper horizon.

The upper horizon of the palaeosol does contain rare to occasional, partial to complete channel infills composed of dense, very fine quartz sand, silt and amorphous organic matter. This fabric is similar to fabric (2) of the overlying ploughsoil/occupation horizon, and is probably indicative of the leaching of ploughsoil material and its deposition in channels lower down the soil profile.

Both the upper and lower horizons are subject to considerable amounts of sesquioxide impregnation. This characteristic becomes most pronounced in the lower horizon. Therefore the palaeosol became subject to both periodic flooding and a rising, but fluctuating, local groundwater table, but mainly as post-depositional events.

The strong influence of sesquioxides and the relative paucity of textural features and organic matter suggest that the soil fabric of both horizons is a leached B/Bg or gleyed B horizon. Given the relatively substantial depth of the buried soil, further analysis of the lower horizon might detect other lower soil horizons which are not visible in the field.

It is important to stress that the overlying alluvium protects a complete soil profile, both beneath the rampart and within the interior of the ringwork enclosure. The only other known example of such excellent prehistoric soil preservation in the area occurs beneath the upper peat on the southwestern edge of Northey 'island'. This is another indication of the exceptional archaeological preservation of this Iron Age site.

Molluscan Analysis of Features 2 and 3, Profile 3, Site BoF 7
(Fig. 44; Tables 10–12)
by Charles French

During the cleaning down of the dyke-side which runs from south to north across the eastern third of the monument, one section (Profile 3) revealed two small pits sealed beneath the buried soil. They were spot sampled for molluscs. One kilogram of soil from each pit was processed. The results are presented in tabular form by absolute numbers of each species (Table 10), by ecological groups (Tables 11 and 12) and in the form of rank-order curves (Fig. 44) (Appendix II).

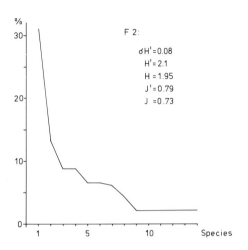

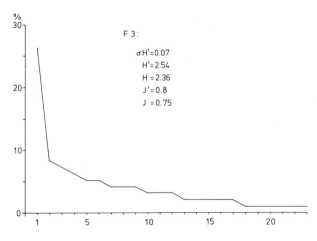

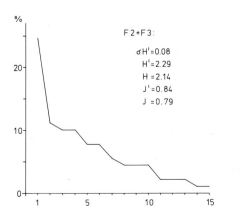

Figure 44 BoF Site 7 molluscan diversity indices and rank order curves.

Dry weight 1.0 kg

Sample	F2	F3
Valvata cristata (Müller)	3	4
Bithynia tentaculata (Linnaeus)	1	1
B.leachii (Sheppard)	-	4
Lymnaea truncatula (Müller)	3	25
L.palustris (Müller)	1	-
L.auricularia (Linnaeus)	-	2
Anisus vortex (Linnaeus)	-	1
Bathyomphalus contortus (Linnaeus)	-	1
Armiger crista (Linnaeus)	-	1
Carychium tridentatum (Risso)	6	3
Succinea oblonga (Draparnaud)	-	5
Cochlicopa spp.	2	2
Pupilla muscorum (Linnaeus)	1	1
Vallonia costata (Müller)	4	5
V.pulchella (Müller)	-	1
V.excentrica Sterki	4	3
Vallonia spp.	-	2
Vitrea contracta (Westerlund)	14	8
Aegopinella nitidula (Draparnaud)	-	2
Oxychilus spp.	1	3
Deroceras sp.	1	-
Helicella itala (Linnaeus)	3	7
? Monacha cantiana (Montagu)	-	4
Trichia hispida (Linnaeus)	1	6
Pisidium milium Held	-	2

Table 10. Molluscs from Features 2 and 3 in Borough Fen, site 7.

Rank-order curves and the diversity indexes of the species assemblages were determined for each sample separately, and as one combined sample with only the land molluscs considered. The 'regularly curved' to 'intermediate' graphs suggest that the assemblages represent a diverse and relatively mature environment with a wide range of habitats (J. Evans unpublished paper). But the rather low numbers of species and individuals suggest that some part of the assemblage is derived. The medium H1; H values and the small diferences between the diversity (H1; H) and evenness values (J1; J) suggest that the species present in greater abundance (*e.g. Lymnaea truncatula, Vitrea contracta, Carychium tridentatum, Vallonia costata, V. excentrica, Helicella itala*) are probably *in situ* and representative of a relatively simple environment. There is also the possibility that at least some of the land species reflect the micro-habitats of the pits in which they were found. Most of the freshwater species are probably derived from elsewhere.

The ecological aspects of both assemblages are considered together. Land molluscs dominate the assemblages in both pits, comprising 77% and 50.5% respectively of the total number of snails recovered.

Vallonia costata, V. excentrica and *Helicella itala* are the principal open-country species present, which together comprise 26% and 20.5% of the assemblages (Tables 11 and 12). These species suggest the presence of relatively dry, open, undisturbed, short-turved grassland (Evans 1972). It should be pointed out that *V. costata* avoids

Sample	F2	F3
Freshwater:	17.0	17.25
Catholic	2.25	7.5
Ditch	6.6	4.3
Moving water	2.25	5.3
Freshwater slum/Marsh:	6.0	32.25
Land:	77.0	50.5
Shade-loving	15.0	8.7
Shade/scrub/waste ground	28.0	13.0
Catholic	8.0	8.7
Open-country	26.0	20.5

Table 11. Molluscs arranged by percentage in ecological group from Borough Fen, site 7.

pasture which is disturbed by cattle, but may occur in close association with man as a synanthropic species (Evans 1972). These three species are often found in grassland grazed by sheep (Evans 1972).

Although the arrangement of the species into conventional ecological groups appears to favour the shade-loving/scrub/waste ground group (43%; 21.7%) (Table 11), none of these species specifically requires woodland habitats. *C. tridentatum* (13.3%; 3.15%) favours leaf litter, although it is equally at home in ungrazed grassland as on woodland floors (Evans 1972). *V. contracta* (31.1%; 8.4%) is more or less ubiquitous in its habitat preferences (Evans 1972). Cameron and Morgan-Huws (1975) have suggested that both these species should be re-classified as catholic species. If these two species are combined with *Aegopinella nitidula*, *Oxychilus* and *Trichia hispida* and the other catholic species (51%; 30.4%), they are more suggestive of unkempt vegetation or a possible scrub element against the background of an open environment. Nevertheless, the absence of any species more closely confined to woodland such as *Acanthinula aculeata* (Paul 1975, 1978a and b) attests to the extent of open ground, at least within the interior of the monument.

The freshwater species comprise a minority of the assemblages (17.0%; 17.25%) (Table 11). Although the most abundant species, *Lymnaea truncatula* (6.0%; 26.0%), is characteristic of freshwater slum conditions; it may be found in marsh habitats (Boycott 1936; Evans 1972). Together with the obligatory marsh species *Succinea oblonga* (5.4%), they suggest the presence of localised wet ground, but which was generally unsuitable for sustained freshwater molluscan life. It is probable that the other few freshwater species have been incorporated in the features as a result of the occasional overspill of water from the adjacent fen or River Welland to the north.

After considering all these factors, the land molluscs suggest relatively dry, open ground covered with a combination of grass and patches of weeds, and a possible scrub element. There may be very localised marshy conditions, and occasionally freshwater overspill from the adjacent fen. Thus, although these two small assemblages are somewhat restricted in species variety and numbers, they are probably a fairly reliable indicator of the immediate environment within the interior of the ringwork.

The presence of *Monacha cantiana* appears to be somewhat of an enigma at first glance. It prefers grassy

Ecological Group		Molluscan Species
Freshwater:	Slum:	*Lymnaea truncatula*
	Catholic:	*Lymnaea palustris*
		L.auricularia
		Bathyomphalus contortus
		Armiger crista
		Pisidium milium
	Ditch-living:	*Valvata cristata*
		Anisus vortex
	Moving water:	*Bithynia tentaculata*
		B.leachii
Marsh:		*Succinea oblonga*
Land:	Shade-loving:	*Carychium tridentatum*
		Aegopinella nitidula
		Vitrea contracta
		Oxychilus
	Catholic/Intermediate:	*Cochlicopa*
		Deroceras
		Trichia hispida
	Open-country:	*Pupilla muscorum*
		Vallonia costata
		V.pulchella
		V.excentrica
		Helicella itala
	Alien:	*Monacha cantiana*

Table 12. Molluscan species ecological groups.

areas, on banks amongst nettles, in hedgerows and waste ground (Kerney and Cameron 1979), and it does not like excessively wet ground (Chatfield 1968, 1972). Although these habitat preferences suit the envisaged Middle/Late Iron Age environment within the monument, this species is an alien species of western European origin which is first thought to occur in Britain in post-glacial times in the Roman period (Kerney *et al.* 1964). It is considered unlikely that the samples are contaminated by modern molluscs which are living on the adjacent dyke-side; rather, it is more probable that the buried soil/occupation surface had a life of several centuries which continued into the Roman period. Only future excavation will provide a definitive answer; but there is certainly evidence of early Roman occupation about 300m to the northeast on the same gravel ridge (BoF site 1).

Archaeological Survey: Roman

1. Borough Fen Site 1 (BoF1)

The Survey
(Figs 2, 11, 45, 46)
This site (TF 5196 3074) is situated some 300m to the east of the Middle Iron Age ringwork, just described, on the highest point of the same First Terrace deposits (Figs 2, 11, 45). The site appears as a dark soil mark, and as a discrete scatter of Romano- British pottery (Fig. 45). Hall's survey (1987) discovered the site initially. A northwest to southeast mapping transect illustrates that the site is situated on a rise in terrace deposits, from *c.* 3.6m OD

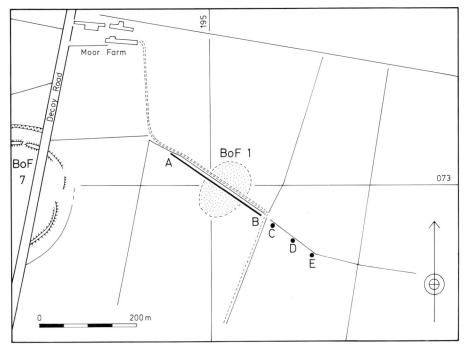

Figure 45 The area of the pottery scatter at BoF Site 1, and the phosphate and magnetic susceptibility sample locations.

at the northwest to *c.* 4.4m OD in the centre of the site to *c.* 2.1m OD at the southeast side of the site. Pottery collected along the same transect suggests a first half of the 2nd century to early/mid 3rd century AD date for the site (see Gurney below).

Stratigraphy generally representative of the site was obtained from field observation and a geological survey borehole log:

Depth in m OD

3.3–2.9	Black humic loam. 10YR5/1. Narrow boundary.
2.9–2.5	Silt loam. 10YR4/2. Narrow boundary. First Terrace deposits which consist :
2.5–1.8	Clay which is silty in patches, with some gravel pebbles. 10YR4/2; 2.5YR4/4.
1.8–0.2	'Clayey' pebbly sand. 10YR6/4.
0.2+	Oxford Clay.

Dr R. Evans (pers. comm.) suggests that the post-Roman peat cover was very thin, or about 30cm thick, and has now become incorporated with the silty clay alluvium, primarily as a result of intensive arable agriculture.

The artefacts mainly come from this A horizon. The range of pottery types suggests that this was probably a habitation site. This hypothesis is corroborated by the high phosphate and magnetic susceptibilty values (see Gurney below). This location was probably chosen because of its relatively upstanding and dry situation despite being surrounded by peat fen and areas prone to freshwater flooding. The surrounding fen would also have provided rich seasonal pasture.

The Romano-British pottery from Site BoF 1
by D.A. Gurney
(Figs 45–47)

All sherds from a 3m wide transect on the southern edge of the dyke were collected (Fig. 45). These were plotted so that the distribution of pottery along the transect could be related both to the dykeside profiles (from which phosphate samples were taken) and the positions at which magnetic susceptibility readings were taken. The number

of sherds collected along the transect was 165, and these have a total weight of 1782g. The distribution has been plotted by sherd count and by sherd weight (Fig. 46).

The pottery recovered suggests that the site was occupied by at least the mid 2nd century AD, until the early or mid 3rd century AD (Fig. 47). The wares represented are as follows :

samian	6 sherds	22g
Nene Valley colour-coated	7 sherds	117g
oxidised wares	3 sherds	37g
Nene Valley grey ware	78 sherds	738g
other reduced wares	27 sherds	210g
calcite-gritted ware	43 sherds	618g
mortaria (Nene Valley)	1 sherd	40g

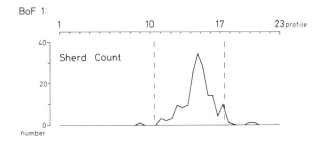

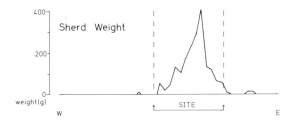

Figure 46 BoF Site 1 pottery distribution.

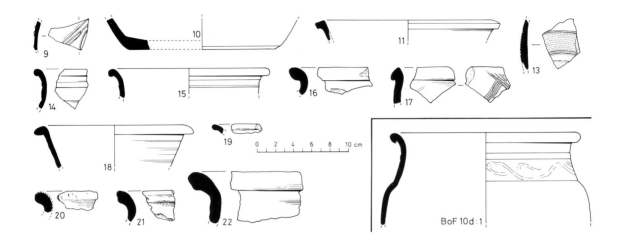

Figure 47 BoF Sites 1 and 10d pottery.

Roman pottery catalogue
(Fig. 47)

Samian (not illustrated)
1. Form 18 or 18/31 rim, South Gaulish.
2. Form 27 rim, South Gaulish.
3. Body sherd, South Gaulish.
4. Flake, South Gaulish.
5. Flake, South Gaulish.
6. Form 38, body sherd with flange, Central Gaulish.
7. Rim scrap, Central Gaulish.

Mortarium (not illustrated)
8. Body sherd from junction of wall and base. Hard off-white fabric, grey core, brownish buff slip. Black slaggy trituration, worn, Castor-Stibbington area of the lower Nene valley. AD 200–400.

Nene Valley colour-coated wares (illustrated)
9. Body sherd of a scroll-decorated beaker. White with a dark grey colour-coat.
10. Dish with a chamfered base. White with an orangey-brown colour-coat.
11. Bowl. White with a brown colour-coat.
12. Not illustrated. Roughcast body sherd. White with a dark brown colour-coat.

Self-coloured ware (illustrated)
13. Body sherd from a flagon. Off-white to pinkish fabric. Rouletted.

Nene Valley grey wares (illustrated)
14– Jars.
16
17. Bowl. Combed decoration internally.
18. Bowl.

Calcite-gritted wares (illustrated)
19– Jars.
21
22. Storage jar.

Soil pH, Phosphate and Magnetic Susceptibility Analyses, Site BoF 1
by D.A. Gurney
(Figs 45, 48–51)

The site is cut by a modern dyke, and the north face of this dyke was sampled at 23 locations at *c.* 10m intervals (Fig. 45, A to B), and at three locations at *c.* 50m intervals in the fen to the east (Fig. 45, C, D, E).

Soil pH
(Figs 48 and 49)
Figure 48 illustrates the vertical variation within each profile, and Figure 49 illustrates the horizontal variation across the site plotted by depth. In profiles 1 to 23 there is little variation across the site, and little variation down the profile. All horizons are neutral to alkaline (7.0–9.1). In profiles 24 to 26 to the east, there is a distinct fall in the pH, with the peat becoming slightly acidic (5.5–6.5) to neutral (6.5–7.5) in profile 26.

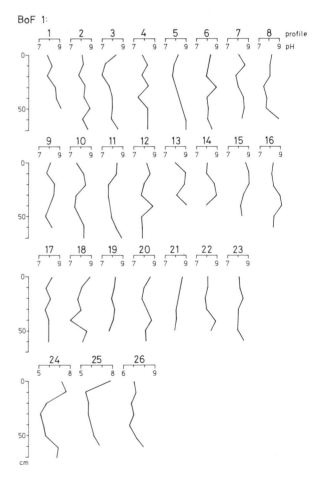

Figure 48 BoF Site 1 vertical variation in pH.

Four profiles (1, 5, 10, 15) were cut back a further 25cm to check any 'dyke edge' effects and variation between the original profile values. This varied between ± 0.9, but values were not consistently higher or lower than those from the original sampling points. This sort of variation within these pH values should have no effect upon the fixation or leaching of phosphates from soils exposed in dyke sections.

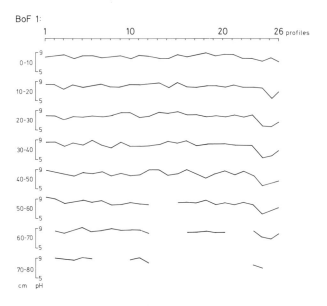

Figure 49 BoF Site 1 horizontal variation in pH.

Soil Phosphate Analysis
(Fig.50)
Up to seven samples were taken at *c.* 10cm vertical intervals down each of the 23 profiles, *c.* 10m apart, for laboratory analysis. The results to a depth of 40–50cm are illustrated (Fig. 50). At all levels, higher values (up to 300mg) were obtained from the area of the soil mark and sherd scatter (profiles 10–17), with lower values to the east and west of the site.

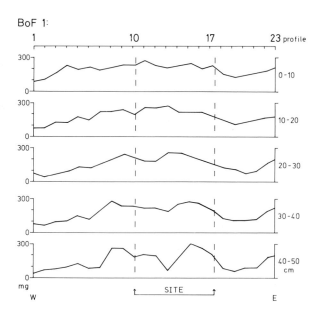

Figure 50 BoF Site 1 phosphate results.

Magnetic Susceptibility Analysis
(Fig. 51)
The ploughsoil was tested in the field using both senors along a transect south of and parallel to the dyke. Readings were taken at *c.* 10m intervals, corresponding with the locations of the dykeside profiles. The results show the highest readings from both sensors were coincident with the soil mark and sherd scatter. Sensor A located a single peak at profile 13, while Sensor B located two peaks at profiles 11 and 14, with a 'trough' between. In this instance, Sensor B appears to hae been the more sensitive of the two, providing the highest readings from the area of the site, and lower readings than Sensor A beyond the limits of the soil mark.

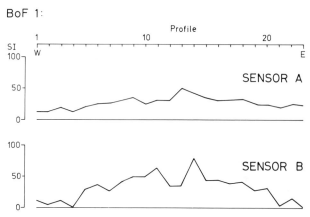

Figure 51 BoF Site 1 magnetic susceptibility results of the ploughsoil, sensor A above, sensor B below.

II. Morris Fen

Introduction
(Figs 2, 52–54; Pl. XI)
Morris Fen is situated to the east of Borough Fen in the northern part of Thorney parish (Figs 2, 52). This fen is approximately defined by the Cat's Water to the west, Thorney village and the A47 highway to the south, the B1167 to the east and French Drove and the New South Eau to the north.

A series of dykes have been cleaned that cut an almost complete section across the fen from southwest to northeast (Dykes 56, 52/51, 50, 44, 43, 41 and 42) (Figs 52–54). The stratigraphic sequence revealed will be discussed below. Within Morris Fen several areas of relatively high ground suitable for earlier prehistoric settlement were observed, but only one 'island' in Dyke 41 produced artefactual material and is discussed in detail below (Pl. XI).

Stratigraphy
(Figs 52–57; Tables 1 and 3)
Morris Fen and the sequence of dykes surveyed reveal stratigraphy representative of the complete fenland sequence. The section through this fen consists of Dykes 56, 52, 50, 44, 43, 41 and 42; it begins on the northernmost extremity of Thorney 'island' and dips northeastwards into

Figure 53 Location of Dykes 40-43.

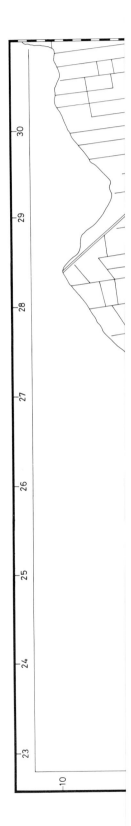

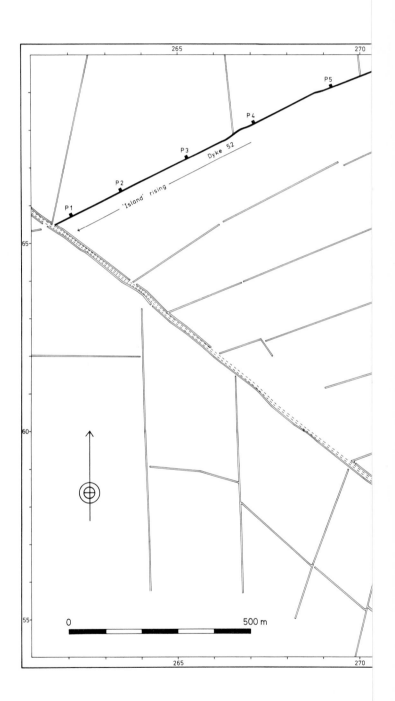

Figure 52 Mo

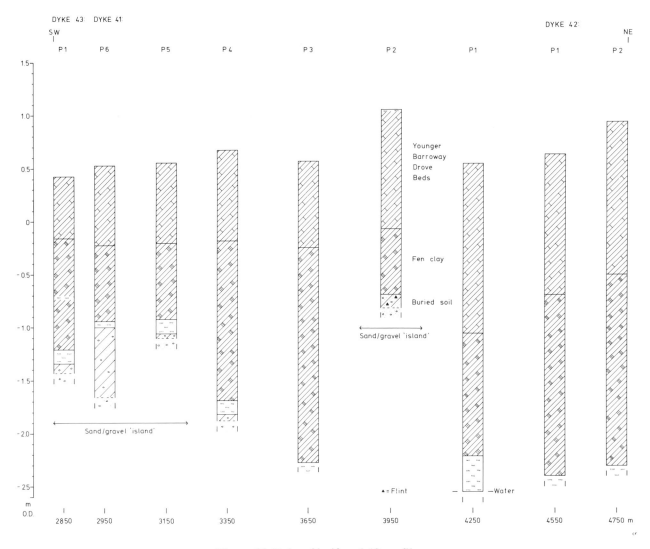

Figure 56 Dykes 41, 42 and 43 profiles.

the deepest part of the fenland basin, over a distance of *c.* 6km (Figs 52–56; M. Pls 22–27).

The stratigraphic sequence will be discussed working from southwest to northeast, beginning with Dyke 56. The subsoil is composed of March Gravels which dip from *c.* +0.8m to -0.25m OD northeastwards on the northern margin of Thorney 'island'. A relatively thick (*c.* 20–25cm) sandy loam soil is developed on these gravels. This buried soil is overlain by a discontinuous, thin (*c.* 1–2cm thick) organic (peaty) lens, and by a thin (*c.* 5–30cm thick) deposit of Barroway Drove Bed silty clay. Both of these deposits thin out and disappear to the southwest as the gravel subsoil rises. On the basis of the height above sea level of these deposits, and their correlation with the deposits in the succeeding dykes, the silty clay probably equates with the younger Barroway Drove Bed material, or the later Bronze Age/early Iron Age marine phase of the fen in the Thorney area. A humified upper peat mixed with marine silt, about 30–50cm thick, completes the sequence.

In Dyke 52 to the northeast, the gravel subsoil continues to dip from *c.* -0.25 to -0.60m OD from southwest to northeast on which a similar palaeosol to that observed in Dyke 56 is developed. The buried soil is overlain by a peat lens, probably the lower peat, which thickens from *c.* 2 to 8cm; older Barroway Drove Bed, grey to greyish brown silty clay with oxidation mottles, which thickens

from *c.* 5 to 45cm; younger Barroway Drove Bed, light brownish grey micaceous silty clay to silt, which thickens from *c.* 35–95cm; but no upper peat remains. Dyke 51 which runs parallel to Dyke 52 but *c.* 1.5km to the south exhibits a similar palaeosol, overlain by younger Barroway Drove Bed material and upper peat as the subsoil rises onto Thorney 'island' (Figs 54 and 55).

Dykes 50, 44 and 43 exhibit similar profiles to Dyke 52. The gravel subsoil continues to dip northeastwards from *c.* -0.6 to -0.9m OD. Although the buried soil is evident, it is thinning and becoming more undulating in nature. The overlying lower peat continues to thicken, from *c.* 20–25cm thick, as does the older Barroway Drove Bed silty clay, from *c.* 100–140cm thick, whilst the younger Barroway Drove Bed silty clay remains approximately the same thickness. But in Dyke 44, a lens of peat *c.* 3cm thick has developed between the older and younger Barroway Drove Bed deposits. No upper peat survives (Figs 55 and 56; M. Pls 22 and 23).

In Dyke 41, the subsoil has dipped sharply from *c.* -0.9 to -1.9m OD, and the overlying sequence of deposits continues as for the previous dykes. Towards the middle of Dyke 41 in the vicinity of profile 2 (Fig. 57), the subsoil rises sharply again as high as *c.* -0.9m to *c.* -1.9m OD, thus creating an 'island' (TF 2980 0740) of about 180 metres width from west to east (Fig. 57; Pl. XI; M. Pls 24–26). A *c.* 15–25cm thick sandy loam soil has developed on this 'island' (see below) at *c.* -1.7 to -0.7m OD which contained flint artefacts of Neolithic character (see Middleton below; Table 3). The basal peat peters out over the lower edges of the 'island', and it in turn is overlain by older and younger Barroway Drove Bed deposits (Fig. 57). A second possible 'island' was observed at the western end of Dyke 41 in the vicinity of profiles 5 and 6 (TF 5298 3074), with the surface of the buried soil at *c.* -1.0 to -1.1m OD, but no artefacts were retrieved from the dykeside (Fig. 53).

Beyond the 'island' at profile 2 in Dyke 41, the subsoil dips below the water table with the lower peat just visible between *c.* -2.2 and *c.* 2.55m OD. The older Barroway Drove Bed silty clay is now up to *c.* 1.7 to 1.8m thick, as is the younger material (up to *c.* 1.35 to 1.45m thick). These deposits are cut by massive roddons, up to *c.* 75–100m across, which are infilled with silt and fine sand.

Although no radiocarbon dates are available for the deposits in Morris Fen, two sets of radiocarbon dates exist from North Fen immediately to the north. At Sycamore Farm (TF 5337 3111) there is a date of (SRR–1763) 6010 ± 200 BP for the basal peat, and a date of (SRR–1762) 4460 ± 80 BP (3370–2915 Cal. BC) for the peat lens within the fen clay sequence (Harkness in press; Table 1; Appendix V.I). At Gedney Hill (TF 5334 3108) to the northeast there is a date of (SRR–1758) 3250 ± 50 BP (1680–1420 Cal. BC) for the base of a peat band within the fen clay sequence which the British Geological Survey have equated with the upper peat. Although these dates are not in verifiable stratigraphic positions, and the dated sites are *c.* 3–5km from the Morris Fen sites, they suggest that the basal peat was forming in the deeper parts of the fen between *c.* 3500 and 2000 BC, and by implication the two 'islands' in Morris Fen must have been dry land throughout the Mesolithic and earlier Neolithic periods. The occurrence of Neolithic flints on one of these 'islands' provides complementary evidence for this (see Middleton below; Table 3). These 'islands' of dry ground were approximately 2.5 to 3.5km to the north and east of the higher ground on the northern margins of Thorney 'island', which was predominantly dry land until later in the Neolithic/Early Bronze Age periods on stratigraphic grounds.

Archaeological Survey: Later Mesolithic/Neolithic

1. Morris Fen 'island' (TF 5298 3074) (Dyke 41)

The Survey
(Figs 52, 53, 57; Pl. XI; Table 3)
Profiles 2 and 5–6 of Dyke 41 (Figs 52, 53, 57) were buried 'islands', but only the former produced artefactual evidence (see Middleton below; Table 3). The former 'island' is about 180m across, and the latter *c.* 250m across from east to west. The northern and southern limits of the 'islands' were not discernible due to the considerable depth of overlying deposits (Fig. 53; Pl. XI; M. Pl. 26).

The buried soil profile at profile 2 is visually similar to the profiles at the previously discussed sites of Crowtree Farm (Chapter 3:I.1) and Oakhurst Farm (Chapter 3:I.2). The palaeosol is an apedal, relatively non-porous (*c.* 5% total porosity), light yellowish brown (10YR6/4) sandy loam with a few scattered flint pebbles, *c.* 15–20cm thick, which is developed on a structureless, brownish yellow (10YR6/8) sand and fine gravel subsoil. No horizonisation

of the buried soil was evident in the field as at the other two sites in Newborough Fen.

The outer, lower edges of the 'island' are covered by a thin accumulation of lower peat (10YR2/1), which may well have been truncated by the subsequent inundation responsible for depositing the fen clay or older Barroway Drove Beds (10YR5/1). Overlying this marine deposit is a second and later marine deposit or the younger Barroway Drove Beds (10YR6/2), with the thin and discontinuous remnants of upper peat at the present day ground surface (Fig. 5).

The Flints from Morrris Fen
by H.R. Middleton
(Fig. 27; Table 3)

Catalogue of illustrated flints
(Fig. 27)
9. Morris Fen: *Truncated Blade.* Dyke 41, profile 2. Archive No. 72.
10. Morris Fen: *Core Fragment.* Dyke 41, profile 2. Archive No. 69.

Dyke 41, profile 2
Four flints were found, all made of good quality, gravel-derived flint with a thin brown cortex. Two pieces were of dark brown flint and two of dark grey. The assemblage is fresh and unpatinated, except for one piece which has a thin, white patina.

The technology involved the production of small blades with a soft hammer off, probably, well-prepared cores. One such blade is present (Fig. 27, no. 9), along with a retouched fragment of a blade core (Fig. 27, no. 10).

The best dating for this assemblage, along with the technological information, is provided by the presence of a truncated blade (Fig. 27, no. 9) which can be paralleled at other fenland sites of late Mesolithic date, such as Peacock's Farm, Shippea Hill (Clark 1955; fig. 4, no. 87), but which are absent from later assemblages such as that from Etton (Middleton in Pryor *et al.* in prep.).

Dyke 44, profile 4
Three waste flakes on good quality grey/brown flint with thin grey or light brown cortex were found, all being in a fresh condition and having a very thin, white patina.

The technology is cruder than that employed for the flints found in Dyke 41 and is therefore suggestive of a later date, although little can be said of the cultural and chronological significance of these finds.

Soil Micromorphology in Morris Fen
by Charles French
(Pl. XI; M. Pls 53–55)

Three contiguous samples were analysed in thin section from a profile through the buried soil *c.* 5m to the east of profile 2 in Dyke 41, at the approximate centre of the 'island' (Pl. XI). The methods of Bullock *et al.* (1985a, b) were used (Appendix I). The detailed soil micromorphological descriptions are found in Appendix VI.

As at Oakhurst Farm, the dense sand-dominated fabric, the absence of organic matter and illuvial clay suggest that the upper one-third of this buried soil (*c.* 0–7cm) is an eluvial or Eb horizon (see above) (M. Pl. 53).

The slightly greater number of textural pedofeatures in the middle one-third of this buried soil (*c.* 7–11cm) as opposed to the overlying Eb horizon suggests that this fabric is probably upper B(t) horizon material. The rare occurrence of limpid clay suggests that little clay translo-

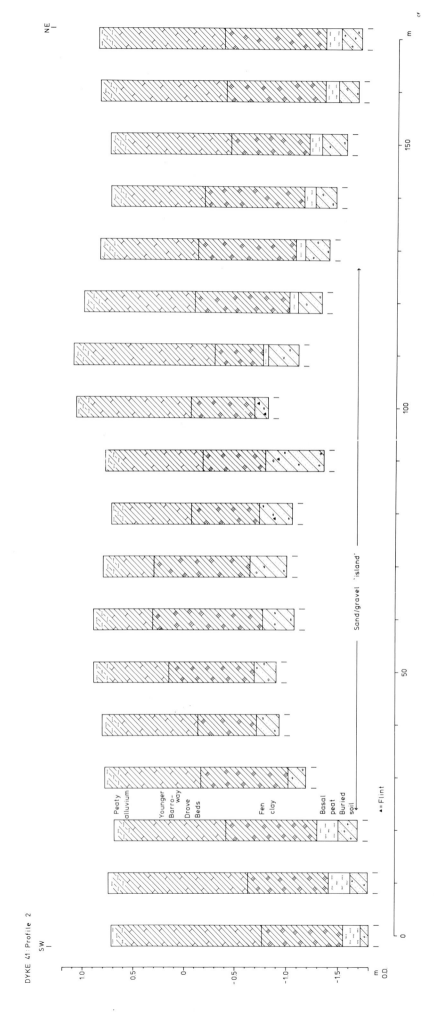

Figure 57 Section through the 'island' at profile 2, Dyke 41.

Plate XI The buried 'island' at Morris Fen, Dyke 41 (Site 3).

cation had occurred. Then the soil exhibits indications of subsequent soil disturbance. These include the rare non-laminated dusty coatings, the fine fragments of limpid clay and the aggregates of fine sand as partial channel infills. Similar features indicative of soil disturbance occurred at Crowtree Farm and Oakhurst Farm (see Chapter 3:I.1), as well as on the northern margin of the Eye peninsula (Chapter 3:I.3). The significance of the soil disturbance is discussed below.

The relative increase in illuvial clay in the lower one-third of the palaeosol (c. 11–15.5cm) suggests that this is a lower B horizon, probably the base of a poorly developed Bt or argillic horizon of an argillic brown earth (Avery 1980; McKeague 1983) (M. Pls 54 and 55).

Two phases of clay illuviation are suggested. First, there are rare limpid and laminated dusty coatings on the grains and in the groundmass. Generally, limpid clay is associated with an undisturbed woodland cover (Fisher 1982; Macphail 1985; Slager and van de Wetering 1977). But at Morris Fen, as at Crowtree and Oakhurst Farm, the relative scarcity of limpid clay suggests that little clay translocation had occurred prior to the next phase of soil disturbance.

In the second phase there are a few non-laminated dusty clay coatings in the groundmass. Although they are not nearly as abundant as at the other sites examined in Borough Fen (Crowtree Farm, Oakhurst Farm and the Eye peninsula), their relative abundance as well as the following indications of soil disturbance are suggestive of tree clearance. As at the Borough Fen sites, very fine sand size fragments of limpid clay occur in the groundmass, as if clay coatings have been broken up. Also the two anoma-

lous fabrics in the upper part of the Bt horizon suggest that either two materials were translocated or they represent two successive phases of soil disturbance. The papule-like aggregate of fine sand and illuvial clay in a former root channel is also indicative of soil disturbance.

These features suggest that the soil was not under well-developed nor established and stable forested conditions for a prolonged period of time. Then the soil suffered some disturbance, probably associated with tree clearance. Unlike the other sites in Borough Fen, 'dirty' clay coatings indicative of 'coarse' illuviation are not evident, and this may suggest that the soil disturbance was not as disruptive, nor possibly as prolonged. Nevertheless, the limited clearance and soil disturbance may be associated with man's use of the 'island' during the Neolithic period.

The prehistoric soil subsequently suffered erosion, as at the other Borough Fen sites. The A and possibly the upper part of the Eb horizons have been truncated at Morris Fen; in this case the soil erosion was probably associated with the marine inundation responsible for depositing the fen clay.

Pseudomorphs of roots or stems are found in the buried soil, in common with the other sites. They may either be relics of *in situ* vegetation, or reflect the rooting of salt marsh plants in the truncated soil. At the Morris Fen 'island' site there is less evidence of sesquioxide impregnation of the soil fabric, although it still affects about one-third of the fabric. This hydromorphic effect (Duchaufour 1982) is probably indicative of alternating wet and dry conditions (Limbrey 1975) which reflects seasonal waterlogging and flooding throughout the later life of the buried soil on this fen 'island'.

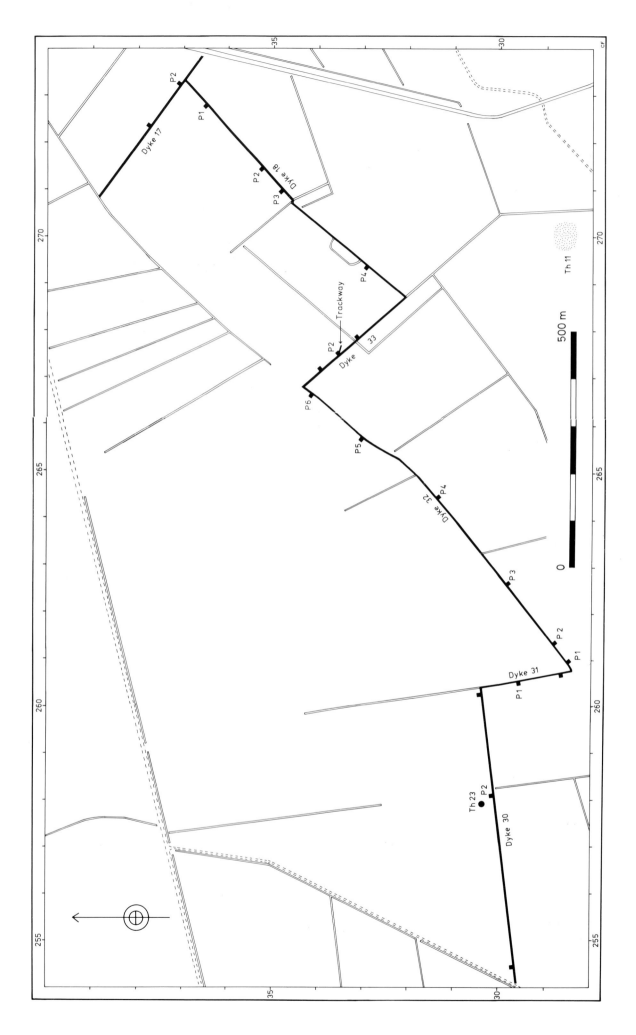

Figure 58 Location of Dykes 17, 18 and 30-33, and the Guy's Fen footpath.

88

III. Guy's Fen

Introduction
(Figs 2, 52, 58)

Guy's Fen is situated to the southwest of Thorney 'island' immediately south of the A47 road (Figs 2, 52, 58). It is bounded by Willow Hall Drove to the west, the Thorney River to the east, and Prior's Fen to the south.

Dykes were examined which cut a section from southwest to northeast across the Fen (Dykes 30–33, 18 and 17) between two areas of high ground: the March Gravels of the Eye peninsula and the Fen gravels of Thorney 'island'. A probable wooden footpath was discovered in Dyke 33 and about a *c.* 14m length of the structure was excavated in the autumn of 1983.

First a general description of the stratigraphy of the Guy's Fen area will be given; this will be followed by a more specific account of the wooden footpath site.

Stratigraphy
(Figs 58–60)

Dykes 30, 31 and the western two-thirds of Dyke 32 are characterised by humified upper peat *c.* 10–40cm thick overlying March Gravels (Figs 58 and 59; M. Pls 28–31). Profiles 1 to 4 of Dyke 32 and profile 2 of Dyke 30 cross the ridge of gravels which extends from the Eye peninsula to Thorney 'island'. One of Hall's (1987) discoveries, barrow site Th 23, is situated on this ridge about 20m to the north of profile 2, Dyke 30 (Fig. 58). The absence of a well-developed buried soil in these dykes is explained by the fact that it is comfortably within the modern plough depth and has become homogenised with the sand/gravel subsoil and the upper peat. It is reasonable to suggest that this southeastern extension of the Eye peninsula remained predominantly dry land until possibly the early 1st millennium BC.

The March Gravels dip eastwards from *c.* 2.15m to *c.* 0.5m OD beyond profiles 5 and 6 in Dyke 32, at which point marine deposits become evident (Fig. 59). By profile 5 the micaceous silty clay marine deposits indicative of the younger Barroway Drove Bed material appear and thicken eastwards. By profile 6, the silty clay marine deposit indicative of the older Barroway Drove Bed or fen clay episode is present. There are no indications of peat growth occurring between the two phases of marine inundation. A thin and thinning humified upper peat overlies the marine deposits.

The stratigraphy exhibited in Dyke 33 is similar to that exhibited in the eastern end of Dyke 32. In profile 2, the wooden trackway or footpath was situated at the base of the fen clay or the older Barroway Drove Bed material. In places there is an underlying lens of lower peat, *c.* 5–10cm thick. This in turn overlies a thin sandy/silt loam buried soil, *c.* 15cm thick.

Between Dyke 33 and the southwestern end of Dyke 18, the subsoil dips away rapidly from *c.* 0.45m to *c.* -1.6m OD, and then gradually rises to *c.* -1.1m OD at the northern end of Dyke 17. A thin, poorly developed buried soil has developed in places, and becomes better developed as the subsoil rises towards Thorney 'island'. Basal peat (*c.* 10–20cm thick), occasionally containing wood and sometimes 'bog oaks', overlies the buried soil. This is overlain by older and younger Barroway Drove Bed material, *c.* 20–100cm and *c.* 70–90cm thick respectively, which thin northeastwards as the ground rises towards Thorney 'island' (Fig. 60; M. Pls 32 and 33).

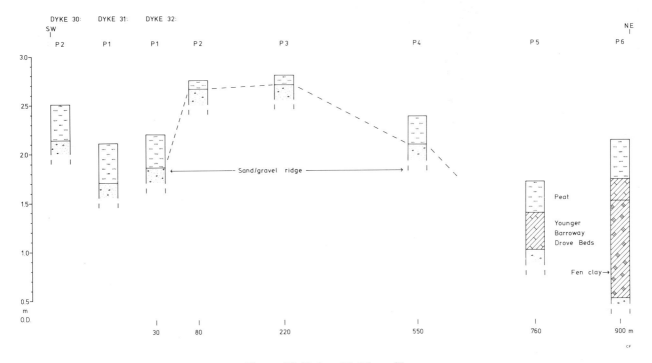

Figure 59 Dykes 30–32 profiles.

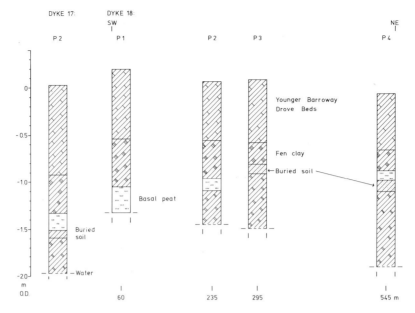

Figure 60 Dykes 17 and 18 profiles.

Plate XII The Guy's Fen footpath, Dyke 33 (Site 4).

Archaeological Survey: Later Neolithic/Early Bronze/Age

1. Guy's Fen footpath (TF 5267 3033) (Dyke 33)

Survey and Excavation
(Figs 58 and 61; Pl. XII)
During the survey of Dyke 33 very degraded wood was seen portruding from the section face at the base of the fen clay sequence at *c.* 0.70–0.75m OD at profile 2. Suspicions aroused, the dyke edge was cleaned by hand to reveal a discrete area of horizontal pieces of wood, emerging at a very obilque angle to the dykeside. Permission to excavate a small trench on the dyke edge was then obtained from the farmer, Mr Flint, and the NLIDB.

Trench 1 was dug by hand and measured 10 × 1.5m; Trench 2 was also dug by hand; it was a narrow slot some 2.5m long and placed some two metres to the southeast of Trench 1 to investigate whether the footpath continued in approximately the same direction (*i.e.* orientated NW–SE) (Fig. 61; Pl. XII). Dyke 18 was re-examined to determine whether the footpath emerged on the same alignment, some 200m away to the southeast, but no traces of it were found. The woodwork of the footpath is descibed by Taylor below.

The footpath appears to have been built as an initial response to wetter conditions, but before they became impassable. Stratigraphically the path is associated with the onset of brackish or marine flooding conditions responsible for the deposition of the older Barroway Drove Bed silty clay, rather than with the freshwater conditions associated with the thin growth of the basal peat. There is every possibility that the footpath was built across shallow salt marsh conditions in the late 3rd or early 2nd millennium BC. The footpath perhaps ran between two ridges of higher ground to the northwest and southeast which 'tongue out' from the western side of Thorney 'island'.

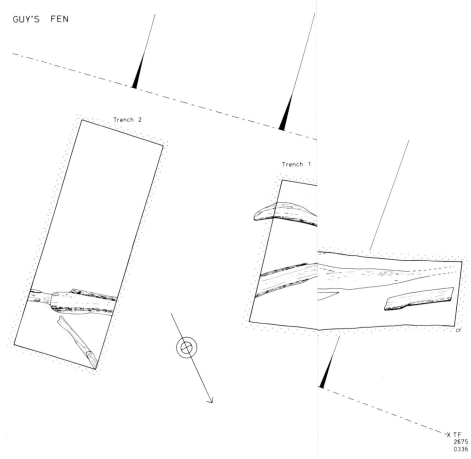

GUY'S FEN

Trench 2

Trench 1

CF

X TF
2675
0336

Figure 61 Plan c

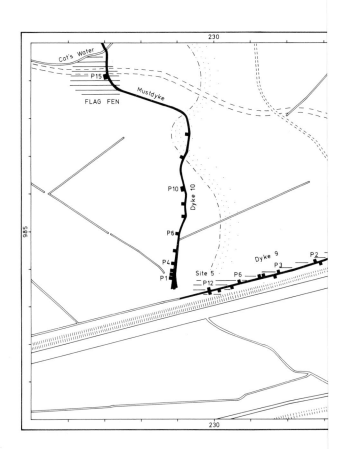

Figure 62 Locatio

9

The Flints from Guy's Fen
by H.R. Middleton
(Table 3)

Dyke 33, Profile 2/3
This profile produced two large pieces of crudely worked flint of rather indifferent quality and probably from a gravel source.

The core appears to have had a few flakes removed which failed to produce the required result, and was then crudely retouched. Several incipient fracture cones are present where flakes have failed to detach.

The technology suggests a date rather late in the Bronze Age although no precision can be guaranteed with such a small assemblage.

The rest of the dyke produced two waste flakes, both of similar materials to those above, and in similar condition. Again, the crude technology would suggest a similar date to the other flints recovered from the dykeside.

Wood and Woodworking of the Guy's Fen Footpath
by Maisie Taylor
(Fig. 61; Pl. XII)

The wood was in a very advanced stage of decay. All pieces were of mature oak (*Quercus* sp.). Fortunately, however, although little structure remained to the wood, the medullary rays were largely intact and distinct. Oak is generally split along or across medullary rays, so their survival enabled split-types to be recognised in the field.

A total of 26 timbers were reliably identified as of oak. All were split radially and where ends survived, they had been dressed square. Although undoubtedly compressed since deposition, the splits were generally thin — perhaps 1/8th or even less. Conditions did not allow the preservation of individual tool-marks, however. Diameters of split timbers fell within a restricted range from 400 to 500mm; tree-ring studies were impossible, but it was considered that no more than two trees had been utilised for the division of the timber.

One piece (Fig. 61, A) had a side branch (diameter about 250mm) trimmed off to a point (about 150mm long). This was positioned below the path, and would have acted as a stabilising peg driven into the underlying clay.

There was only slight evidence (Fig. 61, B) for underlying cross-members, in this case three pieces of oak roundwood, with approximate diameters of 300mm.

Although clearly distorted, displaced and very poorly preserved, the consistent use of thin splits absolutely rules out the possibility that this was a natural feature. Further, the timber was plainly laid down in a linear and non-random manner. Freshly felled timber could be expected to show V-shaped chopped ends (of which there are numerous examples at Flag Fen), but the timbers at Guy's Fen had clearly been deliberately dressed square. Again, bearing in mind the nature of the evidence, it seems probable that Guy's Fen was an informal, perhaps temporary pathway across a deteriorating marshy patch of ground; in this regard it is distinct from the more formal trackways of Somerset (Coles and Orme 1976) and elsewhere; if an analogue must be sought then the estuarine flats of the Hullbridge basin have produced evidence for better preserved, but generally similar types of short-lived structures (Wilkinson and Murphy 1988).

IV. North and Flag Fens

Introduction
(Figs 2, 3 and 62)
North and Flag Fens are situated to the east and west, respectively, of Northey 'island' (Figs 2 and 62). Northey 'island' is composed of Nene First Terrace sands and gravel and March Gravels, and is the westernmost extension of Whittlesey 'island' to the southeast, from which it is now cut off by the modern River Nene (Fig. 3); in reality, therefore, it is more a 'peninsula' than an 'island'.

Cleaning and re-cutting of *c.* 3.5km of the counter drain on the north side of the River Nene revealed an east to west transect across Northey 'island' in Dykes 8 and 9. Dyke 10, or Mustdyke, which runs for *c.* 1km north from the pumping station to the Cat's Water cuts across the western edge of Northey 'island' and into the shallow fen basin beyond (Fig. 62). Dyke 53, in Prior's Fen to the east of North Fen (Fig. 2), is included in this section and it reveals the characteristic tripartite fen stratigraphy (M. Pls 41 and 42).

During the survey two new sites were found, one of which (Flag Fen) is now well-known and elements of the already known Northey site were further examined. Ditches of the Bronze and Iron Age complex on Northey 'island' (Gurney 1980, 1981) were seen in the dykeside of Dyke 8, in the vicinity of Northey Lodge (TF 5238 2985) and south of Four Chimney Farm (TF 5245 2986).

Flints, sherds of pottery, bone, archaeological features and possible areas or features exhibiting phosphatic enrichment and magnetic susceptibility enhancement (see Gurney below) were found along the length of Dyke 9 on the southwestern edge of Northey 'island' (TF 5230 2984). These may or may not be part of the existing complex of sites at Northey. Archaeological features continued to occur along Dyke 10 where it cuts through the western margin of Northey 'island'. About 200m to the west of Northey a large timber settlement of Late Bronze Age date was discovered. The discovery and excavation of the Flag Fen platform is discussed in detail elsewhere (Pryor *et al.* 1986).

Stratigraphy
(Figs 52, 62–65; Pl. XIII; Table 6)
Dykes 8 and 9 cut a transect from east to west across Northey 'island'. The 'island' is mainly composed of March Gravels, as well as Nene First Terrace gravels on its western margin. These gravel deposits have relatively high sand and silt contents (Table 6) with the gravel content not becoming dominant until *c.* 1–2m below the surface of the subsoil. The 'island' rises from a low height of *c.* 1.0m OD at its western end (in the vicinity of the pumping station) to a high point of *c.* 3.15m OD at profile 1 in Dyke 8 (TF 5233 2984), and begins to dip off below -0.3m OD to the east of profile 9 in Dyke 8 (TF 5246 2986). A probable narrow pre-upper peat stream channel, about 25m across, cuts across the edge of the 'island' at profile 2 in Dyke 9 (Fig. 64; M. Pls 34–38).

A generally well-developed buried soil is present across the 'island' (Figs 63 and 64; Pl. XIII). For much of the exposure two horizons are evident: the upper soil horizon is a dark greyish brown (10YR4/2) (organic) sandy clay loam to loam (Table 6). The lower soil horizon is a light yellowish brown (10YR6/4) loam to sandy loam (Table 6). The palaeosol ranges in thickness from *c.* 5–

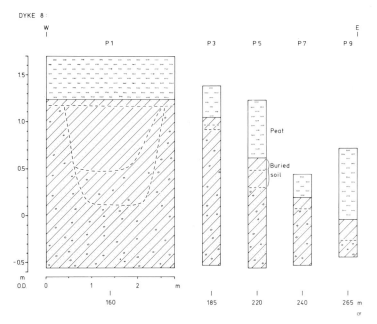

Figure 63 Dyke 8 profiles.

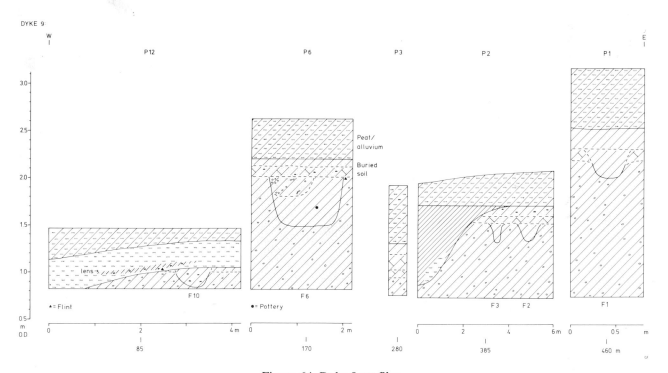

Figure 64 Dyke 9 profiles.

35cm, and is best developed in profiles 1, 2, 3 and 6 in Dyke 9, and profile 5 in Dyke 8. Overlying the buried soil is a well humified upper peat, *c.* 25–65cm thick (Figs 63 and 64; Pl. XIII). This peat generally contains an admixture of alluvial silt and clay.

The stratigraphy of Dyke 10, where the drain cuts across the western margin of Northey 'island' is identical to that observed in Dykes 8 and 9 (Fig. 65; M. Pls 39 and 40), but as the First Terrace silty clay with flint gravel pebbles dips northeastwards (from *c.* +0.25m to *c.* -0.35m OD), and the buried soil narrows to only a thin (*c.* 5cm) layer of weathered subsoil, a series of peat and alluvial deposits are recognisable. Initially wood and detrital peat

formed in a freshwater fen environment, with large bodies of shallow, open water (Chapter 1: III) (Scaife in Pryor *et al.* 1986, 20–21). It was in this environment that the Late Bronze Age settlement of Flag Fen was in use in the earlier 1st millennium BC. A radiocarbon date of (BM–2123) 2610 ± 60 BP was obtained from brushwood within the make-up of the platform; this date was subsequently modified by the laboratory to 2830 ± 120 BP. The date of the first construction of the timber platform is still uncertain, but artefactual evidence would suggest sometime around the Middle Late Bronze Age transition.

The freshwater open fen was followed by deposits of grey silty clay alluvial material which was deposited (at *c.*

93

Plate XIII The southwestern edge of Northey 'island', Dyke 9 (Site 5).

Here the March Gravels which comprise Whittlesey/Northey 'island' are dipping away northwards and northeastwards into the deeper parts of the fen basin. The stratigraphy of the dyke is characterised by an undulating, thin, and in some cases non-existant, buried soil developed on the March Gravels, overlain by a thickening (0–1.3m) deposit of fen clay and a thickening (to the east) growth of upper peat (*c.* 30–50cm).

Archaeological Survey: Bronze Age

1. Northey 'island'

The Survey
(Figs 2, 62–66; Pls XIII and XIV)
The survey of the cleaned Counter Drain (Dykes 8 and 9) produced a variety of archaeological evidence in section, including artefacts and cut features, particularly in Dyke 9.

A large pit or ditch profile was observed at profile 1 in Dyke 8 (Figs 62 and 63; M. Pl. 34). The feature was *c.* 2m across and *c.* 1m deep with a 'U'-shaped profile. It was cut through the buried soil and infilled initially with silty/sandy loam and latterly with a peaty loam. It would seem that this feature was probably dug and remained open prior to the onset of upper peat growth on the southern margin of Northey 'island' — *i.e.* prior to the earlier 1st millennium BC. Indeed it could be contemporary with the Bronze Age system of ditches, droveways and settlement on Northey 'island' (Gurney 1980). Excavations of ditches on the 'island' in 1977 produced pottery contemporary with that found in the 2nd millennium BC ditches at Fengate (Gurney 1980; Pryor 1980a).

0.95–1.0m OD) and was initially intermixed with the growth of (now humified) detrital peats. A further period of alluviation deposited a reddish brown (oxidised) alluvial silty clay, about 30cm thick, between *c.* 1.4–1.7m OD, before peat growth resumed. Although the present day land surface is at *c.* 2.0m OD, at least one metre and probably more of peat has been lost from the modern surface through desiccation and deflation (R. Evans pers. comm.).

Dyke 53 runs west to east for about a kilometre across Prior's Fen, east of North Fen (Fig. 52; M. Pls 41 and 42).

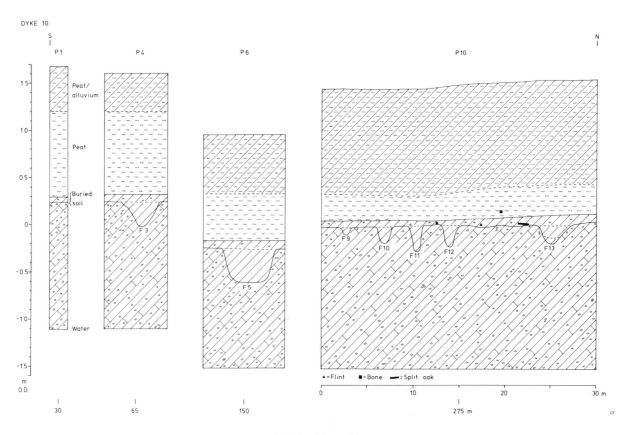

Figure 65 Dyke 10 profiles.

94

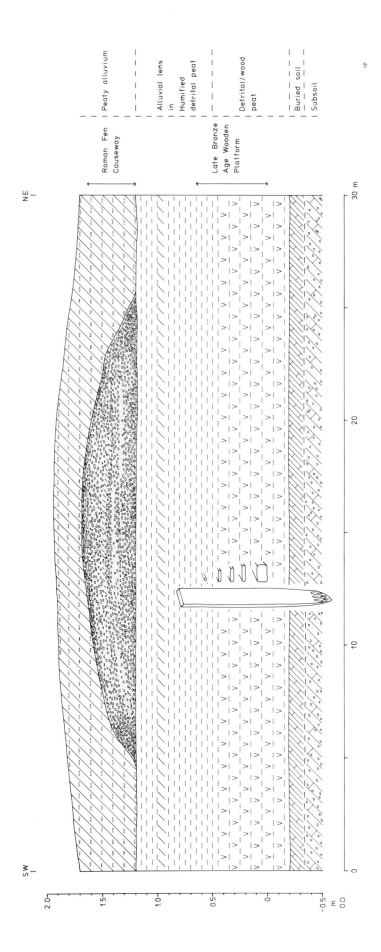

Figure 66 Dyke 10, profile 15 schematic section.

Roman Fen Causeway — Peaty alluvium

Alluvial lens in Humified detrital peat

Late Bronze Age Wooden Platform — Detrital/wood peat

Buried soil

Subsoil

95

Plate XIV Flag Fen, Dyke 10 (Site 6): the Roman Fen Causeway (above), and the Late Bronze Age settlement site below delineated by the tape.

Archaeological features were observed at profiles 1, 2, 4, 5, 6, 7, 9, 11 and 12 of Dyke 9 (Figs 62 and 64; Pl. XIII; M. Pls 36–38). Most were pit- and small post-hole-size, and often contained artefacts and charcoal. All these features were sealed by the growth of the upper peat. A radiocarbon date of (Har–8511) 2800 ± 100 BP (1290–800 Cal. BC) was obtained from charcoal contained in the basal fill of feature 2 at profile 2. Features containing flint occurred at profiles 4, 6, 9, 10, 12 and 13 (flint archive nos 43, 48–50 and 52–4). All of these flints are probably Bronze Age waste flakes, except for the Neolithic irregular retouched flake from profile 12 (see Middleton below). Animal bone was found in features at profiles 6 and 9 (bone archive nos 49, 50). Several fragments of Neolithic pottery were found in the buried soil at profile 8 (pot archive no. 209), and one sherd of later or middle Iron Age 'Scored Ware' (pot archive no. 206) from the buried soil. These artefacts are consistent with the use of the 'island' for settlement during the prehistoric period (see below).

A lens of sandy loam soil, c. 10cm thick and c. 2m in lateral extent, was observed resting on a c. 15cm thickness of peat and overlain by peat, at the southwestern edge of the 'island' adjacent to profile 12 (Pl. XIII). This lens contained one flint (archive no. 44), a waste flake of Bronze Age date. The possible origins of this lens are discussed below.

Sixteen possible features were observed at profiles 2–7, 9, 10 and 12–15, in Dyke 10 (Figs 62 and 65; M. Pls 39 and 40). They were all of small pit/post-hole size, and some contained charcoal. Two Bronze Age flints were found in the buried soil at profile 10 (flint archive nos 56, 58), associated with three, possibly four features. One sherd of later Iron Age 'Scored Ware' pottery (archive no. 208) was found at profile 15, possibly associated with the Roman Fen Causeway.

The Fen Causeway passes across Dyke 10 and above the Flag Fen wooden platform (TF 5227 2989) (Fig. 66; Pl. XIV). It is composed of a sand and gravel dump, c.

40cm thick, between c. 1.3 and 1.7m OD, c. 20m across. A similar section across this Roman road at Fengate suggested a date in the later 1st Century AD (Pryor 1980a, 1984). The upper surface of this road has been disturbed by modern ploughing. Thus at the minimum, c. 70cm of peat growth, with an admixture of alluvium, had occurred between the building of the Flag Fen platform in the Late Bronze Age and the construction of the road in the early Roman period. Only c. 30–40cm of the post-early Roman peat growth survives above the monument and over most of the surrounding fen.

Recent augering surveys by the writer and Dr F. Pryor have suggested that the Flag Fen site is situated in the narrow 'neck' of a peat-infilled basin equidistant between the Fengate 'shore' and Northey 'island', a distance of about 200m to the northwest and southeast respectively. So it can now be shown that the Fengate fen-edge 'plain' or 'flat' extends southeastwards by an additional 200–300m, beneath the overlying later Bronze Age peat. In effect this has doubled the potential usable area of the earlier prehistoric flood-free landscape whose periphery (as we now understand it to be) was excavated in the 1970s (Pryor 1978, 1980a, 1984).

Flints from Flag and North Fens
by H.R. Middleton
(Table 3)

Dyke 9

Twelve fresh and unpatinated flints (not ilustrated) were recovered from the series of features revealed in this dyke, none of which are demonstrably differing in date.

Five of these flints had some thin, light brown cortex remaining, including one primary flake, which shows that local flint nodules from the Nene gravels were used for raw material. This varied from dark brown to light grey and is of good quality with little evidence for internal planes of weakness or other flaws.

All of the flakes have large, unprepared platforms and have been crudely struck with a hard hammer. Many of the flakes have incipient fracture cones where unsuccessful attempts have been made to remove flakes.

Three implements were recovered, all of which were utilised flakes, displaying edge damage on one lateral edge in two cases and on three edges in the other.

The poor technology employed, combined with the casual use of waste pieces would point to a Late Bronze Age date for the whole assemblage, resembling as it does the material from Mildenhall Fen (Clark 1936) and the Newark Road subsite, Fengate (Pryor 1980a).

Dyke 10

This findspot produced three flints (not illustrated) all of which were made of good quality, dark brown flawless flint from the local Nene valley gravels. These were also the products of a relatively crude technology, as indicated by the disc core which has numerous incipient fracture cones on its ventral surface and abraded edges revealing failed attempts to remove flakes.

None of the pieces would be out of place in a later Bronze Age context coming, as they do, from around the Late Bronze Age platform at Flag Fen.

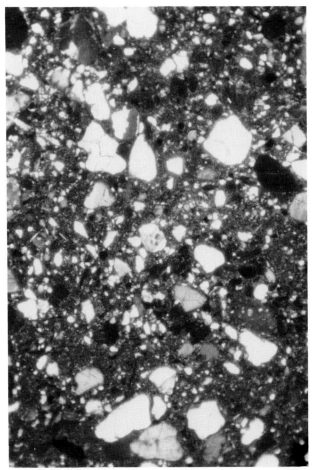

Plate XV A photomicrograph of fabric 1 in the Ap horizon of the buried soil in Dyke 9 (CPL; frame =4.25mm).

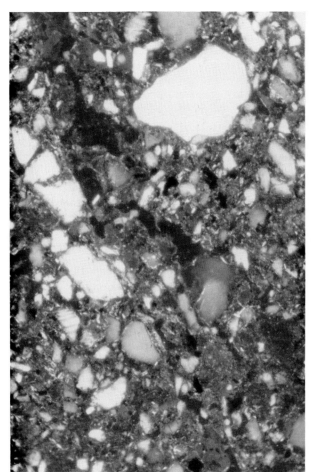

Plate XVI A photomicrograph of fabric 2 in the Ap horizon of the buried soil in Dyke 9 (CPL; frame =4.25mm).

Analysis and Micromorphology of Buried Soils in the Northey Area
by Charles French
(Figs 62–64; Pls XIII, XV and XVI; M. Pls 37 and 38, 43–46; Tables 3, 6–8)

The buried soil on Northey 'island' was examined in detail at two loci: profile 5 in Dyke 8 and profiles 2 and 12 in Dyke 9 (Figs 62–64; Pl. XIII; M. Pls 37 and 38, 43–46).

The textural composition of the buried land surfaces from all of the dykes are generally similar: clay loam, sandy clay loam and loam (Table 6). The four statistical measures (Tables 7 and 8) exhibit no real anomalies or extremes. The sand fraction is well sorted; the silt fraction is poorly sorted. The sand and silt fractions exhibit only slight negative skewness and have kurtosis values around normal. The only exception is the possible 'occupation horizon' in the peat which exhibits extremely poor sorting of the sand fraction (Table 7). This suggests that some of the material composing this lens was previously unsorted and underwent little or no weathering *in situ*.

The severely leached nature of these buried soils testifies to past waterlogging, fluctuations in the water table and more recently very effective drainage. Leaching of the profile is still occurring, as the fresh organic staining with humic acids from the overlying peat indicates. This occurs within a few days of the dyke being cleaned. The severity of the leaching is indicated by slightly acidic pH values, the bleached nature of the sand grains and the absence of any appreciable organic material in the soil matrix. These processes suggest that a considerable degree of physical and chemical weathering continues to occur in these soils.

The now buried soil probably formed under dry land conditions as shallow sandy loam soils of *c.* 30cm depth, developed on sand and gravel deposits which comprise the fen 'islands'. It would probably have been similar to the present day sandy loams developed on the river terrace deposits in the lower Welland valley around Maxey (French in Pryor and French 1985, 205-216).

Dyke 9
The buried soil profile evident in Dyke 9 consists of two visible horizons as in Dyke 8. The upper horizon is a *c.* 10–14cm thick organic sandy loam (10YR4/2), and the lower horizon is a *c.* 10–12cm thick bleached sandy loam (10YR6/4).

One spot sample was taken for thin sectioning from the approximate middle of the upper and lower horizons at profile 2, Dyke 9, at the extreme southwestern edge of Northey 'island'. There were several possible features visible at the base of the palaeosol, and twelve Bronze Age flints were recovered (see Middleton above). As the 'island' dipped westwards into the Flag Fen basin, the overlying upper peat thickens from about 50cm to 1.5m. The previously mentioned lens of soil and charcoal within the peat adjacent to profile 12 (Pl. XIII) on the edge of the 'island' at profile 12 was also sampled for micromorphological analysis. The detailed soil micromorphological descriptions are found in Appendix VI.

The upper horizon of the buried soil at profile 2 in Dyke 9 (Pls XV and XVI; M. Pls 37, 43 and 44) is an heterogeneous mixture of two different soil fabrics. The predominant fabric (1) (c. 80%) is a dense, fine sandy loam containing very little fine fabric and textural coatings, with numerous fine flecks of charcoal throughout its groundmass (Pl. XV). It is suggested that this a combination of leached A horizon material and ash-like, possibly dumped occupation material.

The second, less abundant fabric (2) (c. 20%) is a dense sand/silt which contains abundant amorphous organic matter and many fine flecks of charcoal in the groundmass, with only a few textural coatings (Pl. XVI). This dense, 'dirty' fine fabric is probably ploughsoil or Ap horizon material. The 'dirty' element is dark brown to black, highly humified organic matter, which is probably humified peat.

The heterogeneous and poorly sorted nature of these two fabrics suggests that this horizon has suffered considerable mechanical disturbance as a result of arable agriculture and is in fact the prehistoric ploughsoil. The presence of the peat in the ploughsoil may be explained by one or both of the following reasons. It is possible that the peat was deliberately spread on the ploughsoil as a form of fertiliser; alternatively, at some time during the use of this land for arable, there was a period of limited freshwater flooding and thin peat growth, which was ploughed in at a later date during a drier phase.

There are occasional rolled clay aggregates within fabric (2), which suggests that the ploughsoil had previously received freshwater containing eroded soil, and was receiving an alluvial component. At least three phases of alluvial deposition have been recorded in the adjacent Flag Fen basin, all of post-Late Bronze Age. There are also frequent sesquioxide nodules within the same fabric, as well as zones of sesquioxide impregnation in both fabrics. These features are also suggestive of the periodic influence of freshwater, both in terms of a high local groundwater table and/or flooding, both pre- and post-burial of the soil.

It is important to note that this is only one of two instances in the dyke survey where the upper A horizon of the palaeosol is preserved more or less intact. Consequently, there will have been little post-depositional disturbance of the archaeological record on this part of Northey 'island'.

The lower horizon of this buried soil (M. Pl. 46) is composed of one homogeneous fabric, a relatively dense, very fine sand and silt fabric. It also contains much organic matter including many very fine flecks of charcoal and amorphous organic matter in the groundmass, very few larger flecks of charcoal, and a few ferruginised plant tissue fragments and roots. There are also occasional soil fauna excrements in the channels. These features and the relatively few and poorly developed nature of the textural coatings together suggest that this is A horizon material. But the lack of mixing with other soil fabrics and the absence of evidence for mechanical disturbance of the soil indicates that this soil is the lower A horizon, below the average plough depth. This soil horizon was later subject to some post-depositional waterlogging, as observed in the upper horizon of the buried soil.

The lens within the upper peat just off the southwestern edge of Northey 'island' at profile 12 in Dyke 9 (M. Pls 38 and 45) is composed of two main fabrics in an heterogeneous mixture. Fabric (1) is similar to fabric (1) of the adjacent upper horizon of the buried soil, although it contains even more organic material. It is mainly composed of sand, primarily very fine quartz sand. The relative absence of silt, clay and amorphous organic matter suggests that this soil is severely leached. On the other hand fine flecks of charcoal are abundant in this fabric. This 'ash-like' deposit may result from the dumping of occupation debris.

Fabric (2) is similar to fabric (1) above, except that it contains large amounts of highly humified, black, amorphous organic matter. This organic material is probably peat.

There are also very small amounts of dense, fine fabric present which are similar to the fabric (2) or ploughsoil material of the upper horizon of the buried soil. This ploughsoil material is not yet fully homogenised with the rest of the soil fabric.

Thus this lens is composed of an heterogeneous mixture of A horizon sand, very small amounts of ploughsoil, and organic matter and peat. In most respects, the soil materials composing this lens are similar to that composing the adjacent upper horizon of the buried soil, except for a much greater amount of peat present and a lesser ploughsoil content. There are two possible origins of this lens. First, it could be eroded A horizon material or a form of colluvium, but this is contrary to the impression that the adjacent buried soil is more or less intact and did not suffer any truncation. Second, and more plausibly, it may represent the deliberate dumping of soil and occupation debris off the edge of the 'island'. The general absence of artefactual evidence within the lens suggests that this dumped material is not midden material redeposited. It is also possible that this material was deliberately dumped there by man to extend the area of the arable land available for tillage, particularly during a dry or drier phase in the development of the adjacent growing peat fen. Only its use in this way can satisfactorily account for the large amount of peat incorporated with the other soil materials.

Dyke 8

The buried soil evident in Dyke 8 also exhibited two visible horizons, as in Dyke 9. The upper horizon, c. 7–12cm thick, was composed of a sandy/silt loam (5YR4/2), and the lower horizon was a bleached sandy loam (10YR6/4), c. 8–20cm thick. The detailed soil micromorphological descriptions are found in Appendix VI.

The interpretation of the upper half of the lower horizon of the buried soil in Dyke 8 (c. 0.40–0.45cm) follows on from that given for Dyke 9/profile 2. The relative abundance of organic matter, and the relative paucity and poorly developed nature of the textural coatings suggests that this lower soil horizon is lower A/upper B horizon material. The fine fabric of this sandy loam contains some amorphous organic matter and fine flecks of charcoal. There are also occasional non-laminated dusty/'dirty' coatings in the groundmass and of the sand grains. The micro-contrasted particles in these coatings are probably fine organic matter rather than silt. The homogeneous nature of the single fabric suggests that this soil has not suffered any deep mechanical disturbance. The one channel infill of dense, fine soil fabric is probably an example of groundmass illuviation or intercalation of the overlying Ap or ploughsoil horizon material.

There is little doubt (by analogy with the thin section made of the upper buried soil horizon at profile 2 in Dyke

9) that the upper soil horizon of the palaeosol in Dyke 8 is also Ap horizon material. Also, by implication and in retrospect, the transition zone between the base of the buried soil and the underlying subsoil should also have been sampled and examined micromorphologically.

The common zones of sesquioxide impregnation, of up to one-third of the fabric, suggest that this soil was subject to post-depositional waterlogging. Iron carried in solution was deposited lower down the soil profile, both in the groundmass and occasionally in the void space. The freshwater flooding was probably coincident with encroaching peat growth during the later Bronze Age and Iron Age around the fringes of Northey 'island'. Indeed peat has been observed to form the upper infill of Bronze Age features visible in the dykeside.

As evident in Dyke 9 to the west, the presence of A horizon material suggests that the buried soil on the southern edge of Northey 'island' has suffered little from post-depositional erosion and truncation, as has been frequently observed elsewhere in the North Level area. This is especially important with respect to potential archaeological preservation, given that abundant Bronze and Iron Age material is known to exist on adjacent parts of Northey 'island' (Gurney 1980).

Soil pH, Phosphate and Magnetic Susceptibility Surveys in the Northey Area
by D.A. Gurney

Dyke 9: Soil pH
(Table 5)
Field assessment of the pH indicated that the ploughsoil was alkaline, the buried soil and subsoil neutral.

Dyke 9: Phosphates
(Fig. 67; Table 13)
The buried soil and subsoil were sampled at nine loci between profiles 1 and 2 (at *c.* 5 and 10m intervals). The buried soil was tested in the field and in the laboratory, and

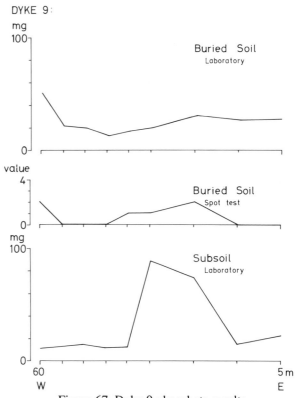

Figure 67 Dyke 9 phosphate results.

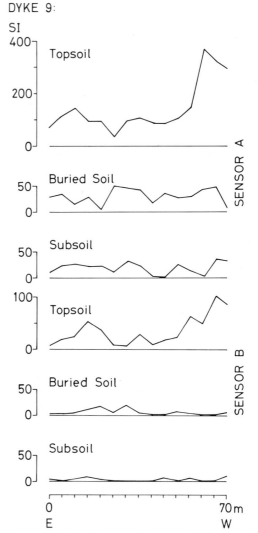

Figure 68 Dyke 9 magnetic susceptibility results.

Feature	Eidt	mg
1	weak	37
2	weak	14
3	trace	17
4 upper fill	weak	82
4 middle fill	weak	91
4 lower fill	positive	320
5	positive	260
6 upper fill	positive	97
6 middle fill	positive	91
6 lower fill	positive	85
7 upper fill	positive	33
7 lower fill	weak	23
8 upper fill	positive	49
8 middle fill	positive	79
8 lower fill	positive	150
11	positive	150
12	weak	76

Table 13. Field and laboratory phosphate results from features in Dyke 9.

the subsoil in the laboratory alone. The results (Fig. 67) from the buried soil are broadly comparable, and generally low. The subsoil analysis in the laboratory gave higher values in one area, up to 88mg.

Ten features (F 1–8, 11, 12) were also sampled, and results obtained in the field and in the laboratory. It was found that the correlation between the field test and the laboratory results was not very precise, with high laboratory values being 'missed' by the spot test, and 'positive' results in the field being contradicted by low values in the laboratory. In the 'weak' range, values in the laboratory varied between 14 and 76mg (6 samples), 'trace' in a single sample was matched by a value of 17mg, and 'positive' values varied between 33 and 320mg (10 samples). The full results are shown in Table 13.

Dyke 9: Magnetic Susceptibility
(Figs 68 and 69)
Fourteen loci between profiles 1 and 2 at *c.* 5m intervals were also surveyed using both field sensors, and values were obtained for the topsoil, the buried soil and the

subsoil. Both sensors provided a similar picture of topsoil variation (Fig. 68), although Sensor A gave significantly higher readings, up to 300 SI. Sensor A also gave higher values for the buried soil and subsoil.

Three features (F 4–6) were also tested using both field sensors and the bridge in the laboratory (Fig. 69). All three methods located an enhanced fill in F 5 (Sensor A, 280 SI; Sensor B, 410 SI; laboratory, 360 SI).

Dyke 10: Soil pH
(Table 5)
The ploughsoil is alkaline, the buried soil moderately to strongly acidic and the subsoil moderately acidic .

Dyke 10: Magnetic Susceptibility
Fifteen profiles were surveyed in the field using both sensors. All results (not illustrated) were low, and no significant patterning was evident. Sensor A generally provided a higher reading than Sensor B. In profile 12, a feature (F 14) provided exceptionally high readings from both sensors (Sensor A, 458 SI; Sensor B, 848 SI).

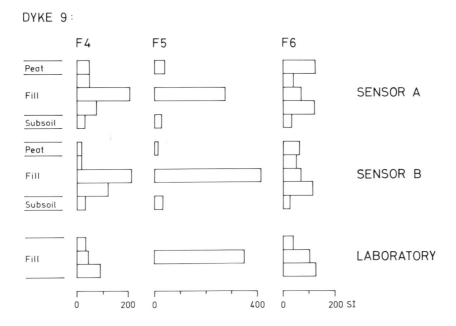

Figure 69 Dyke 9, features 4–6 magnetic susceptibility results.

Chapter 4. Discussion
by C. French and F. Pryor

I. Aspects of archaeology and environment in the North Bedford level

Introduction
This section is arranged by archaeological period and concludes with a brief discussion of soil truncation – a major source of probable post-depositional distortion of the available evidence.

Late Mesolithic/Neolithic
(Figs 2, 3, 70, 71)
Few early prehistoric sites have yet been found in the North Level, but those few that have been discovered are of enormous potential importance; in addition, extensive areas of prehistoric landscape have now been identified and mapped.

Growth of the basal peat was only affecting the eastern half of the study area during the 3rd, and particularly the later 3rd millennium BC. This includes the fen to the east of Northey 'island', east, north and northwest of Thorney 'island' as far west as the vicinity of Newborough village, and encroaching onto the northern edges of the Eye peninsula. This left the whole of the western fen edge beyond the influence of freshwater peat growth. This land includes (from south to north): Northey 'island', the Flag Fen basin, the Fengate area of eastern Peterborough, the Eye peninsula and the western half of Newborough/Borough Fen, as well as the 'islands' of Thorney and Crowland (Figs 2, 70) (Hall 1987, fig. 42). All these areas were essentially dry land throughout the Mesolithic and Neolithic periods. But this does not mean that they were not affected by freshwater influences from inland rivers that were attempting to find new drainage routes through the growing peat fen to the east. Consequently much of the 'skirtland' of this period may only have been seasonally dry land, especially if its elevation was less than one metre above OD. Extensive augering survey of the Flag Fen basin immediately to the southeast of the Fengate fen edge, for example, has revealed that the buried soil continues southeastwards beneath the later Bronze Age peat for 200–300 metres; in effect this survey has almost doubled the potential area available to the 3rd millennium pastoralists at Fengate, and may have served as the 'outfield' summer pasture to the 'infield' winter pasture revealed by earlier excavation (Pryor 1978, 1980a).

Two of the sites found in the eastern part of Borough Fen show that early prehistoric groups were utilising small 'islands' of dry land within the growing peat fen. The Crowtree and Oakhurst Farm sites lie on small dry areas within sight of the contemporary fen edge. Crowtree Farm is c. 0.25km east of Newborough village and Oakhurst Farm is c. 200m north of the dry land of the Eye peninsula (Figs 2, 70, sites 1 and 2). Both appear to have been above the influence of the encroaching (basal) peat for a time. Two other 'island' sites have also been found in Morris Fen to the east, one of which had indications of man's presence (Figs 2, 70, site 3). Unlike the other sites, the Morris Fen 'islands' remained above the growth of the basal peat before being covered by thick deposits of fen clay. The nature of their ancient use is not understood, but it is possible that they were frequented briefly and intermittently — rather than for longer periods. Without more substantial excavation the nature of any settlement or occupation on these 'islands' must remain indeterminate.

The soil micromorphological evidence suggests that there was only limited forest cover on these drier places prior to man's arrival: lengthy, but otherwise minor clearances occurred, and these were associated with considerable soil disturbance; both clearance and disturbance were most probably connected in some way with man's activities. The prehistoric soil does not appear to have been waterlogged when these areas were settled. The 'islands' would also have been visible from the higher ground to south and west; they would have been accessible by canoe or trackway, and were ideally placed to take advantage of the natural resources of the surrounding fen, such as reeds, wood, fish and fowl.

Two pollen sequences have been analysed from buried, truncated soils of late Atlantic/early Sub-Boreal date at Oakhurst and Crowtree Farm. The vegetation of these sites was dominated by lime (*Tilia*) woodland, with oak (*Quercus*) and hazel (*Corylus*) also present. Although both sites produced archaeological evidence for later Mesolithic and earlier Neolithic activity, it is only at Crowtree Farm that this is recorded in the pollen record. Pollen analysis here indicates woodland depletion, with a noted decline in lime, whilst the presence of ruderal herbs suggests open ground. The herbs present, in particular *Chenopodium* type and ribwort plantain (*Plantago lanceolata*), are weeds which can indicate both human occupation and animal husbandry. Grasses and sedges were also present, and a greater diversity of herbs was particularly noted in the upper part of the truncated buried soil at Crowtree Farm.

Micromorphological study of the palaeosol on the northern fen edge of the Eye peninsula indicates a similar picture of lengthy minor tree clearance and soil disturbance — doubtless also associated with human activity. As the ground rises steeply onto the Eye peninsula to the south, the drier land there would have been more suited for permanent settlement. Sadly, most of this land is covered by modern housing. Nevertheless, as Figure 70 illustrates, the available fen edge of the Mesolithic and earlier Neolithic periods amounts to several square kilometres, before it began to be encroached upon by later peat growth and marine deposits around the northern fringes of the peninsula.

Peat growth had begun as early as the later 5th millennium BC in the fenland river valleys in the easternmost part of the North Level. Later, more extensive peat growth was occurring in the northern and eastern areas of the North Level during the second half of the 3rd millennium BC. For example, basal peat growth was well advanced by

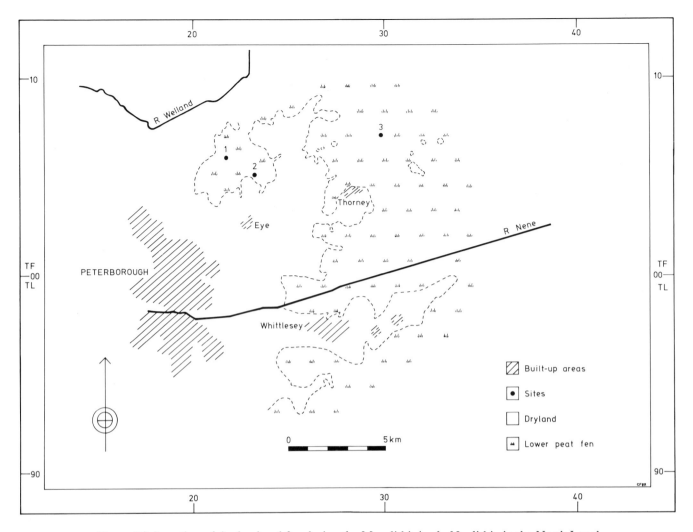

Figure 70 Location of dry land and fen during the Mesolithic/early Neolithic in the North Level.

the time it had overwhelmed the site at Crowtree Farm, that is by (Har–8513) 3660 ± 60 BP (2270–1890 Cal. BC). By this time both Crowtree and Oakhurst Farms must have been covered by peat growth, as was the eastern half of Newborough and Borough Fen; peat growth had also begun to encroach on the 'skirtland' of the Eye peninsula and on the edges of the Morris Fen 'islands'. The first extensive marine inundation, bearing clastic sedimentation occurred in the southern fens in the later 4th or early 3rd millennia BC, but the fen clay episode probably did not begin in the North Level area until earlier in the 2nd millennium BC (Figs 3, 71).

Specific Mesolithic and Neolithic sites and monuments in the North Level area have rarely been found, let alone understood; Hall, however, has found a few scatters of Neolithic lithic material at, for example, Singlesole on the northwestern edge of the Eye gravel peninsula (Hall 1987, fig. 29). Nevertheless, several indications of later Mesolithic or Neolithic activity have been identified by dyke survey. It is possible that the main areas of prehistoric activity in this period lie beneath the late peat and alluvial deposits on the western fen edge. Indeed the 'skirtland' of the western half of Newborough and Borough Fen coalesces with the ceremonial and settlement landscape identified, mainly from cropmark evidence, in the lower Welland valley (Pryor and French 1985; Pryor *et al.* 1986); they merge together about three kilometers beyond the landward limit of the fen 'skirtland' at Peakirk (Figs 2, 3). Almost the whole area, however, is covered by a combi-

nation of modern development and varying depths of alluvium which effectively obscure or destroy a buried landscape of rich archaeological potential.

The Bronze Age
(Figs 2, 33, 36, 71)
The earlier Bronze Age witnesses the marine incursion(s) responsible for the deposition of the fen clay. This tidally influenced salt marsh was drained by creeks oriented SW–NE which are now visible, east of Thorney, as silt-infilled roddons (Hall 1987, fig. 43). Although the rapidity of the marine incursion(s) is not known, it, or they, were probably most disruptive in human terms. The oak, plank-built footpath discovered at Guy's Fen was probably just one, short-lived, example of a community's response to the advancing salt marsh.

Pollen was recovered from the lower part of the fen clay at both Crowtree Farm and Oakhurst Farm. This was remarkable, given the base-status prevailing at each site. More marine conditions are delimited palynologically by the dominance of *Chenopodium* type pollen (glassworts and oraches). This taxon is characteristic of saline environments where halophytic elements of Chenopodiaceae thrive. The regional vegetation of this period is also represented: areas of dry land, presumably to the south and southwest only half a kilometre distant, were dominated by oak and hazel with alder important and growing on the areas fringing the fen and higher ground. In addition pre-Quaternary (Upper Jurassic) spores are frequent

102

within the fen clay and are probably derived from the Oxford Clay beneath, from whence they were removed, before being transported in the fluvial system and re-deposited in this near-shore marine environment. This demonstrates that a substantial degree of erosion was occurring on adjacent land, and that fen clay sediments in this area were derived from sources other than marine transport alone.

Some forty-nine barrows were erected during the earlier Bronze Age on Thorney 'island', the Eye peninsula and the 'skirtland' area of the western half of Newborough and Borough Fens (Figs 2, 33, 71). The principal alignment of the barrows in Borough Fen is NW–SE, along the western fen-edge of the day, immediately beyond (but at right angles to) the western limit of the fen clay (Hall 1987, fig. 10). The one barrow excavated, barrow 10d in Borough Fen (Figs 33, 36), was composed of a primary gravel revetted central turf core with no evident burials, followed by an enlarged secondary mound of sand and gravel, revetted by turves. The buried soil beneath the barrow mound, although severely truncated, had developed under dry land conditions, but subsequently suffered alternating wet and dry conditions, indicative of seasonal waterlogging. By the Roman period the barrow ditch was completely infilled with peat, and the mound was more or less obscured from view by subsequent peat growth.

It could be argued, using traditional archaeological reasoning, that the main criterion for siting the barrow group in this fen-edge location was that the land was considered marginal and prone to at least seasonal flooding. Alternatively, the barrows could have been situated at an important conceptual 'interface' between the worlds of wetland and dryland. The latter hypothesis is discussed by Jane Downes in Chapter 2.

The silting-up of the tidal creek network was probably well underway by the middle of the 2nd millennium BC, and undoubtedly caused considerable disruption to the outfalls of the fen rivers. A consequence of this was the initiation of peat growth on the landward side of the influence of the fen clay, as freshwater began to 'pond-up' behind the salt marsh, especially during the second half of the 2nd millennium BC: upper peat, for example, was beginning to encroach on the fringes of Northey 'island', then a western 'limb' of the much larger 'island' of Whittlesey to the east. Bronze Age features exposed on the higher parts of the 'island' were found to be partially infilled with peat. This process of encroachment must have forced settlement onto the higher parts of the 'island'.

Dyke survey, soil micromorphological analyses and phosphate/magnetic susceptibility tests have revealed Bronze Age occupation and arable use of the southwestern edge of Northey 'island' (Figs 2, 71, site 5: profiles 1–12). It is possible that either the peat from the adjacent fen was used as a form of fertiliser, or that attempts were made to use the land for arable despite the initial encroachment of peat onto the edge of the 'island'. This was achieved both by ploughing-in the peat on the edge of the 'island' and dumping topsoil and occupation debris onto the peat on

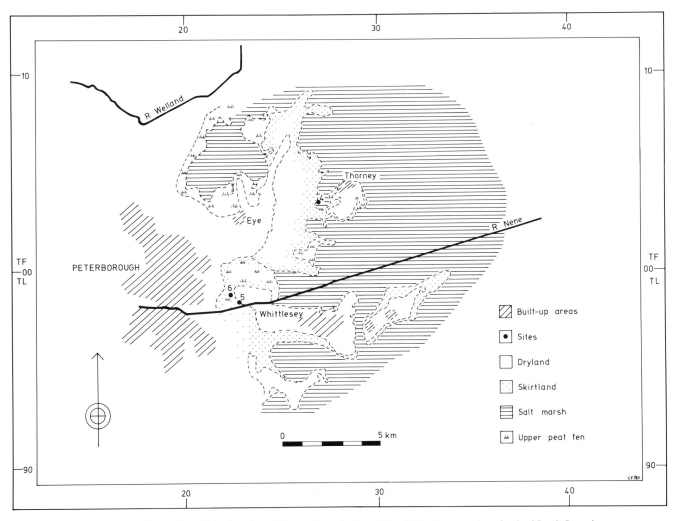

Figure 71 Location of dry land and fen during the later Neolithic/Bronze Age in the North Level.

the fringe of the 'island'. Eventually peat growth gained the upper hand and later, Iron Age, groups were only able to use the higher parts of the 'island' to the east.

The preservation of the complete buried soil profile on the southwestern edge of Northey 'island' is only one of two known instances of such preservation in the North Level area. The other occurs within the interior of the Iron Age ringwork in Borough Fen (see below); consequently, archaeological preservation within this site should prove to be exceptional. Peat growth, in reed swamp conditions with extensive areas of shallow open water, had begun well before c. 1000 BC in the adjacent fen basin to the west. It was in this setting that the Late Bronze Age settlement platform of Flag Fen was constructed (Figs 2, 71, site 6).

The wider archaeological implications of the palaeoenvironmental investigations at Flag Fen are considerable. The shallow and open fen that pertained during the first half of the 1st millennium BC, and earlier, may well have allowed extensive summer grazing; indeed, it probably made the building and habitation of the platform settlement feasible in the first instance.

The archaeological evidence of successive floors and repeated re-building may be a direct manifestation of the gradually rising water table, which was undoubtedly a major contributing factor to the site's abandonment sometime, presumably shortly, before the Iron Age. Coincident with the upper levels of the settlement site, the pollen and diatom evidence suggest that there was a gradual transition from shallow water reedswamp to open water conditions with slight indications of a brackish water content. This change to much wetter conditions probably contributed to the site's final abandonment at the Bronze Age/Iron Age transition. Future radiocarbon and dendrochronological dating may enable a more precise date for this event.

While the water table was rising throughout the second half of the 1st millennium BC, summer grazing in the basin would have become more difficult if not impossible. This in turn would have had implications on the land-use of the Fengate terrace gravel areas. For example, the fen-edge may now have become seasonally prone to flooding, with the consequence that it may have reverted to summer pasture only. The adjacent Cat's Water Iron Age settlement site would have become wetter, as was actually proved to be the case by earlier excavation (Pryor 1974).

The Flag Fen platform aside, settlement during the Bronze Age must have been restricted to higher parts of Fen 'islands', above c. 2.0m OD, and the fen margins — as at Fengate (Pryor 1980a) in the lower Nene valley and possibly in the vicinity of Peakirk, Glinton and Northborough in the lower Welland valley (Fig. 2). Indeed, Hall's (1987) survey suggests that Bronze Age settlement was sparse in the study area: there are, for example, two possible settlements on Thorney 'island', one a lithic scatter (site 11) and another an enclosure (site 26) (Hall 1987, fig. 30). Another site on the Eye peninsula (site 2) (Hall 1987, fig. 15) was composed of a dark 'occupation' layer on a mound with burnt clay 'briquetage' (but not saltern material) and Late Bronze Age pottery, similar to Late Bronze Age sites discovered on the Lincolnshire fen-edge, such as those of the Billingborough area (Chowne 1980). The Billingborough sites are noted for the hardness and durability of their pottery and it must always be questioned whether the apparent rarity of later Bronze

Age sites in the area presently under discussion does not simply reflect poor survival of the evidence.

While the upper peat was growing over most of the North Level, Guy's Fen west of Thorney and Morris Fen north and northeast of Thorney 'island' were subject to further extensive marine incursion(s). These 'younger' Barroway Drove Beds represent a similar tidal salt marsh regime, probably during the earlier half of the 1st millennium BC. The accumulation of these marine silts and silty clays probably prevented effective use of this large area of the North Level by man except for fishing and fowling.

The Iron Age
(Figs 2, 72)

The latter half of the 1st millennium BC witnessed the dwindling influence of marine salt marsh conditions in the north and eastern parts of the North Level, with peat growth continuing to landward and eventually over the bulk of the North Level (Figs 3, 72). The last marine incursions of this part of the Cambridgeshire fens occurred to the north of Thorney immediately to the south of Crowland and the Lincolnshire border during the late Iron Age. They were responsible for depositing silts of the Terrington Beds, which are largely confined to the south Lincolnshire fens (Fig. 3).

Iron Age occupation was again confined to the higher ground on the main fen 'islands' and the fen margins, at sites such as Northey 'island' and Fengate (Figs 2, 72). One notable and exceptionally well preserved example is the rampart enclosure site of Borough Fen site 7 which is situated on a spine of Welland First Terrace river gravels on the northwestern margin of Borough Fen. This site was undoubtedly intensively occupied for a time during the Middle and later Iron Age, and is now corroborated by the radiocarbon date obtained from charcoal within the sealed ploughsoil/occupation deposit of (Har–8512) 2090 ± 80 BP (380 Cal. BC to Cal. AD 80). The defensive ditch and rampart may post-date an earlier phase of the internal settlement (as occupation material has been found on the old land surface beneath the rampart).

The buried 'occupation' deposit within the ringwork exhibited high phosphate values, and contained abundant pottery, bone and charcoal. The animal bone is well preserved, and although fragmentary, it shows distinct signs of butchery which would suggest that domestic refuse was incorporated within this material. Analysis of this deposit in thin section has revealed that it is an heterogeneous mixture of two materials: ploughsoil and dumped occupation debris, mainly wood ash and charcoal. Indeed this horizon has itself been ploughed and is in fact the prehistoric ploughsoil. This is only one of two known examples in the North Level area where the prehistoric ploughsoil and the rest of the soil profile is complete, and unaffected by later erosion and truncation. Although this ploughsoil contained evidence of a minor alluvial component, it did not become waterlogged until later, an event presumably contemporary with the site's abandonment at the end of the Iron Age and possibly coincidental with the onset of alluvial aggradation.

Molluscan analysis of features cut through the base of the buried soil suggests that the site was built in a relatively dry, open, short-turved grassland situation, with the possibility of a minor scrub element in the vicinity. The few freshwater slum and marsh species present indicate a high

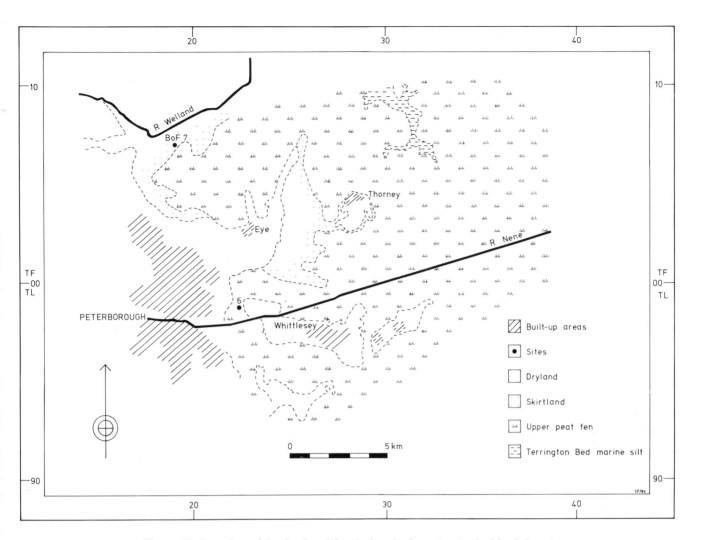

Figure 72 Location of dry land and fen during the Iron Age in the North Level.

ground water table or even occasional flooding; freshwater could never have been far away.

In conclusion, the excellent preservation of bone, artefacts and environmental evidence makes this a prime site for more detailed investigation in the future. It is moreover located in an area of recently improved drainage and desiccation is a very real probability in the next few years.

Hall's (1987) field survey has discovered another five possible Iron Age/Romano-British sites, three on Thorney 'island' and two on the Eye peninsula. The Thorney sites (30, 31, 32) appear to be Middle Iron Age and later settlements set in a network of cropmark enclosures (which may be Iron Age or Roman) on the gravels east of Willow Hall Lane (Hall 1987, fig. 33). Site 4 is a probable settlement situated close to the Late Bronze Age site 2 on the southern edge of the Eye peninsula. Another Eye site (15) has now been destroyed by gravel extraction. It could be attributable to Iron Age or Roman times, and comprises cropmarks of linear ditches and three possible hut circles (Hall 1987, fig.15).

The Roman Period
(Figs 2, 11, 73)
Archaeological evidence for field systems and settlements of the Roman period is more common than for earlier periods, but it is largely confined to Thorney 'island' and the Eye peninsula (Hall 1987, figs. 16 and 33). Aside from the earlier Roman settlement at Fengate (Pryor 1984), the

late 1st century AD Fen Causeway — a gravel dump road which runs across the site at Flag Fen from Fengate to Northey 'island' — the Car Dyke and Borough Fen site 1 (Figs 2, 73), all the other nine sites have been discovered by surface field survey (Hall 1987). On the Eye peninsula there are two possible domestic sites (1 and 5), with another two probable agricultural sites (8 and 9) (Hall 1987, fig. 16). In Thorney parish there is a considerable amount of Roman settlement on the gravels to the west (sites 6, 8, 25, 30 and 31), and also on the now dry Terrington Beds to the north (sites 9 and 10) (Hall 1987, fig. 33). For example, site 9 has cropmarks of paddocks and droveways over c. 8 hectares. Site 6 on the western gravels has extensive earthwork/cropmark paddocks and fields with discrete areas of settlement. The aforementioned sites 30 and 31 probably had Roman as well as Iron Age occupation.

It is suggested that the surface of the peat fen must have undergone a period of relative drying out to enable the Fen Causeway to have been built in the third quarter of the 1st century AD (Potter 1981; Pryor 1984). If the peat surface was actively growing and waterlogged, the simple sand and gravel dump construction of the road would have soon dissipated into the mire. This theory is given further credence by the presence of Roman settlement for the first time on the now dry Terrington Bed silts in the northern part of Thorney parish (Hall 1987, 51). Although this relative drying out of the peat may have enabled some pastoral expansion into the fens, it is unlikely that there was any settlement on the peat areas themselves.

The other main Roman feature of Borough Fen is the Car Dyke (Figs 2, 11). It runs approximately along the western fen-edge in Lincolnshire and the eastern outskirts of Peterborough. Originally believed to be a canal, it is now considered to be a catchwater drain (Simmons 1980), that protected fenland summer grazing by cutting off floodwater from the uplands to the west.

Borough Fen site 1 is situated some 300m to the east of the Iron Age rampart enclosure on the highest point of the same spine of Welland terrace gravels (Fig. 73), and is of mid 2nd to mid 3rd century AD date. Settlement is indicated by a distinct scatter of pottery sherds, as well as high phosphate and magnetic susceptibility values.

Both Borough Fen site 1 and the adjacent Iron Age ringwork site are sealed beneath c. 40–50cm of peaty alluvium; but as most of the later growth of peat has since wasted away, the amount of alluvium is accentuated. The mid 3rd century AD witnessed widespread deposition of alluvium on many fen-edge sites, including Etton, Fengate, Hockwold-cum-Wilton, Grandford, Flaggrass, Stonea, Upwell and Earith; alluvium is also widespread in other parts of England, such as in the upper Thames valley where it occurs throughout the Roman period (Lambrick and Robinson 1979). If nothing else, the initiation of widespread and intensive alluviation indicates a considerable extensification of the open landscape, with land increasingly put under arable cultivation, particularly upstream in lowland river valleys. As a result, vast tracts of

land on the fen margins, for example between Etton and the western edge of Newborough and Borough Fens in the lower Welland valley, and from Fengate over most of the Flag Fen basin at the outfall of the lower Nene valley — these large areas became at least seasonally flooded and subject to alluvial aggradation. As another consequence, these areas also became relatively inaccessible to man except, perhaps, for use as rich spring/early summer pasture. This doubtless explains the apparent absence of ancient settlement over several square kilometres of fen margin and 'skirtland' on the western side of the North Level.

Another probable reason why alluvium is concentrated around the western fen-edge in the North Level is because the upward growth of peat combined with the sluggish outfalls of fenland rivers to impede water flow. This meant that water tended to pond-up between the higher ground of the fen-edge and the upper peat in the deeper fenland basin. Slow-moving water deposits material held in suspension as its pace slackens, and this leads to the gradual accumulation of alluvium: in the Flag Fen basin, for example, there are at least three major phases of alluviation, each separated by the growth of upper peat. The first two phases probably occurred in the latter half of the 1st millennium BC after the platform site was abandoned, and the third phase occurred sometime after the 1st century AD. The latter was possibly associated with the early to mid 3rd century AD alluvial deposition observed at Fengate (Pryor 1984), some 400m to the west.

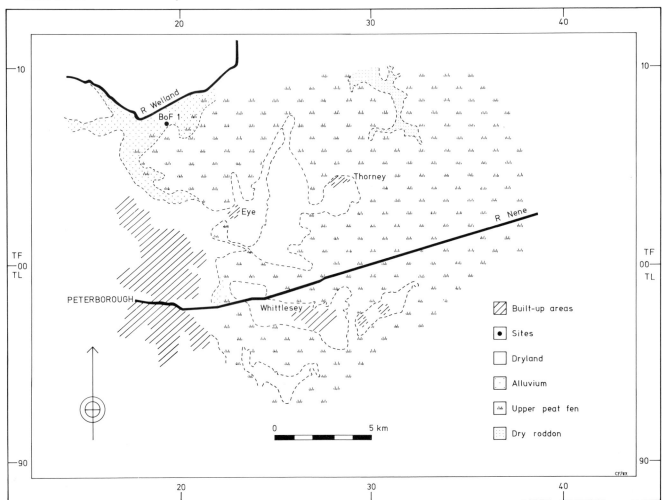

Figure 73 Location of dry land and fen in the Roman period in the North Level.

Soil Truncation: Possible Causes and Effects
One of the major problems to arise from the soil micro-morphological and palynological analyses of the present project and of continuing research (Waller forthcoming), is the recognition of soil truncation. Most of the profiles examined in thin section suggest that up to half the depth of the original, prehistoric, soil has been removed by some form of erosion. On the other hand, fenland pollen analyses completed to date show no evident signs of truncation, nor abrupt changes in the pollen stratigraphy. This contradiction clearly requires explanation.

The most logical explanation might be as follows (Scaife and Waller pers. comm.). First, the original deciduous woodland, dominated by lime (*Tilia*) and oak (*Quercus*), grew on an argillic brown earth with a mull surface horizon. The high biological activity within this mull horizon led to the incorporation of local tree pollen; there may also have been little understorey plant cover in this relatively dense woodland and therefore herbaceous types are not well represented in the pollen record. Second, truncation had generally removed the mull horizon (Ah) and some or all of the eluvial (Ea) horizon (up to *c.* 10cm), leaving only the lower Ea, B and/or the Bt (argillic) horizons at the base of the profile. Although the exact mechanism of truncation is unknown, this stage was probably associated with tree clearance and soil disturbance, both by human and natural agencies. Finally, this truncated soil remained open (and receiving pollen), with some pedogenesis occurring, prior to later waterlogging. This last phase would not have to be long-lived for mixing in the pollen record to obscure the effects of the soil's earlier truncation.

II. Future research

Introduction
The final section of this report will be devoted to future research strategies. The dyke survey will continue in its present form until 1993 when there will have to be a major re-assessment. Shortly thereafter it is hoped to produce the companion volume to the present report. The discussion that follows then will consider two aspects of the next stage of research. It does not cover the continuing dyke survey whose methods will remain substantially the same as those outlined in this report.

Buried Soils and the monitoring of sensitive environmental deposits
The use of the technique of soil micromorphological analysis should be extended, and in conjunction with soil pollen analysis. A major aim of future research would be to construct a palaeosol map of the pre-fen fenland basin. It would, however, require a sufficiently detailed blanket sampling programme with appropriate laboratory back-up. This would undoubtedly be a most innovative and potentially very informative development.

A second fruitful direction for research would be a study of the nature of the soil erosion that resulted from the deposition of the various Flandrian fen deposits; the erosive effects of the fen clay require special attention. This study would help to distinguish between natural and anthropogenic causes of soil erosion, a distinction that is still poorly understood, but is of considerable archaeological significance.

The effects on buried soils of prolonged waterlogging and recent drainage also require investigation, as there is little doubt that waterlogging can deplete palaeosols of various essential interpretive characteristics. Finally, the collaborative nature of future environmental research must be stressed and a variety of different topographical regions should be studied. Emphasis should also be given to sites both unaffected by human activity and those close to or within known ancient settlements.

Site Definition and Management
Hall's (1987) field survey and the present dyke survey have revealed a number of sites and other areas of major importance (Hall 1987, Appendix I) which require further archaeological attention. The next phase of investigation for sites that have been discovered, but whose details are still unknown, involves the type of work that has already been completed at Flag Fen, Crowtree Farm and Borough Fen site 7 (the ringwork). A variety of techniques and procedures can be applied to any individual site, but we would suggest that the following itemised strategy would effectively delimit the size of the site and obtain geophysical and environmental samples. This should be sufficient to determine the nature of the site concerned.

1. hand or powered auger survey using a fixed grid of 5, 10, 20 or 30 metres to establish the extent of the site and its sedimentary context. Properly conducted the auger survey should also:
A. plot contours of the old land surface.
B. sample for phosphates and magnetic susceptibility tests.
C. prospect for areas suitable for later pollen analysis.
D. select areas for test excavation.
2. Small-scale trial excavation, for example in 2 or 5 metre squares. The main aim would be to establish the nature of the archaeological evidence and its survival. Procedures would involve controlled (sieved etc.) artefact recovery, investigative *in situ* soil sampling, macro-botanical and insect bulk sampling.
3. Following 1 and 2, the field data must be integrated with existing information; this might involve correlation with borehole data of the British Geological Survey, aerial photographs and other field survey.
4. Management decisions can only be made at this stage (*i.e.* following 1–3). Preparation of a management plan will involve monitoring and assessment of the site's survival potential. It will lead to recommendations to the land owner, local authorities and English Heritage for future action.

Throughout the assessment process new techniques of investigation must be tried and investigated. In particular, new geophysical survey techniques must be developed which will allow better surface detection and easier prospection. Existing site-specific surface survey techniques are very cumbersome and it is possible to work much faster and more efficiently; post-survey research is particularly slow and could greatly be hastened by adopting computerised procedures that are already in use elsewhere.

The greatest potential for archaeological research in the fens lies well below the rapidly eroding modern surface. The withdrawal of agricultural drainage grants may indeed mean that very large-scale new drainage schemes may no longer happen so frequently, but the damage caused by the schemes of the 1970s and early 1980s has yet to be fully appreciated. Changing ground water tables urgently require monitoring and the effects of de-watering on specific monuments must be investigated over time and at a suitably large scale. Future management decisions cannot afford to ignore what lies, or dries, below the surface.

1 April 1988

Appendix I: Methods of soil/sediment analysis

by C.A.I. French

Field description
(Figs 74 and 75)
Descriptions in the field were based on the criteria of Smith and Atkinson (1975), and the record cards were devised by D.R. Crowther and the writers (Fig. 75).

The main conventions used for the soil/sediment description in all section drawings are given in Fig. 74.

Figure 74 Key to the section drawings.

Sample pretreatment
Sample pretreatment involved the air-drying of each sample for one or two weeks. Then each sample for particle size analysis was quartered, ground with a pestle and mortar, and shaken through a 2mm mesh sieve to remove the gravel fraction. The gravel fraction was weighed and its percentage by weight of the total sample calculated. The sub-gravel fraction (< 2mm) was further sampled for each of the sediment analysis procedures described below (except for the thin sections).

Soil reaction (pH)
Measurements were taken using a pH meter (after Avery and Bascomb 1974). A buffer solution of pH 7 was first prepared to standardise the meter. Dilutions of 10g of less than 2mm air-dried soil were used with 100ml of distilled water. A random number of dilutions was prepared with 0.5NKCl (potassium chloride), which standardises the 'salt effect' and generally gives readings of one unit less than measurements in distilled water.

Particle size analysis
The hydrometer method of particle size analysis was used (Shackley 1975); 40g samples were pretreated by boiling with hydrogen peroxide, allowed to cool, dispersed with 'Calgon' (sodium hexametaphosphate), mixed, and then the suspension poured through a 0.062mm mesh sieve into a 1000ml graduated cylinder. The sand fraction so removed was oven-dried and then fractionated by dry-sieving. Six hydrometer readings of the settling suspension were taken from which the percentage in suspension was calculated as well as the particle diameter and phi (ϕ) value (Page 1955).

The results of the particle size analysis and dry sieving were combined to construct cumulative percentage and frequency graphs, and histograms representing the composition of each sample. The character of the soil or sediment is named by the use of the triangular textural diagram (Limbrey 1975, 261 (b)). The size grades of the United States Department of Agriculture (1951) were used.

Statistical measures based on the particle size analysis were calculated for the mean (Mz), standard deviation (σ,

skewness (Sk) and kurtosis (K_G). The formulae of Folk and Ward (1957) were used to calculate these measures separately for the sand and silt fractions because the phi (ϕ) values at 5% and 16% were generally unavailable due to the presence of unanalysed fines. The mean size reflects the average size of the sediment or grain size fraction, or the central tendency of the distribution curve. The inclusive graphic standard deviation is a measure of the spread of values around the mean, or the degree of sorting. The inclusive graphic skewness is a measure of the symmetry of the distribution curve and the mean, that is, whether the greater part of the material is coarser (Sk = 0 to -1) or finer (Sk = 0 to 1) than the mean. The kurtosis is a measure of the 'peakedness' of the distribution curve. A normal curve has $K_G = 1$. A flat, or platykurtic, distribution will be a bimodal distribution with two more or less equal and widely separated peaks. A peaked, or leptokurtic, distribution will contain one dominant size fraction with coarser or finer 'tails'. An even, or mesokurtic, distribution lies between the previous two types of curve (Folk and Ward 1957; Spiegel 1961).

The results are presented in tabular form. By these exercises one may discern the similarity between sediments, and possibly how deposits were formed and under what environmental conditions. Calculations were made on an Epson QX–10 micro-computer.

The preparation of thin sections (micromorphology)
The former method of impregnation with Autoplax resin and styrene (Bascomb and Bullock 1974) has been superseded by a polyester resin using acetone (Bullock *et al.* 1985a). The descriptive criteria of Bullock *et al.* (1985b) are used throughout.

Air- or oven-dried blocks of soil are impregnated with crystic resin in a fume cupboard for four to six weeks. Slices are sawn from each block and are ground down on diamond plates and the face polished with carborundum paper. After cleaning with deodorised paraffin the slice is mounted face downwards on a microscope slide with a resin mixture. It is then cut to a thickness of 100–200µm, and then ground to a thickness of *c.* 40µm or less on a surface grinding machine. The final grinding and polishing to the 25–30µm required thickness is done by hand using silicon carbide powder and carborundum paper.

The thin section is then examined at various magnifications with various degrees of illumination. Thin sections are useful in the study of soil microstructure and in elucidating pedological processes. Aggregates, concretions and weathered grains are best studied in thin section. Sand and silt grains can be identified mineralogically. Clay translocation and weathering processes may be studied, and clay illuviation may be identified (Bullock in Avery and Bascomb 1974). The study of soil micromorphology examines the hypotheses generated by the previously discussed soil analyses critically, and may elucidate some of the problems. In this study, the micromorphological analyses were used mainly as a descriptive aid and to identify pedogenic processes.

Dr R.I. Macphail of the Institute of Archaeology, London, checked all the micromorphological descriptions. The facilities of the laboratory of the Department of Human Environment, Institute of Archaeology, London, were used for some of the initial preparations of the thin sections.

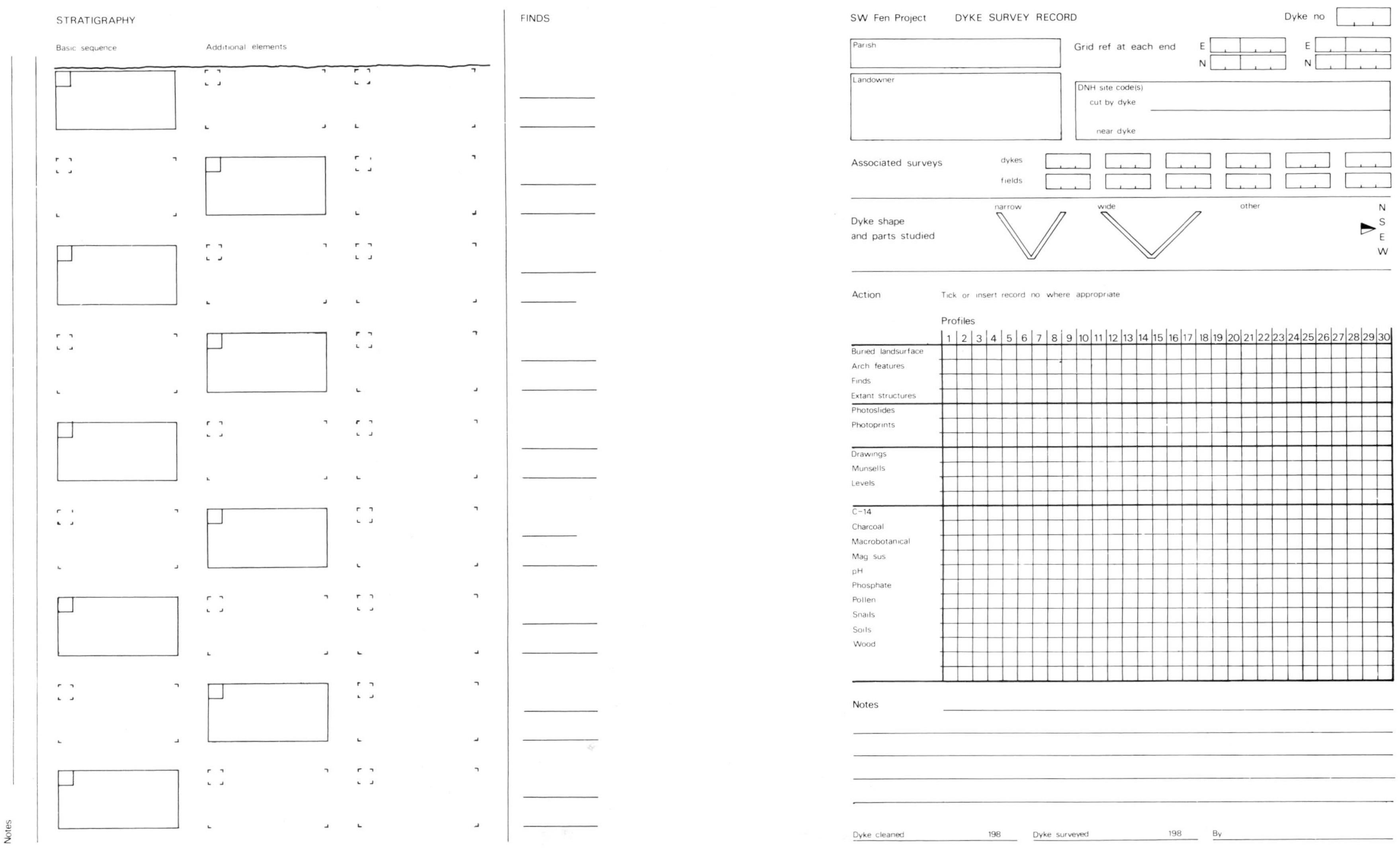

DYKE SURVEY RECORD

SW Fen Project

Dyke no

Parish

Landowner

Grid ref at each end

E
N

E
N

Associated surveys

DNH Site code(s)
cut by dyke
near dyke

dykes
fields

other

N
S
E
W

Dyke shape
and parts studied

narrow   wide

Action   Tick or insert record no where appropriate

Profiles | 1 | 2 | 3 | 4 | 5 | 6 | 7 | 8 | 9 | 10 | 11 | 12 | 13 | 14 | 15 | 16 | 17 | 18 | 19 | 20 | 21 | 22 | 23 | 24 | 25 | 26 | 27 | 28 | 29 | 30 |

Buried landsurface
Arch features
Finds
Extant structures
Photoslides
Photoprints

Drawings
Munsells
Levels

C-14
Charcoal
Macrobotanical
Mag. sus
pH
Phosphate
Pollen
Snails
Soils
Wood

Notes

Dyke cleaned   198   Dyke surveyed   198   By

FINDS

STRATIGRAPHY

Basic sequence   Additional elements

Notes

Figure 75 Dyke survey record card.

Appendix II: Methods of molluscan analysis
by C.A.I. French
(Table 12)

The principles and methods of molluscan analysis given by Evans (1972) have generally been followed. Sample intervals of 10cm or 20cm were used; either as spot samples from individual layers or as continuous sample columns.

Interpretation is based on the work of Boycott (1936) Ellis (1941, 1951), Evans (1972) and Sparks (1961, 1964). The species are listed in their conventional ecological groups in Table 12.

Aside from the conventional ecological methods of dealing with the numbers and species of molluscs represented, two numerical methods were also used to describe the faunas: rank-order or species abundance curves and diversity indexes (Evans pers. comm.; Pielou 1975, 1977).

In rank-order curves the numbers of each species (as a percentage of the total shells in each sample) are plotted in their order of abundance. Each curve illustrates the total number of species and the distribution among the various species. These curves may be considered alone, and with the depositional context and the ecological inferences made from the species assemblage. It is suggested that a regularly curved graph, often with a large number of species, is indicative of diverse and relatively mature habitats. L-shaped curves are indicative of less diverse and often younger environments, and there may be a mixture of *in situ* and derived species in this type of assemblage. Slightly stepped curves are intermediate between these two extreme curves.

Diversity indexes involve the reduction of the information in the rank-order curve to a single figure. In particular, evenness (J1)(3) measures the way in which various individuals are apportioned among the various species. But as this figure does not take account of the number of species and shells in the assemblage, it is a measure applied to samples. Consequently, J1 is compared with an equivalent index, J(4), which is applied to fully censused collections which consider the number of individuals. The difference between J and J1 at any one level is a measure of the closeness of a sample to a fully censused collection.

A second set of diversity indexes, H1(1) (the Shannon-Weiner index) and H(2) (the Brillouin index) incorporates the evenness with the number of species. The divergence of H from H1 is an index of autochthony. When J and J1 and H and H1 are plotted against each other a useful measure of the degree of autochthony or allochthony can be ascertained. The standard deviation (σ) of H1 was also calculated.

1    $H1 = -\Sigma(pi \log_e pi)$ (Pielou 1975)
     where p = proportion of the assemblage belonging to the i–th species
2    $H = 1/N (\log_e N!/TTNi!)$ (Pielou 1975)
     where N = number of individuals in the assemblage
     N!= number in the i–th species for i = 1, . . . s
     s = number of species
3    $J1 = H1/\log_e s$ (Pielou 1977)
4    $J = H/\log_e s$ (Pielou 1977)
     where s = the number of species in the assemblage.

The Shannon-Weiner index originated as a measure of information content or uncertainty obtained from information theory (Krebs 1978). Other measures of diversity include species richness, heterogeneity, Fisher's alpha (α) (Fisher *et al.* 1943) and the log-normal distribution (Preston 1948). For example, Kenward (1978) has used rank-order plots and log-normal distributions with superimposed values of Fisher's alpha as a measure of species structure. This index is well suited to insect assemblages subject to many random variables. It is also suggested that the very abundant species (> 10%) may be used as evidence of breeding, and should be subtracted from the fauna before calculating other statistics. Kenward (1982) has also used close linkages in species-pair analysis of Coleoptera to suggest that this may be a result of the occurrence of insects in the same habitat.

Species diversity in living communities is governed by a complex interaction of factors which are not completely understood (Gould 1981; Krebs 1978). These include the time available for speciation and dispersal; habitat size, range, number and structure; the stability of the primary production; the intensity and frequency of disturbance of an environment; and competition and predation, which may be complementary factors. Thus these factors make the assignment of a number as an indication of species diversity a potentially difficult exercise.

Appendix III: Geophysical and geochemical survey procedures: methods and discussion

1. Summary of methods of pH measurement, phosphate analysis and magnetic susceptibility measurement
by D.A. Gurney

A 1:2.5 solution of soil to distilled water and a Pye model 293 meter were used for the measurement of soil pH.

The spot test method of phosphate analysis, employed the procedure of Eidt (1973); laboratory phosphate analysis used the British Museum technique, based on the molybdenum blue method of Murphy and Riley (1962). For details of this method see Craddock *et al.* (1985).

A Bartington type MSI meter with two field sensors was used for the field measurement of magnetic susceptibility. Sensor A has a circular coil (diameter 20cm) mounted on a sturdy tripod of plastic piping. Sensor B has a coil (type MSIF) mounted at the end of a single pipe. Laboratory measurement involved the use of a Littlemore Type 780 differential inductance bridge.

Results in the text are expressed as follows:
Phosphate spot tests: values after Schwarz (1967):
   0 negative
   1 trace
   2 weak
   3 positive
   4 strong
Magnetic susceptibility measurement: all readings (in the field and laboratory) are in SI / Kg x 10 to the -8 (abbreviated in the text to 'SI').

Assessment
All the phosphate and magnetic susceptibility surveys were carried out by the present writer in 1982. Following the successful application of such surveys at the Maxey excavations (Gurney in Pryor and French 1985, 38–41, 195–205; Gurney 1985b), it was decided during the first season of dykeside survey to conduct limited sampling and measurement on selected dykes, to determine whether or not the techniques were applicable to dykeside work.

The results have been integrated into the descriptions of each dyke survey, but some general conclusions on the phosphate and magnetic susceptibility surveys can be drawn from the results as a whole. Firstly, phosphate determinations in the field (using the Eidt spot test for the first time in our work) were compared with laboratory analyses. At two sites where this was attempted (Borough Fen site 7 and Flag Fen Dyke 9), it was found that there was generally little correlation between the two sets of results, and high values in the laboratory were 'missed' by the spot test and *vice versa*. It is true that in areas of phosphate enhancement, the spot test generally provided some indication of this, but as might be expected, the simple field test proved to be far less reliable than the laboratory analysis.

Secondly, laboratory phosphate analysis at Borough Fen sites 1 and 7 located areas of enhancement corresponding with known archaeological sites. At the former site, the results can be compared with magnetic susceptibility measurements, the observed soil mark and a scatter of Romano-British pottery. The results from the various surveys are closely comparable.

Thirdly, areas of magnetic susceptibility enhancement were successfully located at Borough Fen site 1, and in features in two other dykes (Dykes 9 and 10). Of the two sensors used, A generally provided a higher reading than B, although at Borough Fen site 1, B appeared to be the more sensitive of the two, giving the highest readings from the area of the site, and lower readings than A beyond. When features with burnt fills were tested (Flag Fen), B provided much higher readings, and this sensor is perhaps better suited to testing feature fills or thin buried soils.

If any conclusions are to be drawn from the phosphate and magnetic susceptibility surveys, they are that such surveys may well provide useful locational and interpretative data to supplement 'observed' dykeside archaeological features, that the use of the phosphate spot test in the field provides a quick but not always reliable indication of phosphate levels, and that the use of the portable magnetic susceptibility meter seems as well suited to dykeside survey as it does to conventional ploughsoil survey.

2. Magnetic Susceptibility Methods for the Crowtree Farm Survey
by A. Challands

Basic principles
The most succinct definition of magnetic susceptibility is 'the ratio of the induced magnetic moment of a substance to the applied magnetic field' (Scollar and Graham 1972, 86). Thus, in magnetometry, the detention of, for example, a buried ditch is dependent on a magnetically susceptible ditch filling being contained in an applied magnetic field, which is the earth's magnetic field. Magnetic susceptibility measurements on soils are taken by having a magnetic field applied to them — in the laboratory by means of a coil sensor or in the field by means of a loop or drum sensor.

When carrying out magnetic susceptibility surveys on archaeological sites, it is the enhanced values which are being sought, and these are compared to a normal magnetic susceptibility background which is determined by analytical techniques (Graham 1976; Tite 1972, 55).

Iron oxides are contained in most of the earth's soils usually in the form of weakly magnetic haematite (Fe_2O_3). The naturally occurring haematite is converted, usually by fire, to strongly magnetic magnetite (Fe_3O_4). On cooling and re-oxidation it converts again to a more magnetic haematite known as maghaemite (Fe_2O_3) (Tite 1972, 12).

Where human occupation has taken place over a sufficiently long period of time, the length of time being linked to the intensity of occupation and the concentration of haematite in the soil, the magnetic susceptibility of the soil will have been enhanced by conversion of haematite to maghaemite. Even if the soil has been disturbed, the higher magnetic susceptibility will still stand out against a background of natural magnetic susceptibility. Other occupation activities such as dumping organic rubbish can also enhance the magnetic susceptibility. When organic matter decays in anaerobic conditions any haematite present is reduced to magnetite and converted to maghaemite if the conditions change to aerobic (Tite 1972, 12).

The magnetic susceptibilities to be expected from sites in different geological areas have been investigated by Drs M.S. Tite and C. Mullins and have been shown to vary significantly. For example, there is a wide difference in magnetic susceptibility values between sites situated on post-glacial sands and gravels and those situated on deposits within the Jurassic belt (Tite and Mullins 1971, 209–219).

Field Techniques
It was intially thought that the best method for measuring the depths of the different deposits would be to sink a pilot hole using a 28.58mm diameter screw auger. Thus test pilot holes were sunk in an area adjacent to the survey area, and strata depths were thereby determined. Next, a 70mm diameter bucket auger was used to bore the main holes for taking samples and magnetic susceptibility readings, but this pilot hole and bucket auger method was quickly abandoned because it proved possible to determine the strata depths when using the bucket auger alone, so there was no need to use the screw auger as well. The 70mm bucket auger was also soon abandoned because it proved difficult to insert the 50mm diameter magnetic susceptibility sensor to the appropriate layer, without contamination from other layers. After further trial holes using a 152mm diameter bucket auger head, it was decided that the larger diameter borehole was more practical, and therefore was more suitable for the main survey.

Due to the very friable nature of the peaty alluvium topsoil, the boring technique which proved the most effecient was as follows:

i.) Excavate a pilot hole using a curved drainage spade.
ii.) Insert the 152mm diameter bucket auger to bore through the peaty alluvium to the top of the fen clay, and measure and record their depths.
iii.) Auger down to the base of the fen clay and measure its depth.
iv.) Bore into the palaeosol and remove c. 600g of the palaeosol for laboratory testing.
v.) Auger 5–10cm into the subsoil, and record the depth of the base of the palaeosol.

The field magnetic susceptibility measurements were taken on all the layers, except where ground water rapidly entered the borehole, using the following procedure:

i.) Check the air and soil temperature. Testing must be abandoned if there is too great a difference between the two temperatures.

ii.) Switch the Bartington magnetic susceptibility meter type M.S.I. to C.G.S. units at 1.0 range. Switch the zero/measure switch to zero, and by pointing the field sensor into the air, as far away from any magnetic effects as possible. Bring the switch to the central neutral position while the sensor is still in the air.

iii.) Touch the side of the borehole with the side of the field sensor. Move the switch from the neutral position and record three readings (in order to obtain an average reading) at 5 second intervals, as well as the depth of the sensor, on the proforma.

iv.) Stages (ii) and (iii) are repeated for each layer in the borehole.

Each borehole was backfilled; and a surface level related to Ordnance Datum was measured at each borehole location.

Reasons for Laboratory Magnetic Susceptibility Testing
Laboratory procedures for measuring the magnetic susceptibility of soils can be very accurate. On the other hand field magnetic susceptibility testing, which is commonly carried out using a loop sensor directly placed on the ground surface, is less precise. The reason for obtaining less precision with field measurements is due to variable inclusions in the topsoil, such as stones. Nevertheless, when the readings are taken on a regular grid basis and are processed statistically to establish normal background readings, the results can help to define human settlement areas on archaeological sites (Clark 1983, 128–133).

All of the palaeosol samples collected were laboratory tested in order to compare the accurate laboratory susceptibility values with the field values. This also gave added security, for if the field measurements proved to be unreliable, there would still be a reliable set of laboratory measurements.

Preliminary Sample Processing
The 165 samples obtained from the palaeosol were virtually stone-free and were put into foil containers and heated at low temperature in a drying oven for between 48 and 78 hours, until they were thoroughly dried. After drying, each sample was crushed to a powder, and between 100 and 200g was weighed into a polythene bag (labelled with the site code and borehole number).

Laboratory Magnetic Susceptibility Measurement Procedures
The Bartington magnetic susceptibility meter M.S.I. (which was used in field measurements in conjunction with a borehole sensor) was linked to a laboratory coil sensor M.S.I.B. which carried a 250ml sample bottle.

The laboratory testing procedure was as follows:

i.) Pour the sample of palaeosol into the previously weighed 250ml sample bottle, weigh and record this weight on a proforma.

ii.) Using C.G.S. units at 1.0 range setting, zero the magnetic susceptibility meter by switching the zero/measure switch to zero. The sensor coil is empty at this stage. After a few seconds set the switch to the central neutral position.

iii.) Insert the sample in the sample bottle into the laboratory sensor coil. Switch the meter to measure. Log the reading obtained next to the weight of sample and bottle.

iv.) Clean out the bottle and repeat this procedure for each sample.

Once the testing was completed the absolute magnetic susceptibility values were calculated. As the sensor was calibrated for a 100g sample weight, the formula used to obtain the absolute magnetic susceptibility value was as follows :

$$\frac{100}{nett\ sample\ weight} \times \frac{magnetic\ susceptibility\ reading}{1} \times 1.26$$

which equals an absolute value $\times 10^{-8}$ S.I./kg.

Appendix IV: Selected dykeside profile descriptions

Dyke 14

Profile 1:

Height in metres OD	Description
0.34–0	Upper peat, humified. 10YR2/2.
0 to -1.04	Barroway Drove Beds (fen clay); divided into an upper oxidised horizon (10YR5/2)and a lower reduced horizon (7.5YR4/0).
-1.04 to -1.27	Basal peat; a wood peat. 10YR2/1.
-1.27 to -1.42	Buried soil; bleached sandy loam. 5YR6/2.
-1.42+	Fen gravels; sand and fine gravel. 10YR6/4.

Profile 4:

0.81–0.51	Upper peat.
0.51 to -0.30	Fen clay.
-0.30+	Buried soil.

Profile 5:

0.84–0.40	Upper peat.
0.40 to -0.18	Fen clay.
-0.18 to -0.29	Buried soil.
-0.29+	Fen gravels.

Profile 6:

0.87–0.76	Upper peat.
0.76 to -0.45	Fen clay.
-0.45+	Buried soil.

Profile 8:

0.68–0.38	Upper peat.
0.38 to -0.40	Fen clay.
-0.40+	Buried soil.

Profile 11:

0.54–0.33	Upper peat.
0.33 to -0.44	Fen clay.
-0.44+	Buried soil.

Profile 12:

0.57–0.39	Upper peat.
0.39 to -0.13	Fen clay.
-0.13+	Buried soil.

(The Crowtree Farm peninsula begins to rise westwards from this profile.)

Profile 14:

1.31–0.91	Upper peat.
0.91–0.81	Fen clay.
0.81–0.58	Upper horizon of buried soil; sandy loam (5YR6/2).
0.58–0.50	Lower horizon of buried soil; loamy sand (10YR7/8).
0.50+	Fen gravels.

Profile 17:

1.33–0.63	Upper peat.
0.63–0.50	Fen clay.
0.50–0.34	Buried soil (two horizons).
0.34+	Fen gravels.

Profile 20:

0.82–0.57	Upper peat.
0.57–0.31	Fen clay.
0.31–0.23	Buried soil (one horizon).
0.23+	Fen gravels.

Profile 23:

0.86–0.56	Upper peat.
0.56–0.06	Fen clay.

0.06–0.01   Buried soil (one horizon).
0.01+   Fen gravels.

Profile 24:
1.15–0.57   Upper peat.
0.57–0.15   Fen clay.
0.15–0.07   Buried soil (one horizon).
0.07+   Fen gravels.

Profile 26:
1.15–0.62   Upper peat.
0.62 to -0.05   Fen clay.
-0.05+   Buried soil (one horizon).

Notes:

The basal peat in profile 1 was sampled for pollen analysis.

Dyke 34

Profile 3:
0.84–0.59   Upper peat. 10YR2/2.
0.59 to -0.01   Barroway Drove Beds (fen clay). 10YR5/1.
-0.01 to -0.11   Buried soil; sandy loam. 5YR6/2. (Contained four flints).
-0.11+   Sand and fine gravel of Fen gravels. 10YR6/4.

Profile 5:
0.74–0.39   Upper peat.
0.39–0   Fen clay.
0 to -0.10   Buried soil.
-0.10+   Fen gravels.

Profile 7:
0.92–0.52   Upper peat.
0.52 to -0.43   Fen clay.
-0.43 to -0.63   Buried soil.
-0.63+   Fen gravels.

Dyke 35

Profile 1:
1.09–0.71   Upper peat. 10YR2/2.
0.71–0.05   Barroway Drove Beds (fen clay). 10YR5/1.
0.05–0.02   Basal peat lens. 10YR2/1.
0.02 to -0.18   Sand and fine gravel of Fen gravels. 10YR6/4.

Profile 2:
1.22–0.87   Upper peat.
0.87 to -0.20   Fen clay.
-0.20 to -0.18   Basal peat lens.
-0.18 to -0.30   Buried soil.
-0.30+   Fen gravels.

Profile 3:
1.05–0.75   Upper peat.
0.75–0.18   Fen clay.
0.18 to -0.02   Basal peat.
-0.02 to -0.2   Buried soil.
-0.20+   Fen gravels.

Dyke 37

Profile 1:
1.41–0.86   Upper peat. 10YR2/2.
0.86–0.31   Barroway Drove Beds (fen clay). 10YR5/1.
0.31–0.21   Buried soil; sandy loam. 5YR6/2.
0.21+   Sand and fine gravel of Fen gravels. 10YR6/4.

Profile 3:
1.43–0.64   Upper peat.

0.64–0.41   Fen clay.
0.41–0.17   Buried soil.
0.17+   Fen gravels.

Profile 5:
1.11–0.56   Upper peat.
0.56–0.36   Fen clay.
0.36–0.26   Buried soil.
0.26+   Fen gravels.

Dyke 45

Profile 1:
0.73–0.51   Peaty alluvium. 10YR4/2.
0.51 to -0.95   Barroway Drove Beds (fen clay). 10YR5/1.
-0.95 to -1.11   Buried soil; sandy/silty loam with a few gravel pebbles. 10YR6/6.
-1.11+   Sands and gravels of March Gravels. 10YR7/6.

Profile 2:
0.42–0.10   Peaty alluvium.
0.10 to -0.64   Fen clay.
-0.64 to -0.92   Basal peat with bog oaks. 10YR2/1.
-0.92 to -1.12   Buried soil.
-1.12+   March Gravels.

Profile 3:
0.49–0.18   Peaty alluvium.
0.18 to -0.79   Fen clay.
-0.79 to -1.19   Basal peat with bog oaks.
-1.19 to -1.28   Buried soil.
-1.28+   March Gravels.

Notes:

This dyke reveals the northwards extent of the Oakhurst Farm 'island'; the 'island' dips away beneath deep marine deposits between profiles 2 and 3.

Dyke 46

Profile 2:
0.60–0.30   Peaty alluvium. 10YR4/2.
0.30 to -0.12   Barroway Drove Beds (fen clay). 10YR5/1.
-0.12 to -0.15   Basal peat lens. 10YR2/1.
-0.15 to -0.24   Buried soil; sandy loam with a few scattered gravel pebbles.
-0.24 to -0.96   Sand with some fine gravel (March Gravels). 10YR7/6.
-0.96+   Silty clay with fine gravel and ice wedge cracks (March Gravels). 10YR7/1.

Notes:

The small fen 'island' revealed in this dyke and in dyke 45 is about 100m across. A large roddon delimits its southeastern edge. The basal peat on the western edge of the roddon has been sampled for pollen analysis. The buried soil at profile 2 was sampled for soil micromorphology.

Dyke 47

Profile 2:
0.35 to -0.01   Peaty alluvium. 10YR4/2.
-0.01 to -0.83   Barroway Drove Beds (fen clay). 10YR5/1.
-0.83 to -1.03   Basal peat. 10YR2/1.
-1.03 to -1.10   Buried soil; sandy loam. 10YR6/6.
-1.10+   Sand and gravel (March Gravels). 10YR7/6.

Profile 3:
0.52–0.15   Peaty alluvium.
0.15 to -0.75   Fen clay.
-0.75 to -0.80   Basal peat lens.
-0.80 to -0.91   Buried soil.
-0.91+   March Gravels.

Notes:

The 'island' is not visible in this dyke, indeed the subsoil has dipped steeply to the south (by about 1m). Dykes 48 and 49 continue this section.

Dyke 48

Profile 1:
0.69–0.29	Peaty alluvium. 10YR4/2.
0.29–0.13	Barroway Drove Beds (fen clay). 10YR5/1.
0.13–0.06	Basal peat lens. 10YR2/1.
0.06 to -0.15	Buried soil; sandy loam. 10YR6/6.
-0.15+	Sand (March Gravels).

Profile 2:
0.43–0.29	Peaty alluvium.
0.29–0.19	Fen clay.
0.19–0.14	Basal peat lens.
0.14 to -0.13	Buried soil.
-0.13+	March Gravels.

Profile 3:
0.39–0.14	Peaty alluvium.
0.14 to -0.19	Fen clay.
-0.19 to -0.25	Basal peat lens.
-0.25 to -0.34	Buried soil.
-0.34	March Gravels.

Notes:

The subsoil/buried soil level is beginning to rise as the dyke profile continues southwards to the Eye peninsula. This section is continued in Dyke 49.

Dyke 49

Profile 1:
0.46–0.14	Peaty alluvium. 10YR4/2.
0.14 to -0.20	Barroway Drove Beds (fen clay). 10YR5/1.
-0.20 to -0.31	Basal peat lens. 10YR2/2.
-0.31 to -0.44	Buried soil; sandy loam with a few gravel pebbles. 10YR6/6.
-0.44+	Sand and gravel (March Gravels).

Profile 2:
0.45–0.13	Peaty alluvium.
0.13 to -0.15	Fen clay.
-0.15 to -0.24	Basal peat lens.
-0.24 to -0.41	Buried soil.
-0.41+	March Gravels.

Profile 3:
0.76–0.55	Peaty alluvium.
0.55–0.47	Fen clay.
0.47–0.30	Buried soil.
0.30+	March Gravels.

Profile 4:
0.98–0.60	Peaty alluvium.
0.60–0.48	Fen clay.
0.48–0.36	Buried soil.
0.36+	March Gravels.

Profile 5:
0.98–0.64	Peaty alluvium.
0.64–0.50	Buried soil.
0.50+	March Gravels.

Profile 6:
1.87–1.53	Peaty alluvium.
1.53–1.38	Buried soil.
1.38+	March Gravels.
Notes:

The subsoil/buried soil rises onto the Eye peninsula between profiles 2 and 3 in this dyke.

Dyke 1

Profile 1:
0.95–0.55	Humified upper peat. 10YR2/2.
0.55–0.35	Barroway Drove Beds (fen clay). 10YR5/1.
0.35–0.28	Basal (wood) peat. 10YR2/1.
0.28–0.18	Upper horizon of buried soil; sandy loam. 5YR5/2.
0.18 to -0.52	Lower horizon of buried soil; sandy loam. 7.5YR6/2.
-0.52+	Silty clay with sand and gravel (March Gravels). 10YR7/4.

Profile 2: similar to profile 1

Profile 3:
1.0–0.65	Humified upper peat.
0.65–0.55	Fen clay.
0.55–0.48	Basal peat.
0.48–0.35	Upper horizon of buried soil.
0.35 to -0.52	Lower horizon of buried soil.
-0.52+	March Gravels.
Notes:

Samples for micromorphological analysis were taken from profile 2.

Dyke 2

Profile 2:
0.65–0.40	Humified upper peat. 10YR2/2.
0.40–0.30	Barroway Drove Beds (fen clay). 10YR5/1.
0.30–0.20	Basal (wood) peat. 10YR2/1.
0.20–0.08	Upper horizon of buried soil; sandy loam. 5YR5/2.
0.08 to -0.62	Lower horizon of buried soil; sandy loam. 7.5YR6/2.
-0.62+	Silty clay with sand and gravel (March Gravels). 10YR7/4.

Profile 3:
0.72–0.45	Humified upper peat.
0.45–0.42	Lens of fen clay.
0.42–0.35	Basal peat.
0.35–0.22	Upper horizon of buried soil.
0.22 to -0.62	Lower horizon of buried soil.
-0.62+	March Gravels.

Dyke 3

Profile 1:
0.35 to -0.05	Humified upper peat. 10YR2/2.
-0.05 to -0.30	Barroway Drove Beds (fen clay). 10YR5/1.
-0.30 to -0.45	Basal peat. 10YR2/1.
-0.45+	March Gravels.

Dyke 12

Profile 1:
1.49–0.88	Peaty alluvium, merging with humified upper peat. 10YR3/2.
0.88–0.77	Buried soil; sandy loam with gravel pebbles. 2.5YR5/0; 10YR6/3.
0.77+	Silty clay, sand and gravel of Fen gravels. 10YR6/8.

Profile 3:
1.73–0.93	Peaty alluvium merging with humified upper peat.
0.93–0.83	Fen clay.
0.83–0.81	Organic (peaty) lens.

0.81–0.72	Buried soil.
0.72+	Fen gravels.

Profile 6:

1.75–0.88	Peaty alluvium merging with humified upper peat.
0.88–0.75	Fen clay.
0.75–0.73	Organic (peaty) lens.
0.73–0.60	Buried soil.
0.60+	Fen gravels.

Profile 8:

1.83–0.89	Peaty alluvium merging with humified upper peat.
0.89–0.78	Fen clay.
0.78–0.76	Organic (peaty) lens.
0.76–0.66	Buried soil.
0.66+	Fen gravels.

Profile 10:

1.92–0.92	Peaty alluvium merging with humified upper peat.
0.92–0.80	Fen clay.
0.80–0.78	Organic (peaty) lens.
0.78–0.62	Buried soil.
0.62+	Fen gravels.

Dyke 15

Profile 1:

1.98–0.79	Peaty alluvium merging with humified upper peat. 10YR3/2; 10YR2/1.
0.79–0.55	Barroway Drove Beds (fen clay). 10YR5/1.
0.55–0.52	Organic (peaty) lens. 7.5YR2.5/0.
0.52–0.43	Buried soil; sandy loam with gravel pebbles. 10YR4/1.
0.43+	Silty clay with sand and gravel (Fen gravels). 10YR5/6.

Profile 2:

1.53–0.83	Peaty alluvium merging with humified peat.
0.83–0.72	Fen clay.
0.72–0.70	Organic (peaty) lens.
0.70–0.51	Buried soil.
0.51+	
	Fen gravels.

Profile 3:

1.54–0.88	Peaty alluvium merging with humified upper peat.
0.88–0.53	Fen clay.
0.53–0.50	Organic (peaty) lens.
0.50–0.30	Buried soil.
0.30+	Fen gravels.

Profile 4:

1.65–0.75	Peaty alluvium merging with humified upper peat.
0.75–0.38	Fen clay.
0.38–0.35	Organic (peaty) lens.
0.35–0.18	Buried soil.
0.18+	Fen gravels.

Dyke 11

Profile 2:

1.96–1.24	Peaty alluvium. 10YR2/2.
1.24–1.11	Buried soil; sandy loam with scattered gravel pebbles. 10YR4/3.
1.11+	Sand and gravel (Fen gravels).

Profile 5:

1.74–1.13	Peaty alluvium.
1.13–0.95	Buried soil.
0.95+	Fen gravels.

Profile 7:

1.68–1.03	Peaty alluvium.
1.03–0.92	Buried soil.
0.92+	Fen gravels.

Profile 9:

2.0–0.91	Peaty alluvium.
0.91–0.76	Buried soil.
0.76+	Fen gravels.

Profile 10:

2.26–1.18	Peaty alluvium.
1.18–0.90	Buried soil.
0.90+	Fen gravels.

Profile 12:

1.57–0.96	Peaty alluvium.
0.96–0.84	Buried soil.
0.84+	Fen gravels.

Profile 14:

1.77–1.04	Peaty alluvium.
1.04–0.82	Buried soil.
0.82+	Fen gravels.

Dyke 52

Profile 1:

1.25–0.50	Younger Barroway Drove Beds (marine silty clay). 10YR6/2.
0.50–0.04	Older Barroway Drove Beds (fen clay). 10YR5/1.
0.04 to -0.24	Buried soil; sandy loam with gravel pebbles. 10YR5/6.
-0.24+	Sand and gravel (March Gravels).

Profile 2:

0.72 to -0.30	Marine silty clay.
-0.30 to -0.18	Fen clay.
-0.18 to -0.20	Basal peat lens. 10YR2/2.
-0.20 to -0.47	Buried soil.
-0.47+	March Gravels.

Profile 3:

0.74–0.37	Marine silty clay.
0.37 to -0.33	Fen clay.
-0.33 to -0.36	Basal peat lens.
-0.36 to -0.62	Buried soil.
-0.62+	March Gravels.

Profile 4:

0.35 to -0.08	Marine silty clay.
-0.08 to -0.45	Fen clay.
-0.45 to -0.53	Basal peat lens.
-0.53 to -0.73	Buried soil.
-0.73+	March Gravels.

Profile 5:

0.65 to -0.30	Marine silty clay.
-0.30 to -0.91	Fen clay.
-0.91 to -1.05	Buried soil.
-1.05+	March Gravels.

Notes:

From profile 5 to 1, moving from northeast to southwest, the March Gravels subsoil gradually rises towards Thorney 'island'.

Dyke 50

Profile 4:

-0.20 to -0.50	Younger Barroway Drove Beds (marine silty clay). 10YR6/2.
-0.50 to -0.84	Barroway Drove Beds (fen clay). 10YR5/1.

-0.84 to -1.07   Basal (wood) peat. 10YR2/1.
-1.07+   Buried soil; sandy loam; merging with sand and gravel (March Gravels). 10YR6/8.

Profile 5:
-0.03 to -0.33   Marine silty clay.
-0.33 to -0.77   Fen clay.
-0.77 to -1.01   Basal (wood) peat.
-1.01+   Buried soil.

Profile 6:
0 to -0.47   Marine silty clay.
-0.47 to -1.05   Fen clay.
-1.05 to -1.26   Basal (wood) peat.
-1.26+   Buried soil.

Profile 7:
0.27 to -0.40   Marine silty clay.
-0.40 to -0.62   Fen clay.
-0.62 to -0.85   Basal (wood) peat.
-0.85+   Buried soil.

Notes:

The stratigraphy in these profiles is more or less the same as in Dykes 44 and 52. The definition of the boundary between the Younger and Older Barroway Drove Beds is indistinct. The buried soil is at the present day water table.

Dyke 44

Profile 1:
0.63–0.09   Younger Barroway Drove Beds (marine silty clay). 10YR6/2.
0.09 to -0.97   Barroway Drove Beds (fen clay). 10YR5/1; 5YR4/6 (mottled).
-0.97 to -1.07   Basal (wood) peat. 10YR2/1.
-1.07 to -1.23   Buried soil; sandy loam with a few gravel pebbles. 10YR5/6.
-1.23+   Sand and gravel (March Gravels). 10YR6/8.

Profile 2:
0.93–0.28   Marine silty clay.
0.28 to -0.70   Fen clay.
-0.70 to -0.87   Basal (wood) peat.
-0.87 to -1.10   Buried soil.
-1.10+   March Gravels.

Profile 3:
0.72–0.14   Marine silty clay.
0.14 to -1.12   Fen clay.
-1.12 to -1.22   Basal (wood) peat.
-1.22 to -1.53   Buried soil.
-1.53+   March Gravels.

Profile 4:
0.80 to -0.11   Marine silty clay.
-0.11 to -1.10   Fen clay.

Profile 5:
1.4–0.91   Peaty alluvium. 10YR4/4.
0.91 to -0.24   Marine silty clay.
-0.24 to -1.14   Fen clay.
-1.14 to -1.20   Basal (wood) peat.
-1.20 to -1.25   Buried soil.
-1.25+   March Gravels.

Profile 6:
0.98–0.59   Peaty alluvium.
0.59 to -0.15   Marine silty clay.
-0.15 to -0.18   Peat lens.
-0.18 to -0.99   Fen clay.
-0.99 to -1.11   Basal (wood) peat.
-1.11 to -1.31   Buried soil.
-1.31+   March Gravels.

Profile 7:
0.95–0.63   Peaty alluvium.
0.63–0.14   Marine silty clay.
0.14–0.11   Peat lens.
0.11 to -0.63   Fen clay.
-0.63 to -0.76   Basal (wood) peat.
-0.76 to -0.92   Buried soil.
-0.92+   March Gravels.

Notes:

Dyke 44 is a continuation to the southeast of Dyke 41. The subsoil is slowly beginning to rise westwards, as it reaches the northeast of Thorney 'island'. The buried soil/subsoil is at about the same height OD as the 'island' centred on profile 2 in Dyke 41.

Dyke 41

Profile 1:
0.56 to -1.05   Younger Barroway Drove Beds (marine silty clay). 10YR6/2.
-1.05 to -2.21   Barroway Drove Beds (fen clay). 10YR5/1.
-2.21 to -2.55   Basal (wood) peat. 10YR2/1.

Profile 2:
1.1 to -0.30   Marine silty clay.
-0.30 to -0.80   Fen clay.
-0.80 to -0.85   Basal peat lens.
-0.85 to -1.10   Buried soil; sandy loam with a few scattered gravel pebbles. 10YR6/4.
-1.10+   Sand and gravel subsoil of 'island'.

Notes:

This is the Morris Fen 'island' site. Samples for micromorphological analysis were taken from the buried soil at this profile.

Profile 3:
0.48 to -0.24   Marine silty clay.
-0.24 to -2.27   Fen clay.
-2.27+   Basal (wood) peat.

Profile 4:
0.68 to -0.18   Marine silty clay.
-0.18 to -1.69   Fen clay.
-1.69 to -1.82   Basal (wood) peat.
-1.82 to -1.88   Buried soil.
-1.88+   Sand and gravel subsoil.

Profile 5:
0.56 to -0.20   Marine silty clay.
-0.20 to -0.92   Fen clay.
-0.92 to -1.06   Basal (wood) peat.
-1.06 to -1.10   Buried soil.
-1.10+   Sand and gravel subsoil.

Profile 6:
0.53 to -0.22   Marine silty clay.
-0.22 to -0.94   Fen clay.
-0.94 to -1.0   Basal (wood) peat.
-1.0 to -1.66   Buried soil.
-1.66+   Sand and gravel subsoil.

Dyke 43

Profile 1:
0.43 to -0.16   Marine silty clay.
-0.16 to -1.21   Fen clay, with a peat lens at -0.70 to -0.73.
-1.21 to -1.34   Basal (wood) peat.
-1.34 to -1.43   Buried soil.
-1.43+   Sand and gravel subsoil.

Notes:

The rise in the subsoil in this dyke and profiles 5 and 6 in Dyke 41, and the presence of a well preserved buried soil, suggests the existence of another lower 'island' in these two dykes, as well as the one centred on profile 2 in Dyke 41.

Dyke 42

Profile 1:

0.65 to -0.68	Younger Barroway Drove Beds (marine silty clay). 10YR6/2.
-0.68 to -2.40	Barroway Drove Beds (fen clay). 10YR5/1.
-2.40+	Basal (wood) peat.

Profile 2:

0.96 to -0.51	Marine silty clay.
-0.51 to -2.30	Fen clay.
-2.30+	Basal (wood) peat.

Notes:

This dyke is a continuation of Dyke 41.

Dyke 30

Profile 2:

2.51–2.14	Humified upper peat. 10YR2/2.
2.14+	Sand and gravel (March Gravels). 10YR6/8.

Dyke 31

Profile 1:

2.11–1.71	Humified upper peat. 10YR2/2.
1.71+	March Gravels. 10YR6/8.

Dyke 32

Profile 1:

2.20–1.86	Humified upper peat. 10YR2/2.
1.86+	March Gravels. 10YR6/8.

Profile 2:

2.75–2.66	Humified upper peat.
2.66+	March Gravels.

Profile 3:

2.80–2.70	Humified upper peat.
2.70+	March Gravels.

Profile 4:

2.38–2.09	Humified upper peat.
2.09+	March Gravels.

Profile 5:

1.71–1.39	Humified upper peat.
1.39–1.01	Younger Barroway Drove Beds (marine silty clay). 10YR6/6.
1.01+	March Gravels.

Profile 6:

2.13–1.83	Humified upper peat.
1.83–1.61	Marine silty clay.
1.61–0.51	Barroway Drove Beds (fen clay). 10YR5/1.
0.51+	March Gravels.

Notes:

Profiles 1 to 4 of Dyke 32 and profile 2 of Dyke 30 cross the ridge of March Gravels joining the Eye peninsula and Thorney 'island'. Hall's site Th23 is situated on this ridge of high ground, *c.* 20m to the north of profile 2, Dyke 30.

Dyke 32

Profile 2:

1.41–1.16	Humified upper peat. 10YR2/2.
1.16–0.76	Younger Barroway Drove Beds (marine silty clay). 10YR6/6.
0.76–0.69	Barroway Drove Beds (fen clay). 10YR5/1.
0.69–0.61	Basal (wood) peat. 10YR2/1.
0.61–0.46	Buried soil; sandy/silt loam. 7.5YR4/4.
0.46+	Silty clay above sands and gravels (March Gravels). 10YR5/1.

Notes:

The oak, plank-built footpath (Guy's Fen) was discovered at this profile at the base of the fen clay.

Dyke 17

Profile 2:

0.03 to -0.92	Younger Barroway Drove Beds (marine silty clay). 10YR6/6.
-0.92 to -1.33	Barroway Drove Beds (fen clay). 10YR5/1.
-1.33 to -1.51	Basal (wood) peat. 10YR2/1.
-1.51 to -1.59	Buried soil; sandy loam (only evident intermittently). 7.5YR4/4.

Dyke 18

Profile 1:

0.20 to -0.54	Younger Barroway Drove Beds (marine silty clay). 10YR6/6.
-0.54 to -1.50	Barroway Drove Beds (fen clay). 10YR5/1.
-1.50 to -1.32	Basal (wood) peat. 10YR2/1.

Profile 2:

0.07 to -0.56	Marine silty clay.
-0.56 to -0.96	Fen clay.
-0.96 to -1.09	Basal (wood) peat.
-1.09+	Silty clay, sand and gravel subsoil (March Gravels). 10YR5/1.

Profile 3:

0.09 to -0.58	Marine silty clay.
-0.58 to -0.81	Fen clay.
-0.81 to -0.91	Buried soil.
-0.91+	March Gravels.

Profile 4:

-0.06 to -0.66	Marine silty clay.
-0.66 to -0.88	Fen clay.
-0.88 to -0.98	Basal (wood) peat.
-0.98 to -1.10	Buried soil.
-1.10+	March Gravels.

Notes:

Dykes 17 and 18 have stratigraphies representative of much of the fen in Thorney parish. The March Gravels are in places overlain by till or Boulder Clay.

Dyke 8

Profile 1:

1.70–1.24	Humified upper peat. 5YR2.5/1.
1.24–1.18	Buried soil; sandy loam. 5YR4/2.
1.18+	Oxidised sand and gravel (March Gravels). 10YR6/6.

Profile 3:

1.48–1.14	Humified upper peat.
1.14–1.07	Upper horizon of buried soil; a sandy/silt loam. 5YR4/2.
1.07–1.01	Lower horizon of buried soil; a bleached sandy loam. 10YR6/4.
1.01+	March Gravels.

Profile 5:

1.24–0.62	Humified upper peat.
0.62–0.49	Upper horizon of buried soil.
0.49–0.30	Lower horizon of buried soil.
0.30+	March Gravels.

Profile 7:

0.54–0.29	Humified upper peat.
0.29–0.17	Buried soil.
0.17+	March Gravels.

Profile 9:

0.72–0.05	Humified upper peat.
0.05 to -0.31	Buried soil.
-0.31+	March Gravels.

Notes:

The profiles in Dyke 8 illustrate a section through Northey 'island'. A well preserved buried soil, often with two horizons evident, is visible. It was sampled for micromorphological analysis at profile 5.

Dyke 9

Profile 1:

3.17–2.54	Peaty alluvium. 10YR2/1.
2.54–2.31	Upper horizon of buried soil; an organic sandy loam. 10YR4/2.
2.31–2.19	Lower horizon of buried soil; a bleached sandy loam. 10YR6/4.
2.19+	Silt, sand and gravels (undulating) (March Gravels). 10YR6/6.

Profile 2:

2.16–1.71	Peaty alluvium.
1.71–1.60	Upper horizon of buried soil.
1.60–1.54	Lower horizon of buried soil.
1.54+	March Gravels.

Profile 3:

1.91–1.29	Peaty alluvium.
1.29–1.18	Upper horizon of buried soil.
1.18–1.02	Middle horizon of buried soil; a reduced sandy loam. 10YR6/2.
1.02–0.93	Lower horizon of buried soil.
0.93+	March Gravels.

Profile 6:

2.64–2.20	Peaty alluvium.
2.20–2.12	Upper horizon of buried soil.
2.12–2.01	Lower horizon of buried soil.
2.01+	March Gravels.

Profile 12:

1.46–1.35	Peaty alluvium.
1.35–1.07	Humified peat. 10YR2/2.
1.07–1.02	Buried soil.
1.02+	March Gravels.

Notes:

This dyke exhibits similar profiles to those in Dyke 8, which is a continuation of Dyke 9. Numerous archaeological features are evident as the 'island' dips westwards. The buried soil at profile 2 was sampled for micromorphological analysis, as was the lens adjacent to profile 12.

Dyke 10

Profile 1:

1.68–1.30	Humified peat and alluvium. 10YR2/1.
1.30–0.28	Humified peat. 10YR2/1.
0.28–0.24	Buried soil; sandy loam. 7.5YR3/2.
0.24+	Silt loam, sand and flint pebbles (Nene First Terrace). 7.5YR5/8.

Profile 4:

1.61–1.30	Peaty alluvium.
1.30–0.32	Humified peat.
0.32–0.25	Buried soil.
0.25+	Terrace subsoil.

Profile 6:

0.96–0.33	Peaty alluvium.
0.33 to -0.17	Humified peat.
-0.17 to -0.26	Buried soil.
-0.26+	Terrace subsoil.

Profile 10:

0.81–0.32	Peaty alluvium.
0.32–0.05	Humified peat.
0.05 to -0.02	Buried soil.
-0.02+	Terrace subsoil.

Profile 15:

2.0–1.70	Peaty alluvium.
1.70–1.40	Oxidised alluvial silty clay.
1.40–1.0	Humified peat.
1.0–0.95	Alluvial silt lens.
0.95 to -0.20	Peat.
-0.20 to -0.34	Silty clay loam immature buried soil.
-0.34+	Terrace subsoil.

Dyke 53

Profile 1:

-0.16 to -0.64	Humified upper peat. 10YR2/1.
-0.64+	Barroway Drove Beds (fen clay). 10YR5/1.

Profile 7:

0.42 to -0.08	Humified upper peat.
-0.08 to -0.44	Fen clay.
-0.44 to -0.53	Buried soil; silt/sandy loam with even fine gravel. 10YR5/6.
-0.53+	Sand, silty clay and gravel, with ice wedges visible (March Gravels). 10YR6/2; 10YR6/6.

Profile 12:

0.80–0.44	Humified upper peat.
0.44–0.42	Fen clay.
0.42 to -0.26	Buried soil.
-0.26	March Gravels.

Notes:

The fen clay thins and disappears to the west of profile 12.

Appendix V: Radiocarbon dates

Introduction
This appendix is in two parts. The first considers the context of dates obtained prior to the present survey; the second discusses dates obtained as part of the dyke survey.

I. Previously obtained radiocarbon dates: context and significance

Introduction
The following information has kindly been supplied by Dr A. Horton of the British Geological Survey. The dates from Park Farm, Elm Tree Farm and Plash Farm have the most reliable contextual information. All dates discussed below are listed in Table 1, together with the available calibrated dates.

Park Farm
These dates are from peat horizons exposed in a freshly dug pit at Park Farm, Tydd St. Giles (TF 5401631608). Quoted sample depth increments (in metres) relate to the present ground surface. Collected in 1979 and submitted by R.J. Wyatt, Institute of Geological Science, London.

SRR–1755. 2270 ± 50BP
Park   Farm. Basal material in thin peat band *c.* 5–8cm thick.
0.93 to 0.98m
(0.31 to 0.26m
OD)

SRR–1756. 3050 ± 50BP
Park   Farm. Basal material in peat band *c.* 18cm thick.
1.71 to 1.76m
(-0.47 to -
0.52m OD)

Elm Tree Farm
SRR–1757. 7690 ± 400BP
Elm   Tree Peat 9.17 to 9.20m depth (-9.11 to -9.14m OD) in
Farm. borehole no. TF 41 SW/10 Elm Tree Farm, Tydd
St Giles, (TF 54010 31487). Collected in 1980 by
A. Horton, and submitted by R.J. Wyatt.

Gedney Hill
SRR–1758. 3250 ± 50BP
Gedney Hill. Peat at base of band within Flandrian clay sequence exposed at 1.7m depth in dyke section
600m SW of Gedney Hill Church, (TF 53344
31084). Collected in 1979 by C. Wilcox, and
submitted by R.J. Wyatt.

Plash Farm
Wood and peat within Flandrian clay sequence in the vicinity of Plash Farm, Murrow, near Wisbech. Collected in 1979 by J. Zalaciewicz and R.J. Wyatt, and submitted by R.J. Wyatt.

SRR–1759. 2510 ± 50BP
Plash Farm. Wood in 0.5m thick peat band at *c.* 0.8m below the
present ground surface (*c.* 0.10m OD) 300m SW
of Plash Farm (TF5387530525).

SRR–1760. 4520 ± 70BP
Plash Farm. Peat at 4.98m in depth (*c.* -4.13m OD) in borehole
no. TF zone/16 (TF5387330530).

SRR–1761. 6080 ± 60BP
Plash Farm. Peat at *c.* 9.3m depth (*c.* -8.45m OD) in borehole
no. TF zone/16.

Sycamore Farm
Peat in bands within and at the base of Flandrian clays recovered from borehole no. TF 31 SW/12, Sycamore Farm, Gedney Hill (TF 53370 31113). Quoted sample depth increments (in m) relate to present ground surface. Collected in 1980 by A. Horton, and submitted by R.J. Wyatt.

SRR–1762. 4460 ± 80BP
Sycamore
Farm. 5.04 to
5.07m.

SRR–1763. 6010 ± 200BP
Sycamore
Farm. 7.70 to
7.75m.

Guyhirn Wash
Peat in band within Flandrian clay sequence recovered from borehole no. TF 30 SE/43, Guyhirn Wash (TF 53810 30198). Quoted sample depths (in m) relate to the present ground surface. Collected in 1979, and submitted by R.J. Wyatt.

SRR–1764. 3080 ± 200BP
Guyhirn Wash.
2.68m.

SRR–1765. 4340 ± 60BP
Guyhirn Wash.
7.27m.

South Farm
SRR–1766. 4310 ± 140BP
South Farm Wood in the base of a peat deposit exposed at *c.*
2.1m below the present day ground surface in
dyke section 650m SW of South Farm, near Thorney, (TF 53024 30260). Collected in 1979, and
submitted by R.J. Wyatt.

'The Firs', Werrington (Newborough Fen)
Wood in peat bands exposed in dyke section 700m NNE of 'The Firs', Werrington (TF 51953 30524). Quoted sample depths (in m) relate to the present ground surface. Collected in 1977, and submitted by R.J. Wyatt.

SRR–1767. 2220 ± 50BP
'The   Firs',
Werrington.
0.8m.

SRR–1768. 3390 ± 40BP
The Firs', Wer-
rington. 2.0m.

II. Dates obtained for the present survey

Introduction
The following dates have been supplied by the Harwell Laboratory as a part of English Heritage's radiocarbon date quota. In general, the four dates obtained are in agreement with the main series of fenland dates recently produced by Dr R. Switsur of the Godwin Laboratory, University of Cambridge (Waller forthcoming).

Crowtree Farm
Three dates from material in Trench 2 (TF52133061) were submitted. Collected in 1985; and submitted by C. French.

Har–8513.	3660 ± 60 BP
Crowtree Farm	Peat from the thin exposure of basal peat which
0.24-0.28m	overlies the buried soil, and is overlain by fen clay.
OD	

Har–8510	3740 ± 100 BP
Crowtree Farm	Organic matter recovered from the wet-seiving of
0.24-0.19 m	the upper 5cm of the buried soil.
OD	

Har–8913	3190 ± 90 BP
Crowtree Farm	Charcoal from the upper 5cm of the buried soil.
0.24-0.19mOD	

Borough Fen Site 7

One date was obtained from the ploughsoil/occupation horizon at the ringwork site, as exposed in the dykeside (of Dyke 5) at profile 2 (TF19200740). Collected in 1982; and submitted by C. French.

Har–8512 Bo-	2090 ± 80 BP
rough Fen Site	Charcoal recovered by wet-seiving of the plough-
7 3.4–3.0m OD	soil/occupation horizon; and sealed by alluvium.

Northey

One date was obtained from a feature sealed by upper peat as revealed on the southwestern edge of Northey 'island' in Dyke 9, profile 2 (TF52302983). Collected in 1982; and submitted by C. French.

Har–8511	2800 ± 100 BP
Northey 0.85–	Charcoal recovered by wet-seiving of a sealed
0.95m OD	archaeological feature.

Appendix VI: Soil micromorphological descriptions

Crowtree Farm (Dyke 14)

The micromorphological description of the upper half of the buried soil (c. 2–7.5cm) is as follows (Pls II and III):

Structure: apedal; granular to bridged grain; Porosity: c. 20–30%; mainly vughs (c. 15–25%), round to sub-round, smooth to weakly serrate, 100–300µm; few channels (c. 5%), smooth to weakly serrate, 2–3mm, 100–400µm; *Mineral Components*: limit 100µm; coarse/fine fraction: 30/70; coarse fraction: medium quartz (c. 30%), sub-angular to sub-rounded, 150–300µm, well sorted; fine fraction: very fine (c. 20%) and fine (c. 30%) sub- angular to sub-rounded quartz, 50–150µm, well sorted; some silt (c. 10%) and clay (c. 10%); dark reddish brown (PPL), reddish brown (RL); slightly speckled; *Organic Component*: c. 5%; mainly amorphous staining of groundmass, and in some cases obscuring it; very few cell tissue fragments, fine flecks of charcoal; very few ferruginised, non-laminated, weakly birefringent, dusty/dirty clay coating pseudomorphs of roots/stems in groundmass; *Groundmass*: coarse: undifferentiated, porphyric; fine: speckled, low to moderate birefringence; related: porphyric; *Pedofeatures: Excrements*: few, black rounded pellets, c. 50µm, in root/stem pseudomorphs; *Textural*: (1) rare (c. 1%) moderately birefringent, sub-angular fragments of limpid clay in the groundmass and void space, c. 50–100µm; (2) very rare (< 1%) laminated, speckled, moderately birefringent, dusty clay coatings of grains and as infills of former plant roots/stems, and in the groundmass; (3) occasional (c. 5%) dusty, non-laminated coatings of grains, in the groundmass and void space; (4) many of the dusty coatings (c. 50%) in the groundmass

and void space contain amorphous organic matter giving them a 'dirty' appearance; (5) one channel contains successive, 'crescentic' infills of ferruginised dusty clay; *Fabric*: few channels have loose, discontinuous infills of very fine sand; *Amorphous*: very few (c. 1%) sesquioxide nodules, c. 50–150µm; amorphous sesquioxide impregnation of the fine fraction, c. 30–50%.

The micromorphological description of the lower half of the buried soil (c. 8–12cm) is as follows (Pl. II; M. Pl. 59):

Structure: apedal; massive to granular; *Porosity*: c. 10–15%; mainly vughs (c. 8–13%), round to sub-round, smooth to weakly serrate, 50–400µm; few (c. 2%) channels, smooth to weakly serrate, 100–400µm; *Mineral Components*: limit 100µm; coarse/fine ratio: 30/70; coarse fraction: medium (c. 30%) quartz, sub-rounded to sub- angular, 150–300µm, well sorted; few mica grains present; fine fraction: very fine (c. 20%) and fine (c. 25%) quartz, sub-angular to sub-rounded, 50–150µm, well sorted; some silt (c. 10%) and clay (c. 15%); golden reddish brown (PPL), golden brown (RL); slightly speckled; *Organic Component*: < 5%; mainly amorphous staining of fines in groundmass, and often obscuring it; few fine flecks of charcoal in groundmass; few ferruginised, non-laminated, weakly birefringent, dusty/dirty clay coating pseudomorphs of roots/stems; *Groundmass*: coarse: undifferentiated, porphyric; fine: speckled, low to moderate birefringence; some granostriated, 20–50µm thick, moderate birefringence; related: porphyric; *Pedofeatures: Textural*: (1) very rare (< 1%) moderately birefringent, sub-angular fragments of limpid clay in groundmass; (2) very rare (< 1%) laminated, weakly speckled dusty clay coatings of grains and void space; (3) many (c. 5–10%) non-laminated dusty coatings of grains and groundmass; (4) many of the dusty coatings (c. 50%) contain amorphous organic matter giving them a 'dirty' appearance; *Fabric*: few loose, discontinuous infills of channels with very fine and fine quartz grains; very few (1%) medium sand size, sub-rounded aggregates of silt with fine amorphous organic matter and little clay, c. 100µm; *Amorphous*: few sesquioxide nodules, 50–100µm; amorphous sesquioxide impregnation of the fine fraction (c. 50–75%).

Oakhurst Farm (Dyke 46)

The micromorphological description of the upper half of the buried soil (c. 2–7cm) is as follows:

Structure: apedal; massive to granular; *Porosity*: c. 5%; very dense fabric; mainly vughs, sub-round to irregular, smooth to weakly serrate, c. 50–400µm; few channels, smooth, 100–400µm; *Mineral Components*: limit 100µm; coarse/fine ratio: 30/70; coarse fraction: medium (c. 30%) quartz, sub-rounded to sub-angular, 150–250µm, moderately well sorted; fine fraction: very fine (c. 20%) and fine (c. 25%) quartz, sub-rounded to sub-angular, 50–150µm, moderately well sorted; some silt (c. 10%) and clay (c. 15%); golden to amber (PPL), reddish brown (RL); speckled; *Organic Components*: c. 5%; mainly amorphous staining of groundmass; very few fine flecks of charcoal in groundmass; few ferruginised, non-laminated, weakly birefringent, dusty/'dirty' clay coating pseudomorphs of roots/stems in groundmass; *Groundmass*: coarse: undifferentiated, porphyric; fine: mosaic-speckled to random striated, moderate birefringence; related: porphyric; *Pedofeatures: Textural*: (1) very rare (< 1%)

fragments of limpid clay, yellow, moderate birefringence; (2) very rare (< 1%) fragments of laminated dusty clay, yellow to red, high birefringence; (3) few (*c.* 5–10%) non-laminated dusty clay coatings of grains in the ground-mass and void space, with 5% in upper half and most dusty coatings in the lower half of the slide; (4) many of the dusty coatings (*c.* 25–50%) contain fine organic matter giving them a 'dirty' appearance particularly in the lower half of the slide; *Fabric:* very few loose discontinuous channel infills of fine sand size material; *Amorphous:* few (*c.* 2%) sesquioxide nodules, 50–100μm; zones of sesquioxide impregnation of groundmass.

The micromorphological description of the lower half of the buried soil (*c.* 8–14cm) is as follows (M. Pl. 60):

Structure: apedal; granular to massive; *Porosity:* <5%; very dense fabric; mainly vughs, round to sub-round, smooth to weakly serrate, 100–200μm; *Mineral Components:* limit 100μm; coarse/fine ratio: 20/80; coarse fraction: coarse (*c.* 2%) and medium (*c.* 18%) quartz, sub-rounded to sub-angular, 150–350μm, moderately well sorted; fine fraction: very fine (*c.* 25%) and fine (*c.* 30%) quartz, sub-rounded to sub-angular, 50–150μm, moderately well sorted; with *c.* 10% silt and *c.* 15% clay; golden brown (PPL), reddish brown (RL); speckled; *Organic Component:* <2%; very few fine flecks of charcoal in groundmass; small amounts of amorphous organic matter in groundmass; *Groundmass:* coarse: undifferentiated, porphyric; fine: mosaic-speckled, moderate birefringence; related: porphyric; *Pedofeatures: Textural:* (1) rare (< 1%) yellow, moderately birefringent, limpid clay coatings as fragments in the groundmass; (2) rare (< 1%) golden, laminated, moderately birefringent dusty clay coatings in the groundmass; (3) many (< 10%) golden red, non-lami-nated dusty clay coatings of grains, groundmass and void space; (4) about half of the dusty clay coatings contain amorphous organic matter giving them a 'dirty' appear-ance; (5) occasional (< 5%) red/black, 'layered' dusty/'dirty' coatings of the voids; (6) three 'crescentic' infills of a void space with ferruginised dusty clay, *c.* 75μm wide, *c.* 1mm apart; *Fabric:* a root channel infilled with similar groundmass to main fabric, but completely ses-quioxide impregnated, with distinct, irregular boundary, 2mm wide, 11mm long; *Amorphous:* very few (< 2%) sesquioxide nodules, 50–100μm; abundant zones of ses-quioxide impregnation of the groundmass (*c.* 50–75%).

Dyke 1

The micromorphological description of the upper horizon (*c.* 2–8cm) of the buried soil is as follows (M. Pl. 56):

Structure: apedal; massive to granular; *Porosity: c.* 5–10%; dominant (*c.* 75%) random, intrapedal channels, 50–100μm, walls partially accomodated, smooth to weakly serrated; frequent (*c.* 25%) vughs, 100–500μm, rounded to irregular, smooth to weakly serrated; *Mineral Components:* limit 100μm; coarse/fine ratio: 20/80; coarse fraction: medium (*c.* 18%) and coarse (*c.* 2%) quartz, sub-rounded to sub-angular, 150–1000μm, moder-ately well sorted; few opaque minerals and mica grains present; fine fraction: very fine (*c.* 40%) and fine (*c.* 25%) quartz, sub-rounded to sub-angular, 50–150μm, well sorted; little silt (*c.* 5%) and some clay (*c.* 10%); light grey brown (PPL), pale grey to light brown (RL); speckled; *Organic Component: c.* 25%; frequent (*c.* 15%) modern roots; few (*c.* 5%) fragments of plant tissue; many fine flecks of charcoal; very few (< 5%) large fragments of

charcoal, 150–300μm; few partial sesquioxide impreg-nated pseudomorphs of roots/stems; *Groundmass:* related distribution: porphyric; coarse: monic; fine: undifferen-tiated to reticulate striated; *Pedofeatures: Textural:* (1) rare (*c.* 1%) laminated dusty clay coatings of the ground-mass, weakly birefringent; (2) rare (*c.* 1%) fragments of non-laminated dusty clay in the groundmass and void space; *Depletion:* fine groundmass more or less depleted of amorphous organic matter; *Amorphous:* very few (< 5%) sesquioxide nodules, sub-rounded, 50–200μm.

The micromorphological description of the lower hori-zon of the buried soil is as follows (Pl. IV; M. Pls 57 and 58):

Structure: apedal; massive to granular, random; *Poros-ity: c.* 20%; dominant (*c.* 80%) random, intrapedal channels, 50–100μm, walls partially accomodated, smooth to weakly serrated; frequent (*c.* 20%) vughs, 100–1000μm, rounded to irregular, smooth to weakly serrated; *Mineral Components:* limit 100μm; coarse/fine ratio: 20/80; coarse fraction: medium (*c.* 20%) quartz, sub-rounded to sub-angular, 150–250μm, moderately well sorted; very few opaque and non-opaque minerals, flint and mica grains present; fine fraction: very fine (*c.* 35%) and fine (*c.* 20%) quartz, sub-rounded to sub-angular, 50–150μm; with *c.* 10% silt and *c.* 15% clay; medium to dark brown (PPL), light yellowish brown (RL); speckled; *Organic Component: c.* 5–10%; very few fine flecks of charcoal; very few fragments of charcoal, 150–300μm; very few fragments of plant tissue; very few sesquioxide impregnated pseudomorphs of roots/stems; *Groundmass:* related distribution: porphyric; coarse: monic; fine: paral-lel to reticulate striated to undifferentiated; *Pedofeatures: Textural:* abundant (*c.* 10–20%) coatings; (1) rare (< 2%) fragments of limpid clay in the groundmass; (2) occasional (*c.* 3–5%) laminated dusty clay coatings in the ground-mass, moderate birefringence, sharp to diffuse extinction; (3) many (*c.* 5–10%) non-laminated dusty clay coatings in discrete areas of the groundmass; (4) most of the dusty clay coatings (*c.* 50–75%) contain amorphous organic matter giving them a 'dirty' appearance; *Fabric:* rare (1–2%) channel infills of silt and fine sand size material; rare (< 2%) channel infills of fine sand size material in the dusty coatings; *Depletion:* some areas of groundmass depleted of clay coatings leaving predominantly fine sand size grain groundmass; *Amorphous:* zones of sesquioxide impregnation of groundmass; one nodule, *c.* 1800μm in diameter, rounded, with sharp boundaries, composed of silt, clay and fine flecks of charcoal; few (< 5%) rounded ferruginous nodules, 100–600μm.

Borough Fen Site 7 (Dyke 5)

The micromorphological description of the 'occupation horizon' material is as follows (Pls IX and X; M. Pls 47–50):

Structure: apedal; heterogeneous; *Porosity:* in fabric (1): *c.* 30%; 15% vughs, sub-rounded to irregular, smooth to weakly serrated, 100–1000μm; 5% vesicles, sub-rounded to irregular, smooth to weakly serrated, 1–5mm; 10% channels, irregular, walls partially accomodated, smooth to weakly serrated, 25–100μm and 0.5–2.0mm wide, 2–20mm long; in fabric (2): *c.* 10% vughs, sub-rounded to irregular, smooth to weakly serrated, 50–100μm; *Mineral Components:* fabric (1): limit 100μm; coarse/fine ratio: 20/80; coarse fraction: medium (10%) and fine (10%) quartz, sub-rounded to sub-angular,

100–250μm, random, unoriented; fine fraction: very fine (35%) quartz, sub-rounded to sub-angular, 50–100μm, random, unoriented; 35% silt and 5–10% clay; one-third of fines without silt and clay fractions; very weakly speckled; yellowish brown/greyish brown/greyish white (PPL), light greyish brown/orangey brown (RL); *c.* 50–70% of total fabric; other components: few fragments of leached bone, 1–2mm long; few phytoliths, equant or slightly prolate opal bodies, isotropic, <1mm in size; very rare nodule of vivianite, 50–100μm; fabric (2): limit 50μm; coarse/fine ratio: 20/80; coarse fraction: very fine (20%) quartz, sub-rounded to sub- angular, 50–100μm, random, unoriented; fine fraction: 60% silt and 10–20% clay; very weakly speckled; dark amber brown (PPL), light yellowish brown (RL); *c.* 30–50% of groundmass; *Organic Component*: frequent (*c.* 20–30%); 20–25% charcoal equally in fabrics (1) and (2), fine (25–100μm) and coarse (300–1000μm); 5–10% amorphous organic matter in groundmass, especially in fabric (2); *Ground-mass*: related: porphyric, undifferentiated; coarse material: monic; fine material: gefuric; weakly stipple-speckled (in fabrics (1) and (2)) and random striated (in fabric (1)); *Pedofeatures: Textural*: 1) very rare (< 2%) limpid clay in groundmass, yellow to orangey-red (CPL); 2) rare (2%) non-laminated dusty/'dirty' clay coatings of grains, groundmass and voids, yellowish-orange (CPL), micro-contrasted particles are mainly organic matter; *Fabric*: fabric (2) is also present as small aggregates forming loose, discontinuous infills in voids, 100–300μm; one irregular, papule-like aggregate, 2mm in diameter, composed of silty clay and very fine quartz, interrupted by channels and vughs, with many phytoliths; one rectilinear, papule-like aggregate composed of silt and very fine quartz, 1 × 2mm; *Amorphous*: *c.* 5% rolled clay aggregates in fabric (2), 50–100μm; *c.* 5% sesquioxide nodules in fabric (2), 25–100μm; amorphous zones of sesquioxide impregnation of groundmass (*c.* 25–50%), particularly of fabric (2); few amorphous iron infills of voids, partial to complete, orangey-red (PPL); common sesquioxide replacement of plant tissue.

The micromorphological description of the upper horizon of the buried soil is as follows (M. Pls 51 and 52):

Structure: apedal; homogeneous; single to compact grain; *Porosity*: *c.* 20%; vughs (10%), sub-rounded to irregular, 100–500μm, smooth to weakly serrated, random, unoriented; very few (2%) channels, irregular, walls partially accommodated, smooth to weakly serrated, 25–75μm in width, 0.5–20mm long, random, unoriented to perpendicular; *Mineral Components*: limit 100μm; coarse/fine ratio: 20/80; coarse fraction: medium (10%) and fine (10%) quartz, sub-rounded to sub-angular, 100–300μm, random, unoriented; fine fraction: very fine (40%) quartz, sub-rounded to sub-angular, 50–100μm, random, unoriented; 30% silt and 10% clay; yellowish brown (PPL), pale yellowish brown (RL); *Organic Component*: *c.* 5–10%; mainly fine (silt size) amorphous organic matter in fine fraction; and very fine flecks of charcoal in groundmass, 25–75μm; very rare (1%) large fragments of charcoal, 100–150μm; *Groundmass*: related: porphyric, undifferentiated; coarse material: monic; fine material: gefuric; weakly mosaic speckled to reticulate striated, discontinuous streaks, medium (20–100μm) thickness, 50–500μm in length; *Pedofeatures: Textural*: 1) rare (2%) limpid clay, of voids, grains and groundmass, weak bire-fringence, diffuse extinction, reddish orange (CPL); 2)

rare (2%) laminated dusty clay, of voids and groundmass, strong birefringence, diffuse extinction, yellow to reddish orange (CPL); 3) occasional (2–5%) non- laminated dusty clay, especially of groundmass, also grains and voids, yellow to yellowish red; *Fabric*: rare to occasional (2–5%), partial to complete infill of brown silt, very fine sand and amorphous organic matter in channels; *Amorphous*: rare (1%) sesquioxide nodules/silty clay aggregates, sub-rounded to sub-angular, 100–150μm, reddish brown to reddish black (CPL); zones of sesquioxide impregnation of fine fabric, up to *c.* 30% of groundmass.

The micromorphological description of the uppermost part of the lower horizon of the buried soil is as follows:

Structure: apedal; homogeneous; single to compact grain; *Porosity*: *c.* 20%; vughs (15%), sub-rounded to irregular, smooth to weakly serrated, 100–300μm, random, unoriented; occasional channels (5%), irregular, walls partially accommodated, smooth to weakly serrated, 25–100μm in width, 200–500μm long, random, unoriented; *Mineral Components*: limit 100μm; coarse/fine ratio: 20/80; coarse fraction: medium (10%) and fine (10%) quartz, sub-rounded to sub-angular, 100–300μm, random, unoriented; fine fraction: very fine (35%) quartz, sub-rounded to sub-angular, 50–100μm, random, unoriented; 40% silt and 5% clay; reddish brown (PPL), reddish yellow (RL); *Organic Component*: *c.* 2%; few very fine flecks of charcoal in groundmass, 25–75μm; Groundmass: related: porphyric, undifferentiated; coarse material: monic; fine material: gefuric; mosaic speckled to reticulate striated, discontinuous streaks, medium (20–50μm) thickness, 50–100μm in length; *Pedofeatures: Textural*: 1) occasional (2–5%) limpid clay, of grains, groundmass and voids, weak birefringence, diffuse extinction, yellow (CPL); 2) occasional (5%) non-laminated dusty clay, of groundmass, yellow (CPL); *Amorphous*: heavily impregnated with sesquioxides, up to 75% of total fabric.

Morris Fen (Dyke 41)

The micromorphological description of the upper third of the buried soil (*c.* 0–7cm) is as follows (M. Pl. 53):

Structure: apedal; granular; *Porosity*: 5%; very dense fabric; mainly vughs, round to sub-round, smooth to weakly serrate, 50–300μm; *Mineral Components*: limit 150μm; coarse/fine ratio: 20/80; coarse fraction: occasional small, sub- rounded gravel pebbles, 5–14mm; medium (*c.* 20%) quartz, sub-rounded to sub-angular, 150–300μm, well sorted; occasional mica grain present; fine fraction: very fine (*c.* 45%) and fine (*c.* 30%) quartz, sub-rounded to sub-angular, 50–150μm, well sorted; *c.* 3% silt and *c.* 2% clay; brown (PPL), light brown (RL); very slightly speckled; *Organic Components*: <1%; amorphous organic matter in groundmass; very few fine flecks of charcoal in groundmass; *Groundmass*: porphyric, un-differentiated; *Pedofeatures: Textural*: rare (1%) laminated and non-laminated dusty coatings in the groundmass; very rare (< 1%) limpid coatings of grains and groundmass; *Amorphous*: very few (*c.* 2%) sesquiox-ide nodules, 50–100μm, 1–2mm in diameter.

The micromorphological description of the middle one-third of the buried soil (*c.* 7–11cm) is as follows:

Structure: apedal; massive to granular; *Porosity*: 5%; very dense fabric; mainly vughs, sub-rounded to irregular, smooth to weakly serrate, 100μm to 5mm; *Mineral Com-ponents*: limit 150μm; coarse/fine ratio: 20/80; coarse fraction: medium (*c.* 20%) quartz, sub-rounded to sub-angular, 150–300µm, well sorted; fine fraction: very fine (*c.* 40%) and fine (*c.* 30%) quartz, sub-rounded to sub-angular, 50–150µm, well sorted; *c.* 5% silt and *c.* 5% clay; reddish brown (PPL), brown (RL); weakly speckled; *Organic Components*: <2%; amorphous organic matter in groundmass; very few fine flecks of charcoal in groundmass; *Groundmass*: coarse: porphyric, undifferentiated; fine: stipple speckled, low to moderate birefringence; *Pedofeatures: Textural*: very rare (< 1%) limpid coatings of grains, and as fragments in the groundmass and void space; rare (*c.* 2%) non-laminated dusty coatings of groundmass and void space; *Fabric*: few (2%) aggregate fragments of fine fraction with dusty coatings in channels; *Amorphous*: very few (*c.* 1%) sesquioxide nodules, 50–200µm; very small zones of sesquioxide impregnation.

The micromorphological description of the lower one-third of the buried soil is as follows (M. Pls 54 and 55):

Structure: apedal; massive to granular; *Porosity*: *c.* 5%; dense fabric; mainly vughs, round to sub-rounded, smooth to weakly serrate, 50–200µm; *Mineral Components*: limit 150µm; coarse/fine ratio: 20/80; coarse fraction: medium (*c.* 20%) quartz, sub-rounded to sub-angular, 150–250µm, well sorted; fine fraction: very fine (*c.* 40%) and fine (*c.* 30%) quartz, sub-rounded to sub-angular, 50–150µm, well sorted; *c.* 5% silt and *c.* 5% clay; brown (PPL), reddish brown (RL); very weakly speckled; *Organic Component*: <2%; amorphous organic matter in the groundmass; very few fine flecks of charcoal in groundmass; occasional sesquioxide-impregnated root/stem pseudomorph; *Groundmass*: coarse: porphyric, undifferentiated; fine: stipple speckled, low to moderate birefringence; *Pedofeatures: Textural*: (1) rare (*c.* 2%) fragments of moderately birefringent limpid clay in the groundmass; (2) very rare (*c.* 1%) laminated dusty clay coatings of grains and groundmass; (3) rare (*c.* 2%) non-laminated dusty clay coatings of the groundmass; *Fabric*: two anomalous fabrics at the upper edge of the slide: (1) consisting of fine sand (*c.* 70%), void space (*c.* 25%) and clay (*c.* 5%) with amorphous organic matter, disaggregated, unsorted, exhibiting horizontal lamination with fabric (2): consisting of fine sand (*c.* 50%), clay (*c.* 40%) and void space (*c.* 10%) with much amorphous organic matter and sesquioxide impregnation, unsorted; *Amorphous*: aggregate of fine sand with laminated and non-laminated dusty clay in a former root channel, 2mm long, 300–500µm wide; very few (2%) sesquioxide nodules, 50–200µm; zones of fine sand with sesquioxide impregnation (*c.* 25–40% of the groundmass).

Dyke 9

The micromorphological description of the upper horizon of the buried soil at profile 2, Dyke 9, is as follows (Pls XV and XVI; M.Pls 43 and 44) :

Structure: apedal; heterogeneous; single to compact grain; *Porosity*: *c.* 10%; very few (2%) vughs, sub-rounded to irregular, smooth to weakly serrate, 100–300µm, random, unoriented; mainly channels (8%), elongate, walls partially accommodated, smooth to weakly serrate, 50–200µm wide, 100–200µm and 1–4mm long, random, unoriented; *Mineral Components*: two fabrics; fabric (1): limit 100fm; coarse/fine ratio: 20/80; coarse fraction: medium (5%) and fine (15%) quartz, sub-rounded to sub-angular, 100–250µm, random, unoriented; fine fraction: very fine (50%) quartz, sub-rounded

to sub-angular, 50–100µm, random, unoriented; 25% silt and 5% clay, speckled, very light brown to greyish yellow (PPL), light greyish yellow (RL); *c.* 80% of total fabric; fabric (2): limit 100µm; coarse/fine ratio: 30/70; coarse fraction: medium (10%) and fine (20%) quartz, sub-rounded to sub-angular, 100–250µm, random, unoriented; fine fraction: very fine (20%) quartz, sub- rounded to sub-angular, 50–100µm, random, unoriented; 40% silt and 10% clay, weakly speckled, reddish brown to dark amber brown (PPL), light reddish brown (RL); *c.* 20% of total fabric; *Organic Component*: *c.* 30–35%; *c.* 10–15% fine flecks of charcoal in groundmass of both fabrics, especially in fabric (1), 50µm, in amorphous zones of greater and lesser density; *c.* 20% amorphous organic matter, mainly in fabric (2), dark brown to black, highly humified, probably peat; *Groundmass*: related: porphyric, undifferentiated; coarse material: monic; fine material: porphyric; fabric (1): stipple- speckled to weakly random striated, discontinuous to continuous, 25–50µm wide, 100–200µm long; fabric (2): weakly stipple-speckled; *Pedofeatures: Textural*: in fabric (1) : very rare (2%) limpid clay in groundmass, yellow (CPL); rare (2%) non-laminated dusty clay in voids, yellow (CPL); in fabric (2): very rare (< 2%) limpid clay in groundmass, yellow to reddish yellow (CPL); rare (2%) non-laminated dusty/'dirty' clay of grains and groundmass, with micro-contrasted particles of organic matter, yellow to reddish yellow (CPL); *Amorphous*: rare (2%) clay aggregates, rounded to sub-rounded, 50–100µm, in fabric (2) only; few (10%) sesquioxide nodules, sub-rounded to sub-angular, 50–200µm, most common in fabric (2); amorphous sesquioxide impregnation of groundmass, of most of fabric (2) and around the voids in fabric (1).

The micromorphological description of the lower horizon of the buried soil at profile 2, Dyke 9, is as follows (M. Pl. 46):

Structure: apedal; homogeneous; single to compact grain; *Porosity*: *c.* 10%; mainly vughs (8%), sub-rounded to irregular, smooth to weakly serrate, 50–500µm and 1–2mm, random, unoriented; very few channels (2%), elongate, walls partially accommodated, smooth to weakly serrate, 50–200µm wide, 1–4mm long, random, unoriented; *Mineral Components*: limit 100µm; coarse/fine ratio: 25/75; coarse fraction: medium (5%) and fine (20%) quartz, sub-rounded to sub-angular, 100–300µm, random, unoriented; fine fraction: very fine (45%) quartz, sub-rounded to sub-angular, 50–100µm, random, unoriented; 20% silt and 10% clay, weakly speckled, golden to orangey brown (PPL), greyish brown (RL); *Organic Component*: *c.* 15–20%; mainly (*c.* 10%) very fine flecks of charcoal in groundmass, 50µm; and *c.* 8% amorphous organic matter in groundmass; very few (*c.* 2%) large flecks of charcoal, 100–200µm; rare (1%) ferruginised plant tissues/roots; *Groundmass*: related: porphyric, undifferentiated; coarse material: monic; fine material: porphyric; stipple-speckled to very slightly random mosaic-speckled, discontinuous to continuous, 25–50µm wide, 50–200µm long; *Pedofeatures: Textural*: rare (2%) limpid clay of grains and groundmass, yellow (CPL); occasional (2–5%) non-laminated dusty/'dirty' clay in groundmass, of grains and voids, with organic matter as micro-contrasted particles, orangey-yellow (CPL); *Amorphous*: few zones of amorphous sesquioxide impregnation, *c.* 10–15% of total fabric; *Excrements*: occasional (*c.* 5%) excrements in channels, as loose, discontinuous, fine sand size aggregates with very fine sand, organic matter and silt.

The micromorphological description of the lens within the upper peat just off the southwestern edge of Northey 'island' at profile 12 in Dyke 9 is as follows (M. Pl. 45):

Structure: apedal; heterogeneous; single to compact grain; *Porosity*: *c.* 15%; mainly (10%) vughs, irregular to sub-rounded, smooth to weakly serrate, 100–200µm, random, unoriented; few (5%) channels, elongate, walls partially accommodated, smooth to weakly serrate, 100–200µm wide, 1–5mm long, approximately parallel and perpendicular; *Mineral Components*: two fabrics; fabric (1): limit 100µm; coarse/fine ratio: 30/70; coarse fraction: medium (10%) and fine (20%), sub-rounded to sub-angular, 100–250µm, random, unoriented; fine fraction: very fine (45%) quartz, sub-rounded to sub-angular, 50–100µm, random, unoriented; 15% silt and 10% clay, weakly speckled, dark brown to yellowish grey (PPL), black to light grey (RL); *c.* 50% of total fabric; fabric (2): limit 100µm; coarse/fine ratio: 20/80; coarse fraction: medium (10%) and fine (10%) quartz, sub-rounded to sub-angular, 100–250µm, random, unoriented; fine fraction: very fine (25%) quartz, sub-rounded to sub-angular, 50–100µm, random, unoriented; 10% silt and 5% clay, dark yellowish brown (PPL), dark yellowish grey to black (RL); up to 40% organic matter; *c.* 50% of total fabric; *Organic Component*: *c.* 40-60%; very few (2%) plant tissue remnants with cell structure evident; frequent (10–20%) fine flecks of charcoal in groundmass of both fabrics; up to 40% dark brown to black, highly humified, amorphous organic matter, probably peat, especially in fabric (2); *Groundmass*: related: porphyric, undifferentiated; coarse material: monic to porphyric; fine material: porphyric; stipple-speckled in fabric (1); *Pedofeatures: Fabric*: rare (< 2%) areas of Ap fabric (2) of the upper horizon of the buried soil, impregnated with sesquioxides; *Textural*: very rare (1%) limpid clay in groundmass and on grains, yellow to orangey-yellow (CPL); very rare (2%) non-laminated dusty clay coatings in groundmass and of voids, very thin, yellow (CPL); *Amorphous*: few (< 10%) zones of amorphous sesquioxide impregnation of ground-

mass of fabric (1); rare (2%) sesquioxide nodules, sub-rounded, 100–150µm; rare (1%) amorphous iron partial infills of voids.

Dyke 8

The upper half of the lower horizon was sampled for thin sectioning, *c.* 0.45–0.40m OD. The micromorphological description is as follows :

Structure: apedal; homogeneous; single to compact grain to intergrain channel; Porosity: *c.* 5%; rare vughs (< 1%), irregular to sub-rounded, smooth to weakly serrate, 100–250µm, random, unoriented; few channels (4%), elongate, walls partially accommodated, smooth to weakly serrate, 25–75µm wide, 0.5–2.0cm long, parallel and perpendicular; *Mineral Components*: limit 100µm; coarse/fine ratio: 20/80; coarse fraction: medium (5%) and fine (15%) quartz, sub-rounded to sub-angular, 100–300µm, random, unoriented; fine fraction: very fine (40%) quartz, sub-rounded to sub-angular, 50–100µm, random, unoriented; 25% silt and 15% clay, weakly speckled, light yellowish brown (PPL), yellowish brown (RL); *Organic Component*: *c.* 15%; very rare (1%) sesquioxide impregnated pseudomorph of root/stem; few (5%) fine flecks of charcoal in groundmass, 25–50µm; mainly (10%) amorphous organic matter in groundmass; *Groundmass*: related: porphyric, undifferentiated; coarse material: monic; fine material: porphyric; random striated, continuous, 25–50µm wide, 50–300µm long; *Pedofeatures: Textural*: rare to occasional (2–5%) limpid clay of groundmass and grains, yellow (CPL); occasional (5%) non-laminated dusty/'dirty' clay coatings in groundmass and of grains, yellow to yellowish red (CPL); *Fabric*: 1 × 3mm zone acting as channel infill, of very fine sand, silt and clay, bridged grain structure; *Amorphous*: rare (1%) partial to complete infills of amorphous iron; very few (2%) sesquioxide nodules, sub-rounded, 50–100µm; very few (2%) rolled clay aggregates, 50–100µm, reddish black (CPL); large zones of sesquioxide impregnation, up to 35% of groundmass, and in former root channels and around voids.

Bibliography

Abbott, G.W. and Smith, R.A., 1910 'The Discovery of Prehistoric Pits at Peterborough, and the Development of Neolithic Pottery', *Archaeologia* 62, 333–352

Addyman, P.V. and Fennell, K.R., 1964 'A Dark-Age settlement at Maxey, Northants.', *Medieval Archaeology* 8, 20–73

Alderton, A., 1983/84 'Environmental Report', *Fenland Research* 1, 19–22

Alderton, A., 1984/85 'Palaeoenvironmental Report', *Fenland Research* 2, 62–66

Atkinson, R.J.C., Piggott, C.M. and Sandars, N.K., 1951 *Excavations at Dorchester, Oxon. First Report* (Oxford)

Avery, B.W., 1980 *Soil Classification for England and Wales*, Soil Survey Monograph 14 (Harpenden)

Avery, B.W. and Bascomb, C.L., 1974 *Soil Survey Laboratory Methods*, Soil Survey Technical Monograph 6 (Harpenden)

Baker, C.A., Moxey, P.A. and Oxford, P.M., 1979 'Woodland Continuity and Change in Epping Forest', *Field Studies* 4, 645–669

Bamford, H.M., 1985 *Briar Hill: Excavations 1974-78*, (Northampton)

Bascomb, C.L. and Bullock, P., 1974 'Sample preparation and stone content', in Avery, B.W. and Bascomb, C.L. 'Soil Survey Laboratory Methods', 5–13, *Soil Survey Technical Monograph 6* (Harpenden)

Barker, G. and Webley, D., 1978 'Causewayed camps and early Neolithic economies in central southern England', *Proc. Prehist. Soc.* 44, 161–186

Barrett, J.C., 1980 'The Evolution of later Bronze Age settlement', in Barrett, J.C. and Bradley, R.J. (eds) 'Settlement and Society in the British Later Bronze Age', Brit. Archaeol. Rep. 83, 77–100 (Oxford)

Barrett, J.C., 1987 'The Glastonbury Lake Village: Models and Source Criticism', *Archaeol. J.* 144, 409–423

Barrett, J.C. and Bradley, R.J. (eds), 1980 *Settlement and Society in the British Later Bronze Age*, Brit. Archaeol. Rep. 83 (Oxford)

Barrett,, J.C. and Gourlay, R., 1984 'Dail na Caraidh', *Current Archaeology* 94, 347–349

Bibby, J.S. and Mackney, D., 1969 *Land use capability classification*, Soil Survey Technical Monograph 1 (Harpenden)

Biddick, K., 1980 'Animal Bones from Second Millennium Ditches, Newark Road', in Pryor (1980), 217–232

Booth, S.J., 1982 'The sand and gravel resources of the country around Whittlesey, Cambridgeshire: description of 1:25000 sheets TF20 and TL29', *Miner. Assess. Rep. Inst. Geol. Sci.* 93

Bouma, J., 1969 'Microstructure and stability of two sandy loam soils with different soil management', *Agricultural Res. Rep.* 724 (Wageningen)

Boycott, A.E., 1936 'The Freshwater Mollusca in Britain', *J. Animal Ecol.* 5, 116–187

Bradley, R.J., 1978 *The Prehistoric Settlement of Britain*, (London)

Bradley, R.J., 1982 'The destruction of wealth in later British prehistory', *Man* 17, 108–22

Bradley, R.J., 1984 *The Social Foundations of Prehistoric Britain*, (London)

Brandt, R.W., Groenman-van Waateringe, W. and van der Leeuw, S.E., 1987 *The Assendelver Polders Papers*, 1 (Amsterdam)

Bromwich, J., 1970 'Freshwater flooding along the Fen margins south of the Isle of Ely during the Roman period', in Phillips (1970), 114–126

Buckley, D.G, Major, M. and Milton, B., 1988 'Excavation of a possible Neolithic long barrow or mortuary enclosure at Rivenhall, Essex, 1986', *Proc. Prehist. Soc.* 54, 77–92

Bullock, P, Murphy, C.P. and Waller, P.J., 1985a *The Preparation of Thin Sections of Soils and Unconsolidated Sediments*, (Harpenden)

Bullock, P., Fedoroff, N., Jongerius, A. and Stoops, G., 1985b *Handbook for Soil Thin Section Descriptions*, Waine Research (Wolverhampton)

Bullock, P. and Murphy, C.P., 1979 'Evolution of a Palaeo-Argillic Brown Earth (Palendalf) from Oxfordshire, England', *Geoderma* 22, 225–252

Bullock, P., and Murphy, C.P. (eds), 1985 *Soil Micromorphology*, 2 vols (Berkhamstead)

Burgess, C., 1974 'The Bronze Age', in Renfrew, C. (ed.) *British Prehistory* 165–222 (London)

Burton, R.G.O., 1981 *Soils in Cambridgeshire II*, Soil Survey Record 69 (Harpenden)

Cameron, R.A.D. and Morgan-Huws, D.I., 1975 'Snail fauna in the early stages of a chalk grassland succession', *Biol. Journ. Linnean Soc. London* 39, 215–229

Challands, A.C., 1974 'The Lynch Farm Complex: Recent Work', *Durobrivae* 2, 23

Champion, T.C., 1975 'Britain in the European Iron Age', *Archaeologia Atlantica* 1, 127–45

Charnley, P.R., 1977 *A History of the Drainage of Knarr Lake*, North Level Internal Drainage Board (Thorney)

Charnley, P.R., 1979 *A History of the Drainage of Wisbech Northside*, North Level Internal Drainage Board (Thorney)

Charnley, P.R., 1980 *A History of the Draining of Tydd, Newton and Gorefield Fens*, North Level Internal Drainage Board (Thorney)

Charnley, P.R., 1983 *A History of the Drainage of Pode Hole, The Gores, North and Priors Fens and Grounds East of Peterborough*, North Level Internal Drainage Board (Thorney)

Chatfield, J.E., 1968 'The life history of the helicid snail *Monacha cantiana* (Montagu), with reference also to *M. cartusiana* (Muller)', *Proc. Malacological Soc. Lond.* 38, 233–245

Chatfield, J.E., 1972 'Observations on the ecology of *Monacha cantiana* (Montagu) and associated molluscan fauna', *Proc. Malacological Soc. Lond.* 40, 59–69

Chatwin, C.P., 1961 *British Regional Geology: East Anglia and Adjoining Areas*, HMSO (London)

Cherry, J.F., Gamble, C. and Shennan, I. (eds), 1978 *Sampling in Contemporary British Archaeology*, British Archaeological Reports 50 (Oxford)

Chowne, P., 1980 'Bronze Age settlements in south Lincolnshire', in Barrett, J.C. and Bradley, R.J. (eds) *'Settlement and Society in the British Later Bronze Age'*, Brit. Archaeol. Rep. 83, 295–305 (Oxford)

Churchill, D.M., 1970 'Post-Neolithic to Romano-British Sedimentation in the southern Fenlands of Cambridgeshire and Norfolk', in Phillips (1970), 132–146

Clark, A.J., 1983 'The Testimony of the Topsoil', in Maxwell, G.S. (ed.) *The Impact of Aerial Reconnaissance on Archaeology*, Coun. Brit. Archaeol. Res. Rep. 49, 128–135

Clark, J.G.D., 1933 'Report on an Early Bronze Age site in the South-Eastern Fens', *Antiq. J.* 13, 264–296

Clark, J.G.D., 1936 'Report on a Late Bronze Age site in Mildenhall Fen, West Suffolk', *Antiq. J.* 16, 29–50

Clark, J.G.D., 1955 'A Microlithic Industry from the Cambridgeshire Fenland and other Industries of Sauveterrian affinities from Britain', *Proc. Prehist. Soc.* 21, 3–20

Clark, J.G.D. and Clifford, M.H., 1935 'Report on recent excavations at Peacock's Farm, Shippea Hill, Cambridgeshire', *Antiq. J.* 15, 284–319

Clark, J,G.D. and Godwin, H., 1962 'The Neolithic of the Cambridgeshire Fens', *Antiquity* 36, 10–23

Clark, J.G.D., Higgs, E.S. and Longworth, I.H., 1960 'Excavations at the Neolithic Site at Hurst Fen, Mildenhall, Suffolk', *Proc. Prehist. Soc.* 26, 202–245

Clarke, D.L., 1970 *Beaker Pottery of Great Britain and Ireland*, (Cambridge)

Coles, J.M., 1984 *The Archaeology of Wetlands*, (Edinburgh)

Coles, J.M. and Hall, D.N., 1983 'The Fenland Project', *Antiquity* 57, 51

Coles, J.M. and Harding, A.F., 1979 *The Bronze Age in Europe*, (London)

Coles, J.M. and Orme, B., 1976 'A Neolithic hurdle from the Somerset Levels', *Antiquity* 50, 57–60, (Cambridge)

Cotterell, B. and Kamminga, J., 1987 'The Formation of Flakes', *American Antiquity* 52, 675–708

Courty, M.- A. and Fedoroff, N., 1982 'Micromorphology of a Holocene dwelling', *Nordic Archaeometry* 2, PACT 7 (II), 257–277

Craddock, P.T., Gurney, D., Pryor, F.M.M. and Hughes, M.J., 1985 'The Application of Soil Phosphate Analysis to the Location and Interpretion of Archaeological Sites', *Archaeol. J.* 142, 362–376

Craddock, P.T., 1980 'Metal analysis of the spearhead', in Pryor (1980a) 128–9

Crowther, D.R., French, C.A.I. and Pryor, F.M.M., 1985 'Approaching the Fens the Flexible Way', in C. Haselgrove, M. Millett and I. Smith (eds) *Archaeology from the Ploughsoil*, 59–76 (Sheffield)

Dallas, C., 1975 'A Belgic Farmstead at Orton Longueville', *Durobrivae* 3, 26–27

Darby, H.C., 1940a *The Medieval Fenland*, (Cambridge)

Darby, H.C., 1940b *The Draining of the Fens*, (Cambridge)

Davey, P.J., 1971 'The distribution of later Bronze Age metalwork from Lincolnshire', *Proc. Prehist. Soc.* 34, 96–111

Davey, P.J., 1973 'Bronze Age Metalwork from Lincolnshire', *Archaeologia* 104, 51–127

Davies, D.B., Eagle, D.J. and Finney, J.B., 1982 *Soil Management*, 4th edition (Ipswich)

Dettman, M.G. and Emerson, W.W., 1959 'A modified permeability test for measuring the cohesion of soil crumbs', *J. Soil Sci.* 26, 215–216

Devoy, R.J., 1980 'Post-Glacial environmental change and Man in the Thames Estuary: a synopsis', in Thompson, F.H. (ed.) *'Archaeology and Coastal Change'*, Soc. Antiq. Lond. Occ. Paper (N.S.) 1, 134–148 (London)

Donaldson, P., 1977 'The excavation of a multiple round barrow at Barnack, Cambs. 1974–6', *Antiq. J.* 57, 197–231

Duchaufour, P., 1982 *Pedology*, (London)

Eidt, R.C., 1973 'A rapid chemical field test for Archaeological Site Surveying', *American Antiquity* 38, 206–210

Ellis, A.E., 1941 'The Mollusca of a Norfolk Broad', *J. of Conchology* 21, 224–243

Ellis, A.E., 1951 'Census of the distribution of British non-marine Mollusca', *J. of Conchology* 23, 171–244

Evans, C., 1987 "Nomads in Waterland'? Prehistoric Transhumance and Fenland Archaeology', *Proc. Cambridge Antiq. Soc.* 76, 27–40

Evans, J., 1881 *The Ancient Bronze Implements of Great Britain and Ireland*, (London)

Evans, J.G., 1972 *Land Snails in Archaeology*, (London)

Evans, J.G., 1978 'Comment (on paper by Barker and Webley)', *Proc. Prehist. Soc.* 44, 185–6

Evans, J.G., unpublished 'New things to do with Snails and Slugs: a study in Diversity and Association', Unpublished paper (1983)

Evans, R., 1979 'The early courses of the River Nene', *Durobrivae* 7, 8–10

Evans, R., 1981 'Assessments of soil erosion and peat wastage for parts of East Anglia, England: a Field Visit', in Morgan, R.P.C. (ed.) *Soil Conservation: problems and prospects*, 521–530 (New York)

Fairbridge, R.W., 1961 'Eustatic changes in sea level', *Phys. Chem. Earth* 5, 99

Fedoroff, N., 1969 'Caracteres micromorphologiques des pedogeneses Quaternaires en France', in *Étude sur le Quaternaire dans le Monde* (8th INQUA Congress)

Fisher, P.F., 1982 'A review of lessivage and Neolithic cultivation in Southern England', *J. Archaeol. Sci.* 9, 299–304

Fisher, R.A., Corbet, A.S. and Williams, C.B., 1943 'The relationship between the number of species and the number of individuals in a random sample of an animal population', *J. of Animal Ecology* 12, 42–58

Folk, R.L. and Ward, W.C., 1957 'Brazos River Bar: a study in the significance of grain-size parameters', *J. Sedimentary Petrology* 27, 3–26

French, C.A.I., 1980 'Analyses of molluscs from two Bronze Age ditches at the Newark Road site, Fengate', in Pryor, F.M.M., 1980 *'Excavation at Fengate, Peterbrough, England: the Third Report'* 204–212 Northants. Archaeol. Soc. Archaeol. Monogr. 1/Royal Ontario Museum Archaeol. Monogr. 6 (Toronto and Northampton)

French, C.A.I., 1983 *An Environmental Study of the Soils, Sediments and Molluscan Evidence Associated with Prehistoric Monuments on River Terrace Gravels in North-West Cambridgeshire.* Unpublished Ph.D. thesis, Institute of Archaeology (University of London)

French, C.A.I., 1988a 'Aspects of buried prehistoric soils in the Lower Welland Valley and the Fen Margin North of Peterborough, Cambridgeshire', in Groenman-van Waateringe, W. and Robinson, M. (eds) *'Man-made Soils',* Brit. Archaeol. Rep. S410, 115–128 (Oxford)

French, C.A.I., 1988b 'Further aspects of the Buried Prehistoric Soils in the Fen Margin Northeast of Peterborough, Cambridgeshire', in Murphy, P. and French, C.A.I. (eds) *'The Exploitation of Wetlands',* Brit. Archaeol. Rep. 186, 193–211 (Oxford)

French, C.A.I., 1990 'Neolithic soils, middens and alluvium in the lower Welland valley', *Oxford J. Archaeol.* 9, 305-311

French, C.A.I. and Pryor, F.M.M, in preparation *Archaeology and Environment of the Etton Landscape,* Fenland Archaeological Trust Monograph

Gallois, R.W., 1979 *Geological Investigations for the Wash Storage Scheme,* Inst. Geological Sci. Rep. 78/19 (London)

Gibson, A., 1980 'Some Beaker Pottery from the G. Wyman Abbott collection in Peterborough Museum', in F.M.M. Pryor (1980a) 234–245

Gibson, A., 1986 *Neolithic and Early Bronze Age pottery,* Shire Archaeology (Princes Risborough)

Godwin, H., 1941 'Studies in the Post-Glacial history of British Vegetation: parts III and IV', *Phil. Trans. Royal Soc. B* 230, 233–303

Godwin, H., 1975 *The History of the British Flora,* 2nd edition (Cambridge)

Godwin, H., 1978 *Fenland: its Ancient Past and Uncertain Future* (Cambridge)

Godwin, H. and Clifford, M.H., 1938 'Studies in the Post-Glacial History of British vegetation: I. Origin and Stratigraphy of Fenland deposits near Woodwalton, Huntingdonshire, II. Origin and Stratigraphy of Deposits in Southern Fenland', *Phil. Trans. Royal Soc. B* 229, 323–406

Godwin, H. and Suggate, R.P. and Willis, E.H., 1958 'Radiocarbon Dating of the Eustatic rise in ocean level', *Nature* 181, 15–18

Godwin, H. and Vishnu-Mittre, 1975 'Flandrian deposits of the Fenland Margin at Holme Fen and Whittlesey Mere, Hunts.', *Phil. Trans. Royal Soc. B* 270, 561–608

Godwin, H. and Willis, E., 1961 'Cambridge University natural radiocarbon measurements, III', *Radiocarbon* 3

Godwin, H., Willis, E.H. and Switsur, V.R., 1965 'Cambridge University natural radiocarbon measurements VII', *Radiocarbon* 7, 210–211

Gould, S.J., 1981 'Palaeontology plus ecology as palaeobiology', in May, R.M. (ed.) *Theoretical Ecology: Principles and Applications* (2nd edition), 295–317 (Oxford)

Graham, I., 1976 'The Investigation of the Magnetic Properties of Archaeological Sediments', in Davidson, D.A. and Shackley, M.L. (eds) *Geoarchaeology: Earth Science and the Past,* 49–63 (Duckworth, London)

Green, F.J., 1985 'Evidence for domestic cereal use at Maxey', in Pryor, F.M.M. and French, C.A.I. 'Archaeology and Environment in the Lower Welland Valley', *E. Anglian Archaeol.* 27, 224–232

Green, M.J., 1977 *Prehistoric Peterborough: a Guide Catalogue to the Prehistoric Archaeological Collections in the Peterborough City Museum,* (Peterborough)

Greenland, D.J. and Rimmer, D. and Payne, D., 1975 'Determination of the Structural Stability class of English and Welsh soils, using a water coherence test', *J. Soil Science* 26, 294–303

Greensmith, J.T. and Tucker, E.V., 1973 'Holocene transgressions and regressions on ther Essex coast, outer Thames estuary', *Geologieen Mynbouw* 52, 193–202

Greig, J.R.A., 1982 'Past and present lime woods in Europe', in Bell, M. and Limbrey, S. (eds) *'Archaeological Aspects of Woodland Ecology',* Brit. Archaeol. Rep. S146, 23–55 (Oxford)

Gurney, D.A., 1980 'Evidence for Bronze Age salt production at Northey, Peterborough', *Northants. Archaeol.* 15, 1–11

Gurney, D.A., 1981 'Romano-British Salt Production on the Western Fen-edge: a re-assessment', *Proc. Cambridge Antiq. Soc.* 71, 81–88

Gurney, D.A., 1985a 'Geophysical and Geochemical Analyses of Subsoil Features', in Pryor, F.M.M. and French, C.A.I. 'Archaeology and Environment in the Lower Welland Valley', *E. Anglian Archaeol.* 27, 195–205

Gurney, D.A., 1985b *Phosphate analysis of soils: a guide for the field archaeologist,* Inst. Field Archaeol. Technical Paper 3 (Birmingham)

Hall, D.N., 1981 *Cambridgeshire Fenland: an intensive archaeological survey,* Fenland Research Committee, unpublished report

Hall, D.N., 1985 'Survey Work in Eastern England', in Macready, S. and Thompson, F.H. (eds) *'Archaeological Field Survey in Britain and Abroad',* Soc. Antiq. Occ. Paper (NS) 1, 25–44

Hall, D.N., 1987 'The Fenland Project No. 2: Cambridgeshire Survey, Peterborough to March', *E. Anglian Archaeology.* 35 (Norwich)

Hall, D.N. and Martin, P., 1980 'Fieldwork Survey of the Soke of Peterborough', *Durobrivae* 8, 13–14

Hall, D.N. and Swistur, V.R., 1981 'A Buried Peat Band at Manea, Cambridgeshire', *Proc. Cambridge Antiq. Soc.* 71, 75–80

Hallam, S.J., 1961 'Wash coast-line levels since Roman times', *Antiquity* 35, 152–154

Hallam, S.J., 1970 — 'Settlement around the Wash', in Phillips, C.W. (ed.) *'The Fenland in Roman Times'*, Royal Geographical Soc. Res. Ser. 5, 22–113 (London)

Halstead, P., 1985 — 'A study of Mandibular Teeth from Romano-British Contexts at Maxey', in Pryor, F.M.M. and French, C.A.I. 'Archaeology and Environment in the Lower Welland Valley', *E. Anglian Archaeol.* 27, 219–224

Harris, L.E., 1952 — 'Sir Cornelius Vermuyden and the Great Level of the Fens: a new judgement', *Proc. Cambridge Antiq. Soc.* 45, 17–27

Hawkes, C.F.C. and Fell, C.I., 1945 — 'The Early Iron Age Settlement at Fengate, Peterborough', *Archaeol. J.* 100, 188–223

Hills, R.L., 1967 — *Machines, Mills and Uncountable Costly Necessities: a short history of the drainage of the Fens* (Norwich)

Hodder, I.R., 1982 — *The Present Past*, (Cambridge)

Hodge, R.D. and Arden-Clarke, C., 1986 — *Soil Erosion in Britain*, Soil Association (Bristol)

Horton, A., Lake, R.D., Bisson, G. and Coppack, B.C., 1974 — *The Geology of Peterborough*, Inst. Geological Sci. Rep. 73/12 (London)

Hutchinson, J.N., 1980 — 'The record of peat wastage in the East Anglian Fenlands at Holme Post, 1848–1978 A.D.', *J. Ecology* 68, 229–249

Imeson, A.C. and Jungerius, P.D., 1974 — 'Landscape stability in the Luxembourg Ardennes as exemplified by hydrological and (micro) pedological investigations of a catena in an experimental watershed', *Catena* 1, 273–295

Jacobi, R. 1984 — 'The Mesolithic of Northern East Anglia and contemporary territories', in Barringer, C. (ed.) *Aspects of East Anglian Prehistory*, 43–76 (Norwich)

Jelgersma, S., 1966 — 'Sea Level changes during the last 10,000 years', in Sawyer, J.S. (ed.) *Proceedings of the International Symposium on World Climate, 8000 to 0 BC*, Royal Meterological Soc. 54–71 (London)

Jelgersma, S., 1979 — 'Sea Level Changes in the North Sea Basin', in Oele, E., Schuttenhelm, R.T.E. and Wiggins, A.J. (eds) *The Quaternary History of the North Sea*, Acta Univ. Uppsala Symposium Annum Quingentesimum Celebrantis 2, 233–248 (Uppsala)

Johnston, A.E., 1973 — 'The effects of ley and arable cropping systems on the amount of soil organic matter in the Rothamstead and Woburn ley arable experiments', *Rep. of Rothamstead Exp. Station for 1972*, pt. 2, 131–167

Jones. M., 1981 — 'The development of crop husbandry', in Jones, M. and Dimbleby, G. (eds) *'The Environment of Man: the Iron Age to the Anglo-Saxon period'*, Brit. Archaeol. Rep. 87, 95–128 (Oxford)

Jongerius, A., 1970 — 'Some morphological aspects of regrouping phenomena in Dutch soils', *Geoderma* 4, 311–331

Juggins, S., 1984 — *Flag Fen Diatom Analysis*, Unpub. M.Sc. thesis, University of London

Keeley, H.C.M., 1982 — 'Pedogenesis during the later prehistoric period in Britain', in Harding, A.F. (ed.) *Climate Change in Later Prehistory*, 103–113 (Edinburgh)

Kenward, H.K., 1978 — 'The value of insect remains as evidence of ecological conditions on archaeological sites', in Brothwell, D.R., Thomas, K.D. and Clutton-Brock, J. (eds) *'Research Problems in Zooarchaeology'*, Inst. Archaeol. Occ. Pub. 3, 25–38 (London)

Kenward, H.K., 1982 — 'Insect communities and death assemblages, past and present', in Hall, A.R. and Kenward, H.K. (eds) *'Environmental Archaeology in the Urban Context'*, Counc. Brit. Archaeol. Res. Rep. 43, 71–78 (London)

Kerney, M.P., Brown, E.H. and Chandler, T.J., 1964 — 'The Late Glacial and Post-Glacial history of the Chalk Escarpment near Brook, Kent', *Phil. Trans. Royal Soc. B* 248, 135–204

Kerney, M.P. and Cameron, R.A.D., 1979 — *A Field Guide to the Land Snails of Britain and North-West Europe*, (Collins, London)

King, E., 1973 — *Peterborough Abbey 1086–1310*, (Cambridge)

Knight, D., 1984 — *Late Bronze Age and Iron Age Settlement in the Nene and Ouse Basins*, 2 vols., Brit. Archaeol. Reps. 130 (Oxford)

Krebs, C.J., 1978 — *Ecology: The Experimental Analysis of Distribution and Abundance*, (2nd Edition) (New York)

Kwaad, F.J.M. and Mücher, H.J., 1977 — 'The evolution of soils and slope deposits in the Luxembourg Ardennes near Wiltz', *Geoderma* 17, 1–37

Lambrick, G. and Robinson, M., 1979 — *Iron Age and Roman riverside settlements at Farmoor, Oxfordshire*, Council Brit. Archaeol. Res. Rep. 32 (London)

Lanting, J.N. and van der Waals, J.D., 1972 — 'British Beakers as seen from the Continent', *Helinium* 12, 20–46

Lawson, A.J., 1984 — 'The Bronze Age in East Anglia', in Barringer, C. (ed.) *Aspects of East Anglian Pre-History*, 141–77 (Norwich)

Leach, E., 1977 — 'A View from the Bridge', in Spriggs, M. (ed.) *Archaeology and Anthropology*, Brit. Archaeol. Rep. S19, 161–176 (Oxford)

Leeds, E.T., 1912 — 'The excavation of a round barrow at Eyebury, near Peterborough', *Proc. Soc. Antiq. Lond.* 24, 80–95

Leeds, E.T., 1915 — 'Further excavations in round barrows near Eyebury, Peterborough', *Proc. Soc. Antiq.* 27, 116–126

Leeds, E.T., 1922 — 'Further Discoveries of the Neolithic and Bronze Ages at Peterborough', *Antiq. J.* 2, 220–45

Limbrey, S., 1975 — *Soil Science and Archaeology*, (London)

Louwe-Kooijmans, L.P., 1974 — 'The Rhine/Meuse Delta: four studies in its Prehistoric Occupation and Holocene Geology', *Oudheid Kundige Mede Delingen*, 53–54 (Leiden)

Louwe-Kooijmans, L.P., 1980 — 'Archaeology and Coastal Change in the Netherlands', in Thompson, F.H. (ed.) *'Archaeology and Coastal Change'*, Soc. Antiq. Occ. Paper (NS) 1, 106–133 (London)

Low, A.J., 1972 — 'The effects of cultivation on the structure and other physical characteristics of grassland and arable soils (1945–1970)', *J. Soil Sci.* 23, 363–380

Mackreth, D.F., 1976 — 'Hall Farm, Orton Longueville', *Durobrivae* 4, 24–25

Mackreth, D.F., 1988
'Excavation of an Iron Age and Roman Enclosure at Werrington, Cambridgeshire', *Britannia* 19, 59–152

Mackreth, D.F. and O'Neill, F., 1980
'Werrington: an Iron Age and Roman Site', *Durobrivae* 8, 23–25

Macphail, R.I., 1985a
'Soil Reports on Hazleton Long Cairn, Gloucestershire', *Ancient Monuments Lab. Archaeol. Rep.* 35P, 186 (London)

Macphail, R.I., 1985b
'Soil Report', in Rudling, D., *'Recent Archaeological Research at Selmeston, East Sussex'*, Sussex Archaeol. Collections 123, 2–3

Macphail, R.I., 1986
'Paleosols in Archaeology: their Role in Understanding Flandrian Pedogenesis', in Wright, V.P. (ed.) *Paleosols: their Recognition and Interpretation*, 263–290 (Blackwell, Oxford)

Macphail, R.I., 1987
'A Review of soil science in archaeology in England', in Keeley, H.C.M. (ed.) *'Environmental Archaeology: a Regional Review 2'*, H.B.M.C. Occ. Paper 1, 332–379 (London)

Macphail, R.I., Romans, J.C.C. and Robertson, L., 1987
'The application of micromorphology to the understanding of Holocene soil development in the British Isles, with special reference to early cultivation', in Fedoroff, N., Bresson, L.M. and Courty, M-A. (eds) *Soil Micromorphology*, I.N.R.A., 647–656

Mahany, C., 1969
'Fengate', *Current Archaeol.* 17, 156–7

McKeague, J.A., 1983
'Clay skins and argillic horizons', in Bullock, P. and Murphy, C.P. (eds) *Soil Micromorphlogy*, vol. 2, 367–388

Megaw, J.V.S. and Simpson, D.D.A., 1979
An Introduction to British Prehistory, (Leicester)

Middleton, H.R., in prep.
'The Flints', in (forthcoming) *'Excavations at the Neolithic Causewayed Enclosure at Etton'*, English Heritage Archaeol. Mono. (London)

Miller, S.H. and Skertchly, S.B.J., 1878
The Fenland Past and Present, (Longmans, London)

Moore, P.D. and Webb, J.A., 1978
An illustrated guide to pollen analysis, (London)

Murphy, J. and Riley, J.P., 1962
'A modified single solution method for the determination of phosphate in natural waters', *Analytica Chimica Acta* 27, 31–36

Needham, S. and Burgess, C., 1980
'The Later Bronze Age in the Lower Thames Valley: the Metalwork Evidence', in Barrett, J.C. and Bradley, R. (eds) *'Settlement and Society in the British Later Bronze Age'*, Brit. Archaeol. Rep. 83, 437–470 (Oxford)

Oldfield, F., Krawiecki, A., Maher, B., Taylor, J.J. and Twigger, S., 1984
The Role of Mineral Magnetic Measurements in Archaeology, unpub. paper, University of Liverpool

Page, H.G., 1955
'Phi-millimeter Conversion Table', *J. Sedimentary Petrology* 25, 4, 285–292

Palmer, R., 1976
'Interrupted ditch enclosures in Britain: the uses of aerial photography for comparative studies', *Proc. Prehist. Soc.* 42, 161–186

Paul, C.R.C., 1975
'The ecology of Mollusca in ancient woodland 1: the fauna of Hayley Wood, Cambridgeshire', *J. Conchology* 25/5, 301–328

Paul, C.R.C., 1978a
'The ecology of Mollusca in ancient woodland 2: analysis of distributions and experiments in Hayley Wood, Cambridgeshire', *J. Conchology* 29/5, 281–294

Paul, C.R.C., 1978b
'The ecology of Mollusca in ancient woodland 3: frequency of occurrence in West Cambridgeshire Woods', *J. Conchology* 29/5, 295–300

Perrin, R.M.S. and Hodge, C.A.H., 1965
'Soils', in Steers, J.A. (ed.) *The Cambridge Region* 1965, 68–84, Brit. Assoc. Advancement of Sci. (Cambridge)

Petrequin, P., 1984
Gens de L'eau, Gens de la Terre, Hachette (Paris)

Phillips, C.W., 1970
The Fenland in Roman Times, Roy. Geograph. Soc. Res. Series 5 (London)

Pielou, E.C., 1975
Ecological Diversity, (London)

Pielou, E.C., 1977
Mathematical Ecology, (New York)

Potter, T.W., 1965
'The Roman Pottery from Coldham Clamp', *Proc. Cambridge Antiq. Soc.* 58 12–37

Potter, T.W., 1975
'Excavations at Stonea, Cambs.', *Proc. Cambridge Antiq. Soc.* 66, 23–54

Potter, T.W., 1976
'Valleys and Settlement: some new evidence', *World Archaeol.* 8, 207–19

Potter, T.W., 1981
'The Roman occupation of the central Fenland', *Britannia* 12, 79–133

Potter, T.W. and Jackson R., forthcoming
Excavations at Stonea Grange, Brit. Mus. Archaeol. Mono. (London)

Potter, T.W. and Potter, C.F., 1982
A Romano-British village at Grandford, March, Cambridgeshire, Brit. Mus. Occ. Paper 35

Preston, F.W., 1948
'The commonness and rarity of species', *Ecology* 29, 254–283

PRO1/301
'1637 Plan of Borough Fen and Eye by Nicklaus Lane', *Land Revenue Record Office* 1/301 (PRO, London)

Pryor, F.M.M., 1974
Excavation at Fengate, Peterborough, England: the First Report, Royal Ontario Mus. Archaeol. Monogr. 3 (Toronto)

Pryor, F.M.M., 1978
Excavation at Fengate, Peterborough, England: the Second Report, Royal Ontario Mus. Archaeol. Monogr. 5. (Toronto)

Pryor, F.M.M., 1980a
Excavation at Fengate, Peterborough, England: the Third Report, Royal Ontario Mus. Archaeol. Monogr. 6/Northants. Archaeol. Soc. Monogr. 1 (Toronto and Northampton)

Pryor, F.M.M., 1980b
'Will it all come out in the Wash? Reflections at the end of eight years' digging', in Barrett J.C. and Bradley, R.J. (eds) *'The British Later Bronze Age'*, Brit. Archaeol. Rep. 83, 483–500 (Oxford)

Pryor, F.M.M., 1983a
'Gone but still respected: some evidence for Iron Age house platforms in lowland England', *Oxford J. Archaeol.* 2, 189–98

Pryor, F.M.M., 1983b
'South-west Fen-edge survey, 1982/3, an interim report', *Northants. Archaeol.* 17, 165–70

Pryor, F.M.M., 1984
Excavation at Fengate, Peterborough, England: the Fourth Report, Royal Ontario Mus. Archaeol. Monogr. 7/Northants. Archaeol. Soc Monogr. 2 (Toronto and Northampton)

Pryor, F.M.M., 1985
'Dyke Survey: an Imperfect Approach to the Invisible', *Archaeol. Rev. Cambridge*, 4, 5–14

Pryor, F.M.M., 1986 '"...Earth Spuing, Unfast and Boggie" – Rescue Archaeology in the Peterborough Fens', *History and Archaeology Review*, i, 5–20

Pryor, F.M.M., 1987 'Etton 1986: Neolithic Metamorphoses', *Antiquity* 61, 78–80

Pryor, F.M.M., 1988 'Earlier Neolithic Organised Landscapes and Ceremonial in Lowland Britian' in Barrett, J.C. and Kinnes, I.A. (eds), *The Archaeology of Context in the Neolithic and Bronze Age: Recent Trends* (Dept. of Prehistory and Archaeology, Sheffield), 63-72

Pryor, F.M.M., forthcoming 'Fengate, Site 11', in Simpson *et al.*, forthcoming (Backlog), *E. Anglian Archaeol.*

Pryor, F.M.M. and French, C.A.I., 1985 'Archaeology and Environment in the Lower Welland Valley', *E. Anglian Archaeol.* 27

Pryor, F.M.M., French, C.A.I. and Taylor, M., 1985 'An Interim Report on Excavations at Etton, Maxey, Cambridgeshire, 1982–1984', *Antiq. J.* 65, 275–311

Pryor, F.M.M., French, C.A.I. and Taylor, M., 1986 'Flag Fen, Fengate, Peterborough I: Discovery, Reconnaissance and initial excavation', *Proc. Prehist. Soc.* 52, 1–24

Pryor, F.M.M., French, C.A.I. and Taylor, M., in prep. *Excavations at the Neolithic Causewayed Enclosure at Etton, Maxey, Cambridgeshire*, English Heritage Archaeol. Monogr. (London)

Pryor, F.M.M. and Palmer, R., 1982 'Aerial Photography and Rescue Archaeology: a case study', *Aerial Archaeology* 6, 5–8

Raban, S., 1977 *The Estates of Thorney and Crowland*, (Cambridge)

Ravensdale, J.R., 1974 *Liable to Floods*, (Cambridge)

R.C.H.M., 1960 *A Matter of Time: an Archaeological Survey.* Royal Commission on Historical Monuments (England)

Richardson, S.J. and Smith, J., 1977 'Peat Wastage in the East Anglian Fens', *J. Soil Sci.* 28, 485–489

Rowlands, M.J., 1976 *The Production and Distribution of Metalwork in the Middle Bronze Age in Southern Britain,* Brit. Archaeol. Rep. 32 (Oxford)

Rowlands, M.J., 1980 'Kinship Alliance and Exchange in the European Bronze Age', in Barrett, J.C. and Bradley, R.J. (eds) *'Settlement and Society in the British later Bronze Age'*, Brit. Archaeol. Rep. 83, 15–56 (Oxford)

Rudling, D., 1985 'Recent Archaeological Research at Selmeston, East Sussex', *Sussex Archaeol. Collections* 123, 1–25

Salway, P., 1967 'Excavations at Hockwold-cum-Wilton, Norfolk, 1961–62', *Proc. Cambridge Antiq. Soc.* LX, 39–80

Salway, P., 1975 'The Roman Fenland', in Phillips, C.W. (ed.) *'The Fenland in Roman Times'*, Royal Geogr. Soc. Res. Ser. 5, 1–21 (London)

Saville, A., 1981 'Honey Hill, Elkington: a Northamptonshire Mesolithic Site', *Northants. Archaeol.* 16, 1–16

Scaife, R.G., 1980 *Late Devensian and Flandrian palaeoecological studies in the Isle of Wight* (unpublished PhD thesis, London University)

Scaife, R.G., 1987 'A review of later Quaternary plant microfossil and macrofossil research in Southern England; with special reference to environmental archaeological evidence', in Keeley, H.C.M. (ed.) *'Environmental Archaeology: a Regional Review'*, H.B.M.C. Occ. Paper 1, 125–203 (London)

Scaife, R.G. and Macphail, R.I., 1983 'The Post-Devensian development of heathland soils and vegetation', in Burnham, P. (ed.) *'Soils of the heathlands and chalklands'*, *Seesoil* 1, 70–99

Schwarz, G.T., 1967 'A simplified chemical test for archaeological work', *Archaeometry* 10, 57–63

Scollar, I. and Graham, I., 1972 'A Method for the determination of the total magnetic moment of soil samples in a constant field', *Prospezioni Archaeologiche* 7, 85–92

Seale, R.S., 1975 *Soils of the Ely District*, Soil Survey Memoire (Harpenden)

Seale, R.S. and Hodge, C.A.H., 1976 *Soils of the Cambridge and Ely District*, Soil Survey Special Survey No. 10 (Harpenden)

Shackley, M.L., 1975 *Archaeological sediments: a survey of analytical methods* (Butterworth, London)

Shennan, I., 1980a *Flandrian sea-level changes in the Fenland* (Unpub. PhD thesis, University of Durham)

Shennan, I., 1980b 'The nature, extent and timing of marine deposits in the English Fenland during the Flandrian Age', in Konigson, L-K and Paalo, K. (eds) *Florilegium Florinis Dedicatum Striae* 14, 177–181

Shennan, I., 1982a 'Problems of correlating Flandrian sea-level changes and climate', in Harding, A.F. (ed.) *Climatic Change in Later Prehistory* 52–67 (Edinburgh)

Shennan, I., 1982b 'Interpretation of Flandrian sea-level data from the Fenland', *Proc. Geological Assoc.* 83, 53–63

Shennan, I., 1986a Flandrian sea-level changes in the Fenland I: the geographical setting and evidence of relative sea-level changes', *J. Quaternary Sci.* 1, 119–154

Shennan, I., 1986b 'Flandrian sea-level changes in the Fenland II: tendencies of sea-level movement, altitudinal changes, and local regional factors', *J. Quaternary Sci.* 1, 155–179

Simmons, B.B., 1980 'Iron Age and Roman coasts around the Wash', in Thompson, F.H. (ed.) *'Archaeology and Coastal Change'*, Soc. Antiq. Occ. Papers 1, 65–73

Simmons, I.G. and Tooley, M.J., 1981 *The Environment in British Prehistory*, (Duckworth, London)

Simpson, W.G., 1966 'Romano-British settlement on the Welland gravels', in Thomas, C. (ed.) *'Rural Settlement in Roman Britain'*, Counc. Brit. Archaeol. Res. Rep. 7, 15–25

Simpson, W.G., 1967 'Three painted objects from Maxey, near Peterborough', *Antiquity* 41, 138–9

Simpson, W.G., 1976 'A Barrow Cemetery at Tallington, Lincs.', *Proc. Prehist. Soc.* 42, 215–39

Simpson, W.G., 1981 'Excavations in Field OS 124, Maxey, Cambridgeshire', *Northants. Archaeol.* 16, 34–64

Simpson, W.G., Gurney, D.A., Neve, J. and Pryor, F.M.M., forthcoming 'Excavations in Peterborough and the Lower Welland Valley, 1960–69', *E. Anglian Archaeol.*

Sims, R., 1973 · 'The anthropogenic fact in East Anglian vegetational history: an approach using A.P.F. techniques', in Birks, H.J.B. and West, R.G. (eds) *Quaternary Plant Ecology* 223–236 (Oxford)

Skertchly, S.B.J., 1877 · *The Geology of the Fenland*, Mem. Geol. Survey (London)

Slager, S. and van de Wetering, H.T.J., 1977 · 'Soil formation in archaeological pits and adjacent loess soils in southern Germany', *J. Archaeol. Sci.* 4, 259–267

Smith, T.S. and Atkinson, K., 1975 · *Techniques in Pedology*, (London)

Spiegel, M.R., 1961 · *Theory and Problems of Statistics*, (London)

Sparks, B.W., 1961 · 'The ecological interpretation of Quaternary non-marine Mollusca', *Proc. Linnaean Soc. London* 172, 71–80

Sparks, B.W., 1964 · 'Non-marine Mollusca and Quaternary Ecology', *J. Animal Ecology* 33, 87–98

Spratling, M.G., 1974 · 'The dating of the Iron Age swan's neck pin from Fengate, Peterborough, Cambridgeshire', *Antiq. J.* 54, 268–9

Spratt, D.A. and Simmons, I.G., 1976 · 'Prehistoric activity and environment on the North York Moors', *J. Archaeol. Sci.* 3, 193–210

Steers, J.A. (ed.), 1965 · *The Cambridge Region*, Brit. Assoc. for the Advancement of Sci. (Cambridge)

Stratham, I., 1979 · *Earth Surface Sediment Transport*, (Oxford)

Stuart, A., 1976 · *Basic ideas of Scientific Sampling*, 2nd edition (London)

Switsur, V.R. and Waller, M., forthcoming · 'Radiocarbon and calibration lists', in Waller, M. 'Fenland Environments', *E. Anglian Archaeol.* forthcoming

Taylor, C.C., 1969 · *Peterborough New Town: a Survey of Antiquities in the Areas of Development*, Pt. 1 (R.C.H.M. London)

Taylor, M., 1985 · 'The Transect Survey', in Pryor, F.M.M. and French, C.A.I. 'Archaeology and Environment in the Lower Welland Valley', *E. Anglian Archaeol.* 27, 15–23

Taylor, M., 1986 · 'Notes on the wood and timber used', in Pryor, F.M.M., French, C.A.I. and Taylor, M., 'Flag Fen, Fengate, Peterborough 1: Discovery, Reconnaissance and Initial Excavation (1982–85)', *Proc. Prehist. Soc.* 52, 1–24

Thomas, K.D., 1982 · 'Neolithic enclosures and woodland habitats on the South Downs in Sussex, England', in Bell, M. and Limbrey, S. (eds) 'Archaeological Aspects of Woodland Ecology', Brit. Archaeol. Rep. S146, 147–170 (Oxford)

Thompson, F.H. (ed.), 1980 · *Archaeology and Coastal Change*, Soc. Antiq. Occ. Paper (New Series) 1 (London)

Thorley, A., 1981 · 'Pollen analytical evidence relating to the vegetational history of the Chalk', *J. Biogeography* 8, 93–106

Thorpe, I.J. and Richards, C., 1984 · 'The Decline of Ritual Authority and the Introduction of Beakers into Britain', in Bradley, R. and Gardiner, J. (eds) 'Neolithic Studies: a Review of Current Research', Brit. Archaeol. Rep. 133, 67–84 (Oxford)

Tite, M.S., 1972 · *Methods of Physical Examination in Archaeology*, (London)

Tite, M.S. and Mullins, C., 1971 · 'Enhancement of the Magnetic Susceptibility of Soils on Archaeological Sites', *Archaeometry* 13, 209–219

Trump, B.A.V., 1968 · 'Fenland Rapiers', in Coles, J.M. and Simpson, D.D.A. (eds) *Studies in Ancient Europe*, 213–226 (Leicester)

U.S.D.A., 1951 · *Soil Survey Manual*, U.S. Dept. Agric. Handbook No. 18

Wainwright, G.J., 1972 · 'The excavation of a Neolithic settlement on Broome Heath, Ditchingham, Norfolk', *Proc. Prehist. Soc.* 38, 1–97

Waller, M., 1985/86 · 'Palaeoenvironmental Report', *Fenland Research* 3, 20–23

Waller, M., 1986/87 · 'Palaeoenvironmental Report', *Fenland Research* 4, 11–17

Waller, M., forthcoming · 'Fenland Environments', *E. Anglian Archaeol.*

West, R.G., 1987 · 'A note on the March Gravels and Fenland sea levels', *Bull. Geolog. Soc. Norfolk* 37, 27–34

Whittle, A.R., 1981 · 'Later Neolithic Society in Britain: a realignment', in Ruggles, C. and Whittle, A.R. (eds) 'Astronomy and Society During the Period 4000–1500 BC', Brit. Archaeol. Rep. 88, 297–342 (Oxford)

Wild, J.P., 1974 · 'Roman settlement in the lower Nene valley', *Archaeol. J.* 131, 140–170

Wilkes, J.J. and Elrington, C.R. (eds) 1978 · *A History of the County of Cambridge and the Isle of Ely: Roman Cambridgeshire (Volume VII)*, Victoria County History

Wilkinson, T.J. and Murphy, P., 1988 · *The Hullbridge Basin Survey 1987: Interim Report No. 8*, Essex County Council (Chelmsford)

Willis, E.H., 1961 · 'Marine Transgression Sequences in the English Fenland', *Annals New York Academy of Science* 95, 368–376

Wilson, D.G., 1980 · 'Palaeobotany', *Nene Valley Research Committee Annual Report for 1979–1980*, 5–7

Wilson, D.G., 1984 · 'A report on plant macrofossils from Fengate', in Pryor, F.M.M., *Excavation at Fengate, Peterborough, England: the Fourth Report*, microfiche pages M242–M244

Zalaciewicz, J.A., 1985/86 · 'Sedimentological evolution of the Fenland during the Flandrian: problems and prospects', *Fenland Research* 3, 45–49

Zalaciewicz, J.A. and Wilmot, R.D., 1986 · 'Conductivity mapping in facies analysis of the Holocene deposits of the Fenland', *Bull. Geolog. Soc. Norfolk* 36, 89–95

Index

Places are in Cambridgeshire unless otherwise indicated.

Fletton, Peterborough, 26
flint(s)
from barrows and pits, 23, 53 (Fig.27), 68
blades and cores, 40, 52, 57, 59, 68, 85, 92, 96
from dykes, 36–7 (Table 2,Fig.15), 38 (Table 3), 39 (Fig.16), 52–3 (Fig.27), 59–61
flakes and chips, 40–1, 52, 92, 96
gravel derived, 85, 93, 96
scrapers, 68
technology, 40–1, 52, 68, 85, 92, 96
typology, 37–8 (Tables 2–3), 40
flint(s), periods
Bronze Age, 18, 20, 68, 92, 94, 96–7
Iron Age, 71
Levalloisian, 17
Mesolithic/early Neolithic, 17, 34, 36, 39–40 (Fig.16), 85
Neolithic, 52, 57, 79, 85, 96
prehistoric, 20
flooding
of fens, 6, 17, 26, 104, 106
freshwater, 16, 18, 47–8, 54, 61, 74, 77, 98, 99, 105
marine, 90
of soils, 11, 47, 74, 87, 107 .
see also water
footpath, Guy's Fen, 3, 88–90 (Fig.58,Pl.XII), 91 (Fig.61), 92, 102, 117
forests
Atlantic/sub-Boreal, 46–8, 54, 56, 60–1, 101
clearance *see* clearance episodes
fen woods, 13–14, 54, 56
Neolithic, 15, 18
see also trees and hedges
Fourth Drove, 16, 18

geology
British Geological Survey, 5–6, 7, 10 (Table 1), 11–12, 77, 119
of North Level, 5–8, 12 (Fig.3)
Geophysical/geochemical survey, 2, 5, 110–12
glacial drift, 6
Glinton, lower Welland valley, 18, 104
Godwin Laboratory, 8, 119
Grandford, 19, 106
grasses (gramineae), 48, 54, 56, 101
grassland, 16, 75–6, 104
grave goods, 26
gravels, 2–6, 19, 20, 97
Fen, 6, 31, 33, 57, 61, 64, 96
March, 6, 11, 51, 84, 89, 92–4, 115, 117
terrace, 6, 8, 11, 15, 19, 33, 61, 64 68, 73, 76, 92–3, 96, 104
Guyhirn Washes, North Level, 11, 119
Guy's Fen, 31, 88–92, 104
dykes, 88–9 (Figs 58–9), 90 (Fig.60, Pl.XII), 91 (Fig.62)
footpath, 3, 88–90 (Fig.58,Pl.XII), 91 (Fig.61), 92, 102, 117

habitats, 75–6, 110
Haddenham, 19
hammers
hard, 96
socketed, 25, 27 (Fig.8), 29
soft, 68, 85
Harwell Laboratory, 119
Hazelton long cairn, 47
hedges *see* trees and hedges
henges, 15, 17–18, 64
herbs, 48
pollens, 54, 56, 101
High Rocks, Sussex, 54
hoards, 25–6, 27–30 (Figs 8–10)
Hockham Mere, Norfolk 18
Hockwold-cum-Wilton, 8, 19, 106
Holme Fen, 7, 11, 13–14, 18, 26
Honey Hill, Northants, 40
horizons, soil, 92, 118–19
A, 15, 47, 54, 56, 61, 77, 87, 98–9
Ap in buried soils, 97 (Pls XV–XVI), 98–9
apedal, 57, 60, 85
B, 15, 46, 54, 64, 74, 87, 98, 107
Bt, 46, 47, 48, 54, 59, 60, 61, 87, 107
Eb, 47, 53–4, 56, 60, 61, 85, 87
occupation, 71 (Pl.VIII), 73–4
truncated, 47, 48, 54, 87, 107

upper/lower, 85, 98–9
Hullbridge basin, 92
human activity, evidence for, 5, 25–6, 29, 48, 51, 54, 56–7, 59, 61, 76, 79, 92, 104–5
Humber valley, 23

illuviation, 46, 47–8, 54, 60, 98, 108
ingots, plano-convex, 25, 29 (Fig.10), 30
insect remains, 16, 110
pollination by, 56
Institute of Archaeology, 108
Institute of Geological Science, 119
iron, 74, 99, 111
Iron Age
pottery, 20, 68, 71–2 (Fig.43), 96, 104
ringwork, Borough Fen, 20, 68, 71–4 (Pls VIII–X), 76–7, 104–5, 106, 120
sites/settlements, 4, 15, 19, 20, 46, 73, 74, 104–5 (Fig.72)
surveys, 68–76
ironstone,6
'islands'
buried, 4, 51 (Pl.IV), 85, 87 (Pl.XI)
Crowland, 101
Crowtree Farm, 4, 33 (Fig.12), 54, 101–2
dykes, 51 (Pl.IV), 79, 84–5, 86 (Fig.57), 87 (Pl.XI)
Eye, 6, 19
fen, 6, 15–16, 51, 104, 113–14
Maxey, 15, 17–18, 97
Morris Fen, 84–7 (Fig.57,Pl.XI), 101–2, 116
Northey *see* Northey 'island'
Oakhurst Farm, 51 (Pl.IV), 54, 56, 101–2, 113
Thorney, 6, 19, 79, 84–5, 89, 101, 103–5, 115–17
Whittlesey, 6, 92, 94, 103

Jurassic period *see* upper Jurassic period

Kellaways Sand, 6

laboratory measurements, 41, 46, 59, 73
phosphate and magnetic susceptibility survey *see*phosphate and magnetic susceptibility survey
soil analysis, 78–9, 99–100, 108, 110–12
landscapes, 8, 18, 23, 26
arable, 3, 5, 12, 16
buried, 1–4, 102
dry land and fen, 5, 102–6 (Figs 70–3)
Etton Landscape Project, 17
open, 15, 16, 106
pasture, 12, 106
landscapes, periods
Bronze Age, 1, 103 (Fig.71)
Flandrian, 4, 12 (Fig.3), 56
Iron Age, 105 (Fig.72)
Mesolithic/Neolithic, 3–4, 18, 31, 102–3 (Figs 70–1)
modern, 32 (Fig.11), 80 (Fig.52)
prehistoric, 95, 101
Roman, 106 (Fig.73)
later Bronze/early Iron Age, 84, 92–3, 95 (Fig.66), 96 (Pl.XIV), 98, 104
later Mesolithic/early Neolithic period
archaeological survey, 33–61, 85–9
flints, 17, 34, 36, 39–40 (Fig.16), 85
sites/settlements, 46, 47–8, 51, 54, 59, 61, 101–2 (Fig.70)
later Neolithic/early Bronze Age, 61, 66–7, 90–4, 103 (Fig.71)
leaching, 66–7, 74, 79, 97–8
lessivage, 46
levelling, 4–5
lime, 6, 14
Lincolnshire, 7, 17, 20, 23, 25, 104, 106
livestock, 15–16, 19, 20, 26, 76, 101
loam, 31, 33, 51, 57, 61, 71
sandy, 73–4, 84–5, 89, 92, 94, 97–8
loomweights, 19
lower Nene valley, 6, 8, 15–16, 104, 106
archaeological survey, 3, 4, 18–20
lower Welland valley
alluviation, 8, 106
archaeological research, 3–4, 18
artefacts, 25, 40
sites/settlements, 15, 19, 23, 102, 106, 108

East Anglian Archaeology

is a serial publication sponsored by the Scole Archaeological Committee Ltd.. The Norfolk, Suffolk and Essex Units, the Norwich Survey and the Fenland Project all contribute volumes to the series. It is the main vehicle for publishing final reports on archaeological excavations and surveys in the region. Copies and information about the contents of all volumes can be obtained from:

Centre of East Anglian Studies,
University of East Anglia,
Norwich, NR4 7TJ

or directly from the Archaeology Unit publishing a particular volume.

Reports available so far:

Report No.1,	1975	Suffolk: various papers
Report No.2,	1976	Norfolk: various papers
Report No.3,	1977	Suffolk: various papers
Report No.4,	1976	Norfolk: Late Saxon town of Thetford
Report No.5,	1977	Norfolk: various papers on Roman sites
Report No.6,	1977	Norfolk: Spong Hill Anglo-Saxon cemetery
Report No.7,	1978	Norfolk: Bergh Apton Anglo-Saxon cemetery
Report No.8,	1978	Norfolk: various papers
Report No.9,	1980	Norfolk: North Elmham Park
Report No.10,	1980	Norfolk: village sites in Launditch Hundred
Report No.11,	1981	Norfolk: Spong Hill, Part II
Report No.12,	1981	The barrows of East Anglia
Report No.13,	1981	Norwich: Eighteen centuries of pottery from Norwich
Report No.14,	1982	Norfolk: various papers
Report No.15,	1982	Norwich: Excavations in Norwich 1971-1978; Part I
Report No.16,	1982	Norfolk: Beaker domestic sites in the Fen-edge and East Anglia
Report No.17,	1983	Norwich: Waterfront excavations and Thetford-type Ware production, Norwich
Report No.18,	1983	Norfolk: The archaeology of Witton
Report No.19,	1983	Norfolk: Two post-medieval earthenware pottery groups from Fulmodeston
Report No.20,	1983	Norfolk: Burgh Castle: excavation by Charles Green, 1958-61
Report No.21,	1984	Norfolk: Spong Hill, Part III
Report No.22,	1984	Norfolk: Excavations in Thetford, 1948-59 and 1973-80
Report No.23,	1985	Norfolk: Excavations at Brancaster 1974 and 1977
Report No.24,	1985	Suffolk: West Stow, the Anglo-Saxon village
Report No.25,	1985	Essex: Excavations by Mr H.P.Cooper on the Roman site at Hill Farm, Gestingthorpe, Essex
Report No.26,	1985	Norwich: Excavations in Norwich 1971-78; Part II
Report No.27,	1985	Cambridgeshire: The Fenland Project No.1: Archaeology and Environment in the Lower Welland valley
Report No.28,	1985	Norwich: Excavations within the north-east bailey of Norwich Castle, 1978
Report No.29,	1986	Norfolk: Barrow excavations in Norfolk, 1950-82
Report No.30,	1986	Norfolk: Excavations at Thornham, Warham, Wighton and Caistor St. Edmund, Norfolk
Report No.31,	1986	Norfolk: Settlement, religion and industry on the Fen-edge; three Romano-British sites in Norfolk
Report No.32,	1987	Norfolk: Three Norman Churches in Norfolk
Report No.33,	1987	Essex: Excavation of a Cropmark Enclosure Complex at Woodham Walter, Essex, 1976 and An Assessment of Excavated Enclosures in Essex
Report No.34,	1987	Norfolk: The Anglo-Saxon Cemetery at Spong Hill, North Elmham, Part IV: Catalogue of Cremations
Report No.35,	1987	Cambridgeshire: The Fenland Project No.2: Fenland Landscapes and Settlement between Peterborough and March
Report No.36,	1987	Norfolk: The Anglo-Saxon Cemetery at Morningthorpe, Norfolk: Catalogue
Report No.37,	1987	Norwich: Excavations at St Martin-at-Palace Plain, Norwich, 1981
Report No.38,	1987	Suffolk: The Anglo-Saxon Cemetery at Westgarth Gardens, Bury St Edmunds, Suffolk: Catalogue
Report No.39,	1988	Norfolk: The Anglo-Saxon Cemetery at Spong Hill, North Elmham, Norfolk, Part VI: Occupation during the 7th-2nd millennia BC
Report No.40,	1988	Suffolk: Burgh: The Iron Age and Roman Enclosure
Report No.41,	1988	Essex: Excavations at Great Dunmow, Essex: a Romano-British small town in the Trinovantian Civitas
Report No.42,	1988	Essex: Archaeology and Environment in South Essex, Rescue Archaeology along the Gray's By-pass 1979-80
Report No.43,	1988	Essex: Excavation at the North Ring, Mucking, Essex: A Late Bronze Age Enclosure
Report No.44,	1988	Norfolk: Six Deserted Villages in Norfolk
Report No.45,	1988	Norfolk: The Fenland Project No. 3: Marshland and the Nar Valley, Norfolk
Report No.46,	1989	Norfolk: The Deserted Medieval Village of Thuxton, Norfolk
Report No.47,	1989	Suffolk: West Stow, Suffolk: Early Anglo-Saxon Animal Husbandry
Report No.48,	1989	Suffolk: West Stow, Suffolk: The Prehistoric and Romano-British Occupations
Report No.49,	1990	Norfolk: The Evolution of Settlement in Three Parishes in South-East Norfolk
Report No.50,	199*	Proceedings of the Flatlands and Wetlands Conference
Report No. 51,	1990	Norfolk: The Ruined and Disused Churches of Norfolk
Report No. 52,	1991	Norfolk: The Fenland Project No. 4, The Wissey Embayment and Fen Causeway
Report No. 53,	1992	Norfolk: Excavations in Thetford, 1980-82, Fison Way
Report No.54,	1992	Norfolk: The Iron Age Forts of Norfolk
Report No.55,	1992	Lincolnshire: The Fenland Project No.5: Lincolnshire Survey, The South-West Fens
Report No.56,	1992	Cambridgeshire: The Fenland Project No.6: The South-Western Cambridgeshire Fens
Report No.57,	1993	Norfolk and Lincolnshire: Excavations at Redgate Hill Hunstanton; and Tattershall Thorpe
Report No.58,	1993	Norwich: Households: The Medieval and Post-Medieval Finds from Norwich Survey Excavations 1971-1978
Report No.59,	1993	Fenland: The South-West Fen Dyke Survey Project 1982-1986